LIFE AND LETTERS OF SAMUEL FISK GREEN

I am, aff'y,

Yr. bro., Samuel F. Green

Oct. 1880.

LIFE AND LETTERS OF SAMUEL FISK GREEN M.D. OF GREEN HILL

An American Medical Missionary in Ceylon during 1847-1873

COMPILED BY
EBENEZER CUTLER

MANOHAR
2021

First published 1891
Reprinted 2021

ISBN 978-81-949912-7-4

Published by
Ajay Kumar Jain *for*
Manohar Publishers & Distributors
4753/23 Ansari Road, Daryaganj
New Delhi 110 002

Printed at
Replika Press Pvt. Ltd.

LIFE AND LETTERS

OF

SAMUEL FISK GREEN, M.D.,

OF

GREEN HILL.

COMPILED BY

EBENEZER CUTLER, D.D.

PRINTED FOR FAMILY FRIENDS.

1891.

INTRODUCTION.

IT can scarcely be hoped that success will attend the attempt to portray the character of one whose life from early manhood was controlled by a fixed purpose to subordinate self, to keep out of notice, and employ with conscientious fidelity the days that were given him in the unostentatious discharge of what he deemed duty, leaving results to take care of themselves. The influence of such a spirit, moving along in its field of activities, may well be likened to that genial warmth which, in the operations of nature silently and without observation, gives form and color to leaf and flower and fruit.

At the brow of a natural depression in a range of smoothly rounded hills, which divides the site of the more compact portion of the growing city of Worcester on the west, from the narrow dale on the east, there stood, nearly a century and a half ago, a plain wooden dwelling of the type then prevalent in the Massachusetts settlement. Two-storied but low in the ceilings, of ample length and breadth, and anchored by a chimney of needless proportions, it afforded, with occasional close packing, accommodations for a numerous family. It stood on a by-road or lane, which though a public way was but little frequented, except by the occupants of the home and their visitors. It was surrounded by trees both of ornament and for fruiting, and, at a near but varying distance, by a rim of the original forest. It came to the Green family in 1754, being purchased by the distinguished clergyman and physician, Thomas Green, of Leicester, for a son whom he had educated for the latter profession.

Here this son, Dr. John Green the first, began the practice of medicine at nineteen years of age, and attained professional distinction. While yet a young man he married his second wife, Mary, daughter of the Hon. and Brig. Gen. Timothy Ruggles, of Hardwick,—a descendant of Thomas Dudley, Governor of the Province of Massachusetts. Gen. Ruggles was President of the First Colonial Congress held at New York in 1765:

his father was a clergyman, and his wife, a granddaughter of the missionary to the Indians at Marshpee whom Dr. Cotton styled, "the godly and gracious Richard Bourn." Dr. Green's family was numerous. Three sons were graduated at Brown University, when the discipline was more after the English fashion. One died an undergraduate of Columbia College – then situated near the City Hall in New York. Two entered the legal profession, two the medical and one the clerical. Some were, for those days, widely travelled men, who at each return from a foreign tour were very sure to bring home some plant, vine, or shrub, or some work of art to add to the modest attractions of their simple but comfortable home. No visitor could look about the premises without readily discovering evidences of taste struggling for a more emphatic manifestation, but confined by imperative demands upon a limited treasury,—for the expenditures were made on the principle that 'the life is more than meat, and the body than raiment.' On the death of Dr. Green, the administration of the place fell to the lot of his son William Elijah,—the father of the subject of this memoir,—who resided upon it, with but brief intervals of absence, till his decease in his eighty-ninth year and in the room where he was born. He was of a fine presence, genial disposition and of an unlimited hospitality, taking active interest in public questions but shunning official life.

The first and second generations of the Greens of Green Hill had passed through the latter stage of the Colonial Period with its institutions framed and guided by the mother country; and the third had entered upon that epoch of conflicting opinions which culminated in the Revolution—in which they were not inactive participants. William E. Green was born in the period between the Declaration of Independence and its consummation and acknowledgement by Great Britain. For several years it was, therefore, undetermined whether he was to remain a British subject or become an American citizen. The Revolution when completed still left unsettled, questions which chafed the patriotic spirits of the infant Republic and led to the hostilities of 1812; and though much bitterness was cherished against England after that time, yet the modes of thought and the habits of domestic and social life were still largely modelled on those of that country. Official life was attended with ancient forms; the sheriff walked the streets with cockade and sword, the judges were conducted to court with marked ceremony, and the clergy were given precedence even in leaving the house of worship.

Mr. William E. Green completed his study of

law, partly in the City of New York, soon after his graduation at Brown University, and in due time was admitted to the Worcester County bar.

His first wife left a son, and the second a daughter, each being commemorated in the name of her child. His third wife was Julia, daughter of Oliver Plimpton, of Southbridge, and granddaughter of Dea. Daniel Fiske, of Sturbridge, – both men of renown in civil affairs. She enjoyed the advantages of "an accomplished family," being of good education, refined tastes, and excellent principles, but of a rather slender constitution.

The family grew in time to the capacity of the house. The father was ever the genial companion of his children. If not as arrows in his quiver, they were as olive-plants round about his table. He took delight in their pleasures, sought their constant improvement, and encouraged their industry. He helped them make the driest study almost a pastime, and had remarkable ability to attach them to himself and to awaken and develop in them a love of literature. Under his conversation and example, they found themselves early possessed of associations which became dearer with the lapse of time. The very trees of the homestead embodied memories which greatly enhanced their value. The once widely-known garden, with its rectangular walks and grassy terraces, its ornamental and medicinal plants and shrubs, bloomed and fruited with traditions of the elders. The spacious "garret" contained a heterogeneous museum of relics of various epochs of the family life, past use but saved in obedience to an economical unwillingness to destroy, and affording inexhaustible amusement, on inclement days, to the inquiring minds and inventive fancies of the children.

The life of a family, so remote from the village and from neighbors, would seem to have been, inevitably, rather monotonous; but it was not without important compensations. The professional life of the head of each of its generations attracted visitors of high cultivation, broad views, instructive and stimulating conversation. There was always at the homestead a library; rather scant it is true, but of standard works, elevating, refining, and well read. The necessity of relying so much upon themselves for social pleasure and culture, may account in part for the remarkable developement of their affection for one another. The seclusion of their early home certainly did not prevent their early attainment to positions of great responsibility and usefulness. William Nelson became a lawyer and for many years Justice of the Police Court of Worcester. Lucy Merriam and her sister, Mary Ruggles, were for thirty years associate proprietors and conductors of a widely-known School for Young Ladies, on Fifth Avenue, New York,—the latter marrying Carl Wilhelm Knudsen, a native of Denmark, educated at the Military College in Copenhagen and at the Royal Academy of Fine Arts. Julia Elizabeth, for many years a teacher, and afterwards head of the family at Green Hill John Plimpton, a physician, for many years resident in South America, having previously practised in New York City and in China. Andrew Haswell, a lawyer, from his youth resident in New York and prominently associated with the educational and material improvements of that City and State. Lydia Plimpton, a teacher in her sister's school. Oliver Bourn, a resident of Chicago, a civil engineer on many important works. Martin, also a civil engineer of wide experience and marked ability, now residing at Green Hill.

It is quite remarkable that for more than a century, the relations of the dwellers in this retired place have been more close and intimate with the City of New York, once, at least a fortnight distant, than with the Capital of the State in which it is situated, though the latter is now distant but an hour's journey. Still the ancestral homestead is the place where the survivors like best to dwell, or to linger in their visits, though realizing more and more pathetically as the seasons come and go the truth of the poet's lines:

> "I see around me here
> Things which you cannot see; we die, my Friend,
> Nor we alone, but that which each man loved
> And prized in his peculiar nook of earth
> Dies with him or is changed, and very soon
> Even of the good is no memorial left."

CHAPTER I.

1822–1846: TO ÆT. 24.

SAMUEL FISK GREEN, son of William E. Green and Julia Plimpton, was born at Green Hill on the tenth of October, 1822. He was the eighth in a family of eleven children, of whom one died in infancy, ten lived beyond middle age, and six survive him.

The child was subject to ills and sufferings of unusual severity, which he barely survived, and from which he but slowly recovered. In his eleventh year he was bereaved of his mother, having been deprived of her care a year and a half by reason of her illness. As his eldest sister had gone from home, it fell to the next, though but in her eighteenth year, to fill the place of a mother to the younger children,—which she did so well as to be cherished by them with filial affection. His natural endowments were not remarkable, except perhaps in the strength of his affections and the quickness of his temper; but however incompatible these traits may seem, the latter did not weaken the former, and the former greatly assisted in subduing and controlling the latter.

Though fond of sport, and freely indulging in it, he was early taught to make himself useful. His aptitude is seen in the fact that before he was fourteen he took the clerkship of his next older brother in New York, while the latter was recovering from a severe illness, and in this and other similar occupations, was away from home and school about ten months. According to his years and strength he was accustomed, while not at school, to such manual labor as boys perform about a farm, and formed habits of industry and economy, from which he ever afterwards derived great advantage. Though he served no apprenticeship, he was handy in the use of tools, and took great delight in what he styled "tinkering," using the word in the most extended signification, and playing the jack-at-all-trades in unconscious preparation for the profession and position to which he was destined.

In the Green Hill Benevolent Society, a household organization for the promotion of the spirit of benevolence in its members, no one seems to have taken more interest, except perhaps his guardian sister, for as secretary he kept it in operation after its originators and early managers had left home.

Its reflex influence was of much more importance than the amount of monthly contributions, and by it he may have been unconsciously "bent" towards the work to which a few years later he was consciously "inclined."

He was educated at the public schools. Though not precocious, he learned with ease, and though often detained at home he kept well up with his classes. Faithful and exemplary, he was naturally a favorite with his teachers and had a high esteem for them. Many years afterwards one of them spoke of him as "the only scholar who tried to do his best, and a perfect gentleman then;" and from his East Indian home he sent to two of them "rulers" of choice wood in token of his friendly remembrance and esteem.

His training at school was supplemented by that at home; his older sisters, and especially his father, aided and stimulated him in his studies and in general literature. He early formed good habits of study, and acquired a taste for good reading; and his acquisitions and discipline were such as to fit him for college, or to lay the foundation for that future improvement which would be a practical substitute for a liberal education.

He was past seventeen before he felt any concern for his spiritual welfare. Free from low associates and vicious habits, he had been satisfied with himself. His first sense of sin was for disobedience to his sister. After this he put a different estimate on other acts. It is remarkable that he seemed to find some of his greatest sins against God in certain slight unbrotherly acts, which would have been entirely forgotten if he had not referred to them years afterwards in his letters. By the time he was eighteen, he had settled the personal question, having surrendered to Christ, and begun to experience that peace which is the witness of the Spirit to adoption into sonship with God.

Having come into the light himself, he desired to lead his brothers into it; but he could hardly help feeling that any premature zeal might be misconstrued, and that any efforts in their behalf would be regarded with more favor after a somewhat longer proof of his own spiritual renewal. From the first, however, he endeavored to live as a light in the world, and it was not long before he rose above his reluctance to plead with others, and became remarkable for his life-long fidelity. "Though naturally of an excitable and fiery nature, through high self-discipline, he converted the fire into central glow and motive power of life, instead of permitting it to waste itself on useless passion."

Early in 1841 he went to New York and took employment under the Rev. Dr. Vaughan, Secretary of the Protestant Episcopal Board of Missions. On the 11th of April he united with the Mercer St. Presbyterian Church, then under the care of the Rev. Dr. Skinner. He attended the evening meetings, took classes in Sunday Schools, conversed with his pupils and associates on spiritual things, though he had not yet the courage to let his voice be heard in public.

Aiming to conform himself to the ideal of Christian life as presented in the Gospel, he found himself greatly favored also by his position; and ever afterwards felt much indebted to his employer for the exemplification of that ideal. Here he gained an insight into the demands and the management of the enterprise of missions, and probably some deeper impressions of his duties to Christ in regard to the heathen.

He seems to have inherited a predilection for the medical profession. As his duties at the Mission House were often light, he found time, not only for study and reading, but also for taking some lessons in dentistry. The fact that a brother was just beginning to practice medicine in the city was not without, at least, a silent influence. When he chanced to hear a lecture on the circulation of the blood, the latent predilection may have been awakened into conscious desire and choice; for by the middle of summer, he gave up his clerkship and became a student in medicine with Dr. John Augustus McVickar. A fortnight sufficed to show him that the study of medicine, in order to amount to anything valuable or desirable, must be something more than a pastime; and he resolutely began his work anew. He embraced opportunities to witness surgical operations, and to hear medical lectures. In October he entered the College of Physicians and Surgeons, of New York, which had a numerous faculty and afforded many advantages. During his course of study, he had also many opportunities to visit hospitals, infirmaries, dispensaries, and to attend clinical lectures and post-mortems,—thus making personal acquaintance with many of the more distinguished men of the profession in the city.

A letter to his aunt shows how ready he was to recognize kindnesses extended to him.

New York, *Oct.* 22, 1841.

Dear Aunt Betsey:

I write you at this time, not to tell any news, for I have nothing of the kind, but to express my gratitude to you for another proof of your friendship toward one so unworthy; if it had not been that you so kindly stepped in to my aid, I fear this winter might have passed without any lectures at all.

This would have put me back a great deal in

my studies, as I should have had to go on without any aid from the light which I shall now derive from them. I shall therefore gain by your liberality, not only the new ideas given by the lecturers, but shall moreover have the aid of those same ideas in helping me onward in the course of my medical pursuits.

For this accept my sincere and hearty thanks, and let me assure you dear Aunt that nothing will serve as a greater spur to me, than the hope of being enabled at some future day to make some slight return for the many favors I have been constantly receiving from you. . . . .

All well. Give my love to all and accept much yourself from your nephew,

SAMUEL F. GREEN.

Soon after his matriculation, he learned that one of his brothers was to sail at once for the Lesser Antilles, to be absent he knew not how long, it might be for years. He could not but feel a deep personal regret at the separation. The following letter, which was to be opened at sea, shows not only the strength of his brotherly affection but also that his single year of Christian experience had been one of thoughfulness and spiritual growth. It is without signature.

DEAR BROTHER ANDREW:

I want to say a few words to you now, even after you have left me far behind, together with all your other earthly friends. You are now among strangers, who have comparatively but little interest in you and who, not having known you before, will take you as you first appear to them. This, then, is the time to take among them and among all a decided stand for Christ. Let the governing influence of His Spirit be seen in all your actions, and strive to glorify Him in all you say and do.

You are going into the midst of thick temptations, and it becomes you to take earnest heed to yourself that you do not fall. Trust not for one single moment to your own strength, but as a little child walk, led by Jesus' hand; if you trust in Him, He will guard and guide you. We have many promises in His word to this effect, and the earth will sooner be removed than that *one* of these should fail. We have also many denunciations against him that "maketh flesh his arm." "It is better to trust in the Lord than to put confidence in princes."

You leave us now with the hope and expectation of getting wealth. If God sees it to be best that you become rich, He will send abundant prosperity; but if not, if He sees that prosperity would be hurtful to you, He will in mercy withhold it, and you should pray that He would, for it will profit nothing to gain the whole world and lose one's soul. If He gives you prosperity, pray that He will at the same time grant you grace to bear it well; and pray that whatever you may gain may be consecrated (as you have consecrated yourself) to His service. Let your light shine brightly amid the moral darkness with which you will be surrounded.

You will doubtless be strongly tempted to follow the practices of those among whom you may be known, in regard to the Sabbath particularly, but do not give way to the temptation. "Remember the Sabbath day to keep it holy." If one becomes accustomed openly to disobey this command, he will lift the flood-gate to a host of sins that before were effectually debarred. Strict observance of the Sabbath and of your private devotions will be to you the chief safeguards, and you ought to be very thankful that, though you leave behind many means of grace, you still have the chief, "the Bible and the throne of grace." These are sufficient, if well used, for any one, and will prove themselves so to you. May we both make good use of them, and never let *carelessness* creep into our Bible readings, nor *formality* into our closets, for they are the death of all vital religion.

NEW YORK, *November* 1, 1841.

The student did not allow his professional course to prevent earnest efforts at general improvement. At the outset he began the study of German, and pursued it under a teacher to whom it was vernacular. He gave attention to Latin, Geometry, and Natural Science; read Philosophy, History, and Poetry. He desired to have his mind so well disciplined that all his powers would be under control. For his age and opportunities, he had a rare perception of what was necessary to such discipline, and a rare determination to attain it. He read with attention, reflected on what he read, and often made his thoughts definite by writing. This practice clarified his mind, and enabled him to take enlarged views and to form quick and accurate judgments. He thus gained a good degree of power to set his mind at work whenever and wherever and on whatever subject he desired.

The first time Mr. Green went into the dissecting-room he was painfully impressed with the repulsiveness of the scene, and with the indifference of the students at work. He said the sight was enough to sicken one, and if it did not remind one of his day of death he knew not what would. Obviously he would have gladly dispensed with this part of his course of study, but he subordinated his feelings to his convictions of duty, and gradually became an enthusiastic student in this department. His interest in the work made him insensible to what at first had been so disagreeable, and probably caused him to appear as indifferent as others.

His scientific interest in the human system, however, instead of inclining him to be sceptical, only made him the more reverent. The adaptation of means to ends throughout the entire organism lifted the work so far above all merely human mechanism, and suggested such unlimited intelligence, that he could not but worship and adore its Author.

On the other hand, instead of making him indifferent to human suffering and reckless towards the patient, his studies rendered him only the more sympathetic, cautious and careful. Though he trained himself to do his duty with a firm hand, he could not forget or slight the claims of the sufferer, nor the dependence of both upon the divine source of health and life.

Having pursued the usual order of study for a year and a half, he met with a new and, as it seemed to him, better method,—that of studying topically and every topic exhaustively,—which he at once adopted, and pursued.

Unable, as the warm season of 1843 drew near, to follow his studies with vigor and without frequent absences from the lectures, he took a vacation of five months to recuperate. Perhaps it was his own experience of debility that suggested the reflection, "There is nothing below the sun that will give us true enjoyment unless we possess a joy-creating spirit within." He was not entirely free from his past infirmities, however, the chief of which he regarded with such aversion that only those who have been similarly afflicted can appreciate his graphic apostrophe: "Oh, Dyspepsia, thou art horrible; it matters not by what avenue thou makest thy approach, none more unwelcome than thou. Why, thou liest concealed, like a lurking robber, in the stomach, and goadest on the appetite, and impartest nice discrimination to the palate, till thou fillest well thy habitation, with fit material, when thou turnest thyself fiendlike against the wretched brain and makest it suffer for its honest credulity in commanding its subordinate functions to obey the mandates of thy despicable self."

He was disposed, however, to find consolation in the possible benefit to be derived from the ills he suffered; for he said that, "Sickness often, though casting a gloom over the mind, makes this serve as a veil to hide the world, that the soul, ever busy, may work upon the future world and thus learn those things which, important as they are, have heretofore remained unheeded."

Before the middle of May, 1844, he again went home to secure the benefit of a vacation. Long before this his thoughts had been occupied occasionally with the question of his duty in respect to foreign missions, but he probably communicated them to no one, except perhaps his friend and classmate, S. R. House, who then thought of going to China, and finally went to Siam. In August he wrote to his sister Mary: "I have some thoughts of going 'missionarying.' Although my health is slim, yet it might improve by change of climate, habits and scenes." Having returned to New York for the last course of lectures, he consulted with his friend House about going to China, having been led to think of that field particularly by the fact that his brother John had gone there to practice medicine; but, on receiving from him some discouragement, he seems to have thought no more of China than any other portion of the heathen world. But he could not rid himself of the sense of personal obligations to the missionary cause; as his health was precarious, he concluded that he would either become a missionary himself, or endeavor to maintain a substitute, as Providence might indicate.

By reason of his two long absences his course in the College was prolonged into the fourth year. That the delay had not been wholly disadvantageous may be inferred from the applause which greeted him at the lecture the morning after his final examination. He graduated on the 13th of March, 1845. A few days afterwards he was nominated to the New York Dispensary, although his credentials had not been presented; but, having been strongly urged to settle in his native town, he declined the nomination.

On the 23d of April he wrote from Worcester, to his sisters and brothers in Nêw York: "Yesterday was my first on professional waters under a regular flag. How shall I ever forget you and your kindnesses. Accept, for all, my thanks, with the hope that these may prove but shadows of coming realities. Though separated here, may our respective roads in life converge, tending heavenward." Young, a novice, and surrounded with physicians of established reputation, he expected that confidence and patronage would be of slow growth; but he regarded his "business," whether "brisk" or "rather dull," "as good as Wisdom saw it best," and therefore he "wished it not better."

The active duties of his profession did not diminish his interest in the question of missionary service, and in March, 1846, he asked himself, "Why is it not better for me to go where I can be very useful, as well in my profession as otherwise, at once—go to a land of darkness and heal the bodies and enlighten the minds of some error-bound people?" It was in this state of mind that he ventured the next day to make some remarks at the prayer meeting, and rejoiced that he had received strength for once to overcome his diffidence. Some months later he recorded his views and feeling as follows:—

"If it prove best that my sphere should be enlarged here, I hope I may be enabled to devote all my influence to the great cause, and make all tell for good upon the welfare (in the broadest sense) of my fellow creatures. For self is not worth living for; such living is not worthy the name of life; it makes one meaner and still more mean; true living—benevolence—is a constant expansion of soul. It is certainly very pleasant to have extended business influence, to have many under one's pay, to be the means of their subsistence, to be the medium of relief to suffering, to have a large share of this world's goods and dispense bounties to all around. But it is as certainly pitiable to see one blessed with all these powers and turning the good to a curse by a grasping, avaricious spirit,—acting the miser, starving his soul, and laboring to tie a golden weight on his neck. John Bunyan's man with the muck rake stood on the lip of a yawning pit, unconsciously heaping gilded dust—that yellow dust which has proved a deadly poison to so many souls. Heartily would I say with Pilgrim,—Deliver me from the muck rake of sordid avarice."

Obviously he still held fast to his resolution to do the work of a missionary either personally or by proxy, though which was to be the way he knew not yet, except that for the present it seemed to be the latter.

He was an ardent lover of Nature. Reared in the midst of rural scenery he was a quick observer of its beauties, and was seldom at a loss to find a suggestion or illustration of some truth or fancy. But his greatest interest in Nature lay in its signs of the Supernatural. He used often in later years to say, "The casual observer looks *at* an object; the scientist looks *into* it; the Christian looks *through* it to its Creator." The spiritual habit of his mind is shown in these extracts from a letter to his youngest sister, to whom he loved to write, though within an easy walk of her.

July 11, 1846.

MY DEAR SISTER:

All around us in Nature calls for gratitude. . . . But do we know, or will reflection assure us, that in the inner world—that world unseen but surely felt—there lie extended fields of thought, luxuriant and sprinkled with angels' flowers? . . . Let us pity those whose eyes seem wholly closed to sentiment, dealing but with the grosser elements of things around them. To such the body of the natural world is dead, for the presence of the spirit is undiscerned. The material world is a set of symbols. . . . As we thread the maze of life, be our ear alert to catch the music of the universal choir,—from the small insect that hums as it sails on gossamer wings, up through the harmonious scale till we catch the music of the spheres, with their note too mighty for our little sense. The little grass that dances with light as the joyous breeze skims over it, the rippling brook with sparkling eye and tone of gladness, the sunbeam that smiles on many a cloud and tinges for us visions of the heavenly land, and the lamps that twinkle with rejoicings,—thick hung throughout the long blue pathway to light imprisoned spirits home,—all, all in more than words sing praise, if but the mind attentive be . . . .

Through calm and tempest, through sunshine and gloom, let us evenly pursue our way, not resting our eye on the present scene, but keeping it fixed on the Star of our destiny till, going before us, it shall stand over the place where . . . death shall give us birth. . . . For us, not through what but to what we pass, it is to look, and we look for a haven of peace.—With love, your brother,

SAMUEL F. GREEN.

He sometimes indulged in rhyming, as a means of obtaining a greater command of language; but did not pretend to be a poet. Yet a remark already quoted about our enjoyment of external things being conditioned upon a joy-creating spirit, and which reminds one of Coleridge's ode to Dejection, again occurs illustrated and embodied, by no means unhappily, in the following stanzas.

Oft have I looked upon the sky
  When all was pure and bright and clear;
As oft within me turned mine eye,
  And almost thought that sky was here.

Again I've watched upon the sky
  The deep black clouds with thunder roll;
Again have turned within mine eye,
  And felt those clouds were in my soul.

Tis in ourselves the sun doth shine,
  Or gloomy shadows throw;
We bear within a power divine
  To work our weal or woe.

CHAPTER II.

1846–1847: ÆT. 24–25.

ABOUT the middle of November, 1846, several missionaries were to sail for India, the Rev. Levi Spaulding and Dr. John Scudder on their return to Ceylon, and the Rev. E. P. Hastings under recent appointment to the same Mission. Dr. Green took the occasion to consult Dr. Scudder and to attend the farewell meeting, and at once offered himself to the American Board. In due time he received appointment to act as missionary physician to the American Mission in Ceylon.

Naturally he began to think of the approaching separation from his friends, of the distant field of labor, and of the future years. This is the record of his revery: "I wandered late beneath the moon, whose pensive light seemed in friendly sympathy with my spirit. I saw her rise from the hazy East, and, awake but dreaming, pictured all those scenes, unknown to me save by description, where my destiny with unwavering finger points my path, and the future is speedily beckoning me away. I looked upon the fair orb of night, and felt myself towards her growing in attachment; for she will surely hereafter, as now, shed beams of softest influence on my soul when lonely I may stray to think on kindred far away, and feed, as I must on memory's shades of scenes too dear, too sacred, it would seem, to leave.—I hear the tones of millions call; I may not stay"

He closed up his affairs in Worcester, and hastened to New York to procure his outfit. As the time for sailing was yet uncertain, he took lessons in drawing and in Daguerreotyping, and began the study of the Tamil language under a returned missionary. Having a good knowledge of Latin and considerable of Greek, French, and German, he was confident he could learn this new tongue, notwithstanding he was told that it was exceedingly difficult, having between thirty and forty characters with about two hundred and forty modifications,—and he had about three months to study it while waiting for a vessel.

It was no idle boast when he wrote one of his sisters that "others have learned it and so can I;" for he was not one to be discouraged by "a lion in the way," but rather one to whom obstacles afforded the greater zeal.

It is interesting to find that after he had given himself to the work of a missionary, he felt no

PORTRAIT OF DR. SAMUEL FISK GREEN.

TAKEN ABOUT 1847.

ARTOTYPE, E. BIERSTADT, N. Y.

regret in view of what he was leaving. To one of his sisters he wrote:

ORANGE, N. J., *Feb.* 24, 1847.

MY DEAR SISTER LYDIA:

. . . . I cannot account for it, that one who does really love his friends as much as I do can yet be away from them as I now am without feeling irrepressible longings for their society; however, I can little tell how I shall yearn to see their faces after a three year's absence from them *all.* I never have been totally divided from them in my life,—but on this theme my pen must stop here. I am not to allow myself in painting dismal hues, I do not believe in them. I believe most cordially that the Lord will cheer any path we may tread if it be pursued with a trustful leaning on Him.

Let us rejoice in that ours is the hope that we both have the Almighty for our Friend, reconciled to us through the beloved Redeemer. We can but cry with the apostle,—"Thanks be unto God for His unspeakable gift." I should be glad, it seems to me, if I could get my heart in a state contented with nothing short of heaven, and I hope I am satisfied with nothing below. I want to be on this footing with all my friends,—to regard all partings with them here as but of very trifling importance, and to look for a full enjoyment of their company above only.

If our eyes were open, what a mere span would

this bound of time present. How surprisingly near would the eternal world seem to us. Our ears, if spiritually opened, could hear glad voices in bliss, and among them might we not perhaps discern some friends calling us thither. Oh, for enlargement of mind and of heart, to see ourselves in our true relation to all around us and beyond us, to feel our condition, what we were, what we are, and what we hope to be. What revelations would an angel's eye, for a moment granted us, present, but, if we "persevere to the end," only a step removed. That vision shall be our own. The gospel, however, has set before us, of that beyond us, an all-sufficiency for our need, in that Christ has developed what was a mystery for ages in the world, what many prophets and righteous men desired to see. Yes, "Life and immortality are brought to light through the Gospel." What a fearful leap must every death in darkness as to the future have been; but now the grave is lighted, and the rays of the Sun of Righteousness dart through the once dark valley, even to the very gates of Heaven. But stop—just as if I could meditate, or should, for you!

. . . Am pursuing the Tamil in earnest. . . . Miss Bull says you taught me the French very correctly indeed. . . . Here I still am, untrammelled or unblessed, as you choose. . . . When I can find one with many of your features of character, I shall be likely to try for a matrimonial arrangement. . .

I am bound for the Seminary at Batticotta, I suppose; but I will write you again, I hope, before

I get there. May God bless you and make us both blessings.

With much love, yours very truly.

SAMUEL F. GREEN.

Among all who had witnessed the life of Dr. Green since his conversion, there was probably not a person who doubted his spiritual fitness for the missionary work. As he was about to bid adieu to his friends in New York an intimate acquaintance, in a note of sympathy to one of his sisters, wrote, "I suppose that the letter which your brother has received from the Board notifying him that the time of his departure draws near, will make you feel now that it is indeed a stern reality—ought we not to say a sweet reality? Should it not be our delight to give of our best to Him who gave Himself for us? I know you would not retract the offering, even in the agony of separation from one who bears about him so much of his Master's likeness as to make it impossible for those who know him well, it seems to me, not to love him. For my own part, I esteem it one of my precious privileges to have known him."

It seemed strange that one so young, so vivacious, so accustomed to society, so ardently attached to his kindred and friends, and to whom the society of friends seemed almost indispensable, should have been willing to go on a foreign mission without a wife. Yet within a few weeks of his departure, and well knowing the solicitude of his friends, he seemed to have no fear of the loneliness that he was sure to experience; saying to one sister that "nobody is more afraid of bad companionship," and to another, "I won't get married, if I can help it, till I have explored the Indies myself alone first."

To relieve the tedium of the voyage and happily surprise him when he arrived at his new home, his friends wrote letters and notes which they either put in his hand to be opened at specified times or places, or hid them in his books and clothing and other goods, where he would never think of looking for them but would sooner or later discover them. The pastor and people with whom he had worshipped in Worcester, and especially the young men of the Sunday School, provided him with useful tokens of esteem. Friends who could do so accompanied him to the ship, to take their leave of him only at the latest possible moment. He sailed from Boston on the 20th of April on the *Jacob Perkins*, sending back the following note by the tug-boat.

JACOB PERKINS, *April* 20, 1847.

MY DEAR SISTER MARY:

I have your two letters, and one inside

from Oliver, to read when I get off. All is bustle now, but I feel like May inside. Thanks for all your kindness. May God bless you all. We are to leave by a tug-boat in a little while. There are about seventeen in the crew. . . .

I have taken my writing desk out, after seeing the last of my friends on the wharf. I hear the bells ringing in Boston. I saw the carriage drive away. We are now at anchor, waiting for the steam-tug with another vessel to go along with us. The sailors are making their usual noise, the steward seems pretty well in liquor, and my room-mate is busily making his arrangements; he has on his sea trim. . . . I have changed my clothes and am ready for sea I believe. Have just read Sister Mary's and Miss Bull's kind letters, for which I cannot too much thank them. . . . Maria's note I have in anticipation. . . . May more such meet me when I arrive at Madras. . . .

I just stepped out of my state room into the Cabin and find the table full, the Captain, Pilot, Mr. Bacon and two young men who returned in the steamboat—I hear them talking—saying how bad it is to leave home etc. The Captain said, as I was swinging my handkerchief to Julia and the rest on the wharf, "Your sister feels real bad to part with you. . . ."

I have much enjoyed a few minutes in commending all of you to our Father in Heaven, and in praying for the ship's company. I feel happy—I see no reason why I should feel otherwise. I hope all the new scenes I am to pass through will teach me more and more the goodness of God. I expect much to enjoy writing you all from time to time.

The wind is fair now. The sails are hoisting and the pilot about to leave. After he has left I am going to open the book Mrs. Sumner handed me this morning. I hope, Julia and Martin, you will have a nice time in Roxbury this evening; I shall be there, and on Green Hill, and at No. 1 Fifth Avenue. I cannot feel too glad that I leave behind me so many friends who have a hope in Christ. Mrs. Sweetser—I must send a message to her, and what can I say but that I can never forget her and her kindness. The singing of the sailors, the calling of the sea terms at the top of the voice, all seem quite like sea; the rigging creaks as if glad. I have just had a smell of the Heliotrope, which stands just where my good friend Mr. Sweetser put it with his own hand. . . . Good Bye—letter called for.

SAMUEL F. GREEN.

Dr. Green had but one fellow-passenger. He found no religious sympathy from him, or from the officers or the crew. Yet he tried "to be the means of good to every one on board." He believed that "faithful dealing towards others is a most powerful means of grace to one's self," and that one can be happy in any circumstances if he is "proficient in Baxter's method of contemplation on heaven." Having finished "Life in Earnest," he hoped to be enabled "one day to say so without quotation marks." For work he studied

Tamil, and read science and literature; for recreation he employed his ingenuity on things for use, ornament, or keepsakes. Sometimes he dissected things taken from the sea.

On the 30th of August he "smelled the spicy breezes," which "seemed like a faint perfume of the heliotrope;" and the next day "the coast of Ceylon gradually revealed itself—the near, low coast, then the line of sand, then the nearer highlands, then the distant mountains, and a few cocoanut trees relieved by a light background—a beautiful green line as far as the eye can reach on our larboard." On the 4th of September he landed at Madras, being rowed from the ship by "about a dozen men naked except a cap or turban, and a piece of cloth around the loins." There he found "notes for reading before leaving Boston or at sea" from missionaries still in America, letters from his brothers and sisters, and "letters of welcome" from missionaries in Ceylon; and there he had the first glimpse of the heathen, and of the methods and success of labor for their conversion to Christ. He visited the Rev. Henry M. Scudder and heard him preach in Tamil; he observed Fast Day with the American Mission, and took part in the services; and in the evening attended a love feast at the Rev. Myron Winslow's with five and twenty natives who were thus renouncing caste for Christ's sake, the women being much abashed to eat with men. He visited the Eye Infirmary, the Dispensary, and the institution for paupers, lepers, idiots, and the insane. Through Mr. Hunt, of the Mission Press, he made the acquaintance of Drs. Appleton, Boyd, Hogg, Johnston, and Wiley.

Having purchased a horse, and other things needed to complete his outfit, he started on horseback for Jaffna on the 20th of September, accompanied by Mr. Hunt and a retinue of necessary servants. After going twenty-seven miles Mr. Hunt returned to Madras. "We kissed at parting," wrote the Doctor, "and I could not help it if I would; he left me, for the first time alone among the heathen." On account of the heat of the sun, it was necessary to travel in the morning, towards evening, and in the night. The way was strange but interesting, leading by villages "like weatherbeaten, long haystacks," across broad streams, over desert plains, by beautiful scenery, and affording many glimpses of native customs. The journey of two hundred and five miles from Madras was finished on the 3d of October; and on the 6th he crossed the straits, landing at Point Pedro, the northernmost point of Ceylon, in season to be driven to Mr. Cope's at Valverty, the nearest missionary station, five miles west, in the evening. The next day he took a lesson in Tamil, and towards evening proceeded west nine miles to Tillipally, where he found Mrs. Spaulding and Mr. Hastings, surprising the latter by instant recognition before his own face was seen in the light of the lantern, he having seen Mr. Hastings' daguerreotype in Boston. On the 8th he rode west from the station of Mr. Poor to Pandeterripo, the station of Mr. Smith; thence south to Mr. Minor's at Manepy, and in the evening west again to Batticotta, having met with the warmest welcome at each of these missionary stations. Here is his first letter from Ceylon to his "Friends in America."

BATTICOTTA, *Oct.* 9, 1847.

DEAR FRIENDS:

Here I am, having been mercifully preserved through a long and tedious voyage and a wearisome journey. Last evening I met a circle of the missionaries at Manepy,—Mr. and Mrs. Minor, Mr. and Mrs. Spaulding, Mr. and Mrs. Fletcher, Mr. Meigs, Mr. Scudder, and Miss Agnew. . . . Am going to investigate what there is here in my department, and get things in train as soon as may be. . . . My next to you will be my Genesis of missionary life.

Just in time to begin my next quarter of a century here,—am twenty-five to-morrow.

Love to all from your son, nephew, cousin, brother, and so forth,

SAMUEL F. GREEN.

CHAPTER III.

1847–1848: ÆT. 25–26.

FORTUNATELY Dr. Green had already seen almost all the missionaries. The welcome they had given him was grateful to his spirit, and he fully reciprocated their fraternal cordiality. Weary almost to illness he enjoyed the sabbath the better for such an introduction to his new home. The record in his journal shows the spirit in which he entered upon his work.

"Spared by Divine Mercy I complete to-day my twenty-fifth year. To-day I commence my second quarter of a century in commencing my missionary life. If permitted to see the close of another period equal to that passed, may it be with the retrospect of diligent, faithful and successful exertion in my great Master's cause. It is my fervent desire that the Lord would make me useful here by giving me an influence as a Christian physician over this darkened people among whom, I cannot but feel, His providence has distinctly called me to dwell; next, that He would give me acceptance with the missionaries here, and their confidence so far as 'creature confidence is proper (and it is so when exercised subordinately to Himself), that I may uphold their hands and be a comfort to them in the great work.

May the flight of time be more clearly attended to by me,—how brief it is, how quickly it passes, and how momentously it terminates."

The day after his arrival at Batticotta he was called to two patients, and had one who called upon him; and on the fourth day he had "several." Whether any of these were Tamils is not certain, but if so they were doubtless connected in some way with the Mission. There is no record of any more patients, except some in the Missionary families, till the 20th of the month, when he was "called to a young man with a large abscess in the left groin." This brief record indicates that Dr. Green was not, at the time, aware of the greatness of his opportunity, and had no suspicion that his success in the case would establish him at once in the confidence of the Tamils; but since the death of Dr. Green, one of his Tamil students, now an Assistant Colonial Surgeon, has communicated many reminiscences, of which the following is one:

"In the year 1847," says Dr. E. Waitillingam, "there were very few English doctors, and none "among the Tamils of Jaffna who had any idea of

"European medical practice. The Jaffnese would "not dare to gainsay their own physicians. . . . So "there was prejudice and ignorance for the new "Doctor to overcome. . . .

"Mr. Mutatamby, a Tamil and Sanskrit Pundit "(my uncle), who was generally the Tamil teacher "of the missionaries, got fever and was suffering "from it for a long time,—under my father who "was a native physician. Fever grew worse and "worse daily, and suddenly turned out to be some-"thing else. The patient was left for a few days "without treatment, to see what was the cause of "the bad state. All hopes of recovery were lost. ". . Other native physicians were equally unable "to solve the difficulty. I suggested to my father "to have recourse to a European doctor, and al-"luded to Dr. Green, who was then in Batticotta a "few days after his arrival.

"After great hesitation and consultation, it was "decided that Dr. Green can be invited, because "he was a missionary. . . . People had crowded "on account of the serious state of the patient and "for curiosity's sake. Dr. Green was taken to the "patient, and the crowd was dispersed. . . . Dr. "Green pronounced that there was an abscess in "the abdomen, and advised immediate operation. "I bravely responded to it, and the patient also was "willing. He discovered the abscess and cut it "open. The patient got free and was a hundred "times better than he was. Dr. Green dressed the "wound, and attended very carefully and cured "him.

"The people heard about the success, and the "fame of the Doctor was spread very soon through-"out the peninsular of Jaffna. The people began "to talk that the English doctor had removed the "bowels out, adjusted them, and refixed them. . . . "From that day forth Dr. Green was considered a "demi-god by the people, who all flocked to him "afterwards from all parts of Jaffna."

On the 25th of the month the Doctor had a dozen patients; afterwards "a few," "enough," "a swarm," "a rush," till he had more than he could attend to, though they came early and waited hours for their turn. Often the night afforded insufficient rest from his labors, so that he longed for the time when the novelty should cease and the discovery be made that he was not infallible. In the course of time, however, he found the number of patients was not so great during the semi-annual harvest, because then attendants on the sick could not so well be spared,—which is one of the milder verifications of the proverb that, "The tender mercies of the wicked are cruel."

In addition to his services as a physician and

surgeon, he applied to every patient the spiritual remedy prescribed in the gospel for the cure of the soul. Until he could get command of the language he was obliged to have an interpreter,—one who could readily apprehend his meaning in English, and communicate it correctly in the vernacular. As this subjection to religious instruction and appeal was well understood to be the condition to receiving aid, and yet did not repel, his experience illustrates the advantage of the medical missionary in getting access to the ears and hearts of the heathen, their relief from physical ills being specially adapted to disarm prejudice and beget confidence in him as a spiritual friend and teacher. He had opportunity not only to explain how all diseases are fundamentally attributable to sin as the cause, but often to show the immediate connection between specific troubles and specific sins. This double work with patients was done mainly at his "back door when they came for medical aid," but sometimes at the houses of the more unfortunate. Thus he daily preached the gospel, and often to as many as a mere evangelist would get to hear him on stated occasions.

This, however, though it may seem enough, was not all his work. It was fortunate that he found relief in a variation of duties,—such as attending the regular business meetings held at each station in turn, visiting every station at the call of the families or persons belonging to the Mission, conducting in his turn the meetings of the church and people who understood English, and addressing the natives assembled on Sundays in "the school bungalows." It was awkward to preach through an interpreter, and, besides, there was the embarrassment of a curious distinction: the people regarded preaching through an interpreter as paid for, and therefore would hear it respectfully for the fortunate interpreter's sake. Fortunately many of the people could read, and the Doctor supplemented his instruction and appeals with religious tracts. His two-fold office was well fitted to increase his influence in each capacity, making him known always as a missionary while he sought to relieve them of physical sufferings, and always as a physician while he sought to lead them to repentance for their sins and to faith in Christ as the only Saviour.

By a vote of the Mission Dr. Green removed early in February to Manepy—about five miles nearer the other stations. He was hardly settled here before patients were again "thronging" him.

Though he had found little time to brood over his separation from friends, yet it was a great satisfaction to have proved that "the line of love that stretches from friend to friend and binds their hearts is truly strengthened by increase of distance." To his sister he wrote:

MANEPY, *Feb.* 5, 1848.

MY DEAR SISTER MARY:

. . . When your welcome package was placed in my hands . . . I took the sheets to a place by myself, and as I read of you all, my heart filled my throat and the water my eyes. I believe I never more fervently thanked God than for this—the assurance that all was well with you and that you knew definitely of my arrival in India. Ere this, I presume, you have learned of my journey from Madras, and my being at last in Ceylon. . . .

Affectionately, your brother,

SAMUEL F. GREEN.

At Manepy stands a celebrated temple of Puliar. Within a few weeks of his settlement there Doctor Green saw the people enclosing it in a hedge, erecting near it temporary sheds, covering a considerable space with little thatched booths for a bazaar, and finally coming "in files over the paddy grounds,—on the banks which separate them one from another,—twisting their bodies and swinging their long arms, staggering under their burdens, here one almost naked, there one enveloped in white cloth, and all shades of clothing between," bringing on their heads baskets filled with things to supply their own wants, and to sell to those who might be obliged to buy, during the stay of the expected concourse. Simple as were their provisions, rude as were their preparations, and scarce as was the money in circulation, it was evident that the people who could avail themselves of the opportunity were determined to turn to pecuniary profit the great festival of the year, which begins about the 25th of March and continues three weeks with evident interest to the end. The method of keeping it appears to be essentially the same from year to year, though in some respects it is probably varied according to circumstances, but always involves a multitude of follies and absurdities, and probably abominations also, with little or nothing which civilization could approve or Christianity fail to condemn. On the second Sunday, his attention being called to a great and noisy crowd in the road, he went to see what it meant. "I saw," he wrote, "a man rolling along on the ground, holding in his hands an offering,—a little brass vessel of milk,—under an arch trimmed with peacock feathers and painting; behind him an old religious beggar ringing a bell; before him another bearing some incense burning. The poor fellow rolled over and over—his black body whitened by the dirt—for about a half a mile, and then around the temple. He had been sick, and made a vow to do this. He got medicine, I understand, of me; but if mine did him any good, he ascribes the virtue to Puliar; so I have been an instrument perhaps of leading this man to serve the devil."

During the progress of the festival, which afforded him a striking exhibition of the follies, degradation, and idolatry of the people,—naturally so repulsive and discouraging to the Christian missionary, Dr. Green wrote as follows:

MANEPY, *April* 1, 1848.

MY DEAR SISTER JULIA:

. . . I feel well in body and happy in heart; feel more and more every day as if I am where I ought to be. . . . As for being homesick, I have not known that feeling since I left. . . . The trials of missionary life are not bodily but of the spirit,—the hardness, deafness, degradedness of the people. All one can say of Divine love and goodness falls unfelt, apparently, on their ear. . . . The work goes on slowly, yet it does advance, and this with the promises of God is encouragement enough to keep one in the field. . . .

Your own brother,

SAMUEL F. GREEN.

With his social culture and refined tastes, Dr. Green might naturally have been expected to feel disheartened in his earlier contact with heathenism. But he had chosen his work, not for the possible romance connected with it, nor from any underestimate of the disagreeable things connected with it, but with conscious self-denial for his Master's sake, and in sympathy with his Master's love for the degraded and ruined for whom He died. In a very short time his interest in it was such that he began to appeal to others to engage in it. To his medical student in Worcester he sent the message, "not to give up the idea of being on mission ground." He expressed a desire that his own youngest brother would study for the ministry and become a missionary.

It was indeed difficult to interest the people in the truth. Their religion was the growth of centuries; like the banyan, it kept the latest generation connected with all the generations preceding, back to its original germ. All their traditions, customs, opinions, remembrances, castes, and pride overlaid their consciences—already defiled—and made them well-nigh invulnerable. With all this their contentment and complacency with their religion enabled them to treat everything else according as it seemed to favor their own selfish ends. Dr. Green wrote of them:

"They will hear patiently, confess that what is said is true, often perhaps out of mere complaisance. If they think it will 'please master,' and they can get anything by his favor, they will even ape an interest in one's advice. They will assent to almost anything which they think you would like to have them. Tell them that as sinners they are in danger of hell, and they will answer, 'Yes, it is so;' and then the subject passes out of their minds. Yes, this people are asleep; and talking to dull ears is wearying to the soul. It requires more faith to work here than I had yet imagined. One sees how vain is all human effort unless God crowns it with success. That is all in His hand, and Christian prayers must call it down."

Missionaries have one advantage even in what is commonly supposed to be a disadvantage; that is the very heathenism around them. A minister of the gospel may be profited himself, by his study of the Bible and his study of the sins and wants of his people, much more than the people themselves. The missionary is excluded from much of the worldliness of Christendom, and is almost obliged to keep the heathen before his mind even in his study of the word, so that his sympathy and pity towards them, and his conviction that only by the gospel can they be raised to a really better condition, keep him very near to the heart of Christ.

As early as November of his first year, Dr.

Green had received two young native Tamils as students in medicine, and in the latter half of the year he had three. One would think he had enough even for a robust man to do without giving medical instruction; but system and perseverance sometimes accomplish the apparently impossible. Besides, it is a part of the missionary policy to raise up a native ministry not only, but native physicians,—with a view to enable the people to carry on the institutions of the Christian religion and its consequent civilization without foreign aid. He had also the superintendence of native assistants, educated by his predecessor, and located at Manepy, Batticotta, Oodooville and Tillipally. All these consulted him, and exhibited their registers of cases treated, when they applied for medicines.

With so much to occupy his time and consume his strength, neglect of the Tamil might seem almost inevitable; but, besides a systematic study of it under instruction, his daily contact with so many natives was favorable to a constant accumulation of words and phrases, and to a rapid advancement in pronunciation. Though he found it a difficult language, and for a time apparently more difficult the more he learned of it, yet, after eight months upon the ground, he was able to speak it, with a good deal of freedom, as learned by the ear, and had advanced in it by the eye "far enough to make it interesting to hear an interpreter twist English into Tamil." A few months later he could understand nearly all of a sermon preached in the vernacular. But much as he had gained, there yet remained very much to acquire.

CHAPTER IV.

1848–1850: ÆT. 26–28.

EXCEPT in such variation as experience suggested, and such additional duties as necessity or expediency imposed, the second year of Dr. Green's missionary life was very much like the first. He gave Tickets, with a synopsis of the gospel and some directions in regard to health printed upon them, to his patients, which he required them to keep and bring to him whenever they should apply again for medical aid,—hoping that by thus keeping them in their possession they might read and heed the instructions for both body and soul. He was this year one of the Committee on the English schools of the Mission, and had special oversight of those in Manepy.

He found the people timid, polite, and servile. A note from an assistant asking for medicine began thus: "Dear Sir, With due reverence and awful fear." Perhaps their servility was an inheritance from the generations oppressed by the Portuguese, when "the law favored the zealous priest and the priest made the most of the law."

Some would bow down and worship without scruple any one who relieved them. A poor person whom he relieved by an operation called him "God."

Though their morality was low, the people scrupulously adhered to their religious customs, no matter how filthy and disgusting. "The cow," he wrote, "is esteemed a sacred animal. I shame the people by asking why they wear that stuff, which they call divine lime on their foreheads and arms—three stripes on the shoulder-joint in front, three halfway between the shoulder and the elbow, three midway between the elbow and the hand, all *across* the arm. The stripes are in threes in honor of the Hindu Triad—Brahma, Vishnu, and Siva [that is, Creator, Preserver, and Destroyer]. They give all sorts of reasons—for beauty, custom, religion," thus betraying either some degree of sensitiveness, or a ludicrous admiration of ashes.

As Siva is the Destroyer he is the one to be feared, and as the religion of the heathen derives its power from fear, it is natural that Siva should be exalted above Brahma and Vishnu in the estimation of the people. It is his favor they desire, and his displeasure they fear; to him they erect temples, and him they serve though under the names of his deputies.

"It is," he wrote, "amusing to see a mop of elf-locks poked over by one in search of those animated ideas that sometimes wander through the human hair. Hunting and killing them for another is a charity. One must not complain of being tired, for that would lesson the merit; must not wash the hands after the work, as that would destroy the merit; must not throw them in the fire, for they will then multiply in the beard. After death God thrusts in and leaves a pin under each finger nail of those who have not been meritorious in this employment. If after death God sees marks of this employment on the nails, he will not torment such by the pins."

Though so careful to avert physical torture in the world to come, however, they think there is great merit in voluntarily afflicting the body in this world. In sickness it is not uncommon to make a vow to perform, in the event of recovery, some special and difficult service to the favoring deity; such as breaking a great number of cocoanuts at the great annual festival without stopping to rest; rolling on the ground a certain distance,—on the road, around some great rock, after the idol car, around the temple,—carrying in the hands all the way an offering to the deity; performing some pilgrimage involving great hardship and fatigue either by the time and distance or by the torturing conditions. Sometimes one walks on edged or pointed irons fastened in his sandals. The Doctor once met a pilgrim returning from the interior of the Island to the Continent, wearing around his neck an iron frame about four feet square—the base of a pyramidal cage formed by eight strips of iron rising from the corners and sides to an apex some distance above the head, which he was to leave at the goal of his pilgrimage. "When asked for his collar to send to America, he replied that to go home without it would be like climbing a cocoanut tree and then coming down part way and falling the rest. When asked about certain things in his ears, he said they were part of his attire as a devotee, and if a dog pretended to be a dog he must wear a tail." These answers sound like ridicule of his own religious service, but were doubtless given in the mistaken sincerity of his defiled conscience. Before biding him adieu the Doctor told him of salvation by grace through Jesus Christ the Son of God.

Their notions of sin are very superficial, distorted and gross. "Murder, killing a cow, and such like things, are sins. I suggested to a drover to kill a beef occasionally for sale; he was horrified at the sinfulness of the act, putting his hand to his head as if the sin would fall there. A man had a finger broken off by his niece: she went off to the coast on a pilgrimage to bathe in holy waters to remove the sin. One man said he had no sin; another replied, 'When you see a fine bullock don't you desire to get him? that is sin.'" This reply seems like a dawning of the notion of the sin of covetousness. But generally they seem to have no notion at all of any sin of the heart, of thought, of intention; though they may admit the fact of such sin when the missionary asserts it. To their apprehensions both sin and religion consist in external acts.

To his brother, long absent from his home, he wrote,

MANEPY, JAFFNA, CEYLON,
27th, *Jan.* '49, *Saturday.*

MY VERY DEAR BRO. JOHN:

I received a letter from you two days ago, dated 4th July, '48, one day off Valparaiso. Last evening I looked at V. on the map and read about it in the Gazetteer, so as to know in what kind of a place you are situated. . . . . You say in your letter, "come home." Now, I can give you more reasons why I should *not* come home, then you can me why I *should* do so. I feel more and more convinced the longer I stay here, that here I ought to stay; that God has shown me it is both my duty and my privilege to remain here so long as I have health to be useful.

That I did not enter on missionary work rashly, without previous sober reflection you may be assured. That I shall not rashly leave it, or so conduct as to be expelled from it, I look for God's help.

I know that missionaries have many faults, and I have seen their faults perhaps clearer than ever you have.

I have not so romantic views concerning the working out of the great scheme of the world's salvation, either in regard to God's chosen instruments, or in regard to the speed with which the task will be completed, as I once had. But I have a growing, deepening conviction, that the only hope of this people or any other heathen people, that they will rise from degradation to that degree of light and privilege which Christian countries enjoy, is in the continued, faithful teaching of the Gospel and Science among them, by such poor instruments as I myself, and others in the missionary work. If it be a small, faint hope, still it is their *only* hope, and we who are blessed by the light of Heaven's salvation are bound to spread that Light so far as lies in our power; and "woe is us" if we do not.

If the instrumentality was perfect; if all missionary operations were carried on without lack of judgement; with the constant observance of the strictest economy; then I would heartily bid the work "God speed," perhaps you say. But hold—God has chosen for the work, not angels but men; and all human action is faulty—the best men are far short of perfection.

If we are about a good work, let us "put in" as hard as we can, and not stand and do nothing, or play among the weeds, because the only hoe we have is somewhat broken and very dull.

Sinful, imperfect men are told to preach the holy Gospel to every creature. If we faithfully declare God's word, our responsibility is fully met; if not one soul is saved in consequence, our duty ought not the less to have been fulfilled. God tells me to do a thing, I do it: He looks out for consequences, not I.

The duty of preaching the Gospel is the duty of every man who has become acquainted with that Gospel; the results of such preaching are to be educed by God. Duty—Mine. Fruits—God's.

So much in defence of my being a missionary, and to induce you to be in fact a missionary wherever you are.

. . . Let me tell you a little what I am doing. I came out here to take medical care of, 1st, the missionaries, and 2ndly, of whoever of the natives applied to me for aid. I began registering the names, residence, diseases, and treatment of these last on the 14th Dec., 1847. The number on the register to-day is two thousand five hundred and forty-four (in thirteen months). Many of these, surgical cases perhaps one-third of them or more.

I have removed lots of tumors, have operated for cataract several times, for strangulated hernia, once, amputated the arm once; . . . removed several cancers; amputated fingers and toes and portions of the hand several times; treated a good many fractures and severe wounds; attended some very bad cases of child-birth, etc. So I am not idle you see, in the way of our *dear profession.*

Together with medical aid, I try to give spiritual. I am one of a committee of two on the English Schools of our Mission, and shall have opportunity to do as much in that line this year as I wish. I do not know the number of these schools precisely, they are as many as a dozen more or less, besides these we have a large number of Tamil schools for boys, and others for girls, and a seminary for boys at Batticotta, with one for girls at Oodooville.

Wednesday 31st. Last Monday I removed the left upper jaw and check bones for a cancerous fungus in the antrum filling the whole mouth and the left nostril. Yesterday couched a cataract, to-day after attending the most necessary cases, have been dissecting a fine subject with my students. . . .

If you could keep a journal of little every day occurrences—trifling incidents, showing us which way the straws blow across your path, and send it to those at home, they could forward it to me and I should be rejoiced to hear from you, at least quarterly.

May the Lord be with you, and may you be inclined to cleave to Him. With Him only is security. I long to hear you breathe the sentiments of a real earnest Christian. In years gone by you once talked with me about my soul, and tried to excite in me desires after Heaven; it is not so of late. Do settle the question in your own mind, guided by the Bible, whether you are serving God, living for Him, or for this world. Dear Brother if you are a Christian, don't be a half-way affair. In the day of death no one ever thought he lived too much for the Lord.

It is a fearful thing to walk through this world. I am dreadfully afraid of falling. But God will keep me safe so long as I hold upon His hand. His aid is my only hope.

Hoping to meet you in Heaven, both of us cleansed, perfected,

I am your loving brother,

3d Feb. '49. SAMUEL F. GREEN.

From MANEPY under date of *Feb.* 7, 1849, Dr. Green wrote:

MY DEAR SISTER MARY:

Since I have received the last packet of letters I feel a great longing to see the writers, and you especially. . . . In many ways you have shown yourself more than a sister; you are my mother-sister. You are my spiritual mother; but for your exertion in my behalf, your earnest prayers, I might now have been a vile open sinner, impenitent, an expectant of hell, a slave of fear, a victim of depravity. God appointed you my angel of deliverance. Your seasons of prayer with the children on Sabbath mornings, your readings of "Pike's Persuasives" during the Sabbath evenings, will be remembered forever. While I used to listen to you with my head laid on the table, apparently drowsy, the truth was working in my heart; and I will be encouraged by my case to tell the truth to those apparently unconcerned;

it may affect them notwithstanding the careless exterior.

. . . Your lot and mine are both appointed of God, and He is leading us both by His own well chosen path to heaven. The thoughts of meeting there with all we love are sometimes almost overpowering. It seems as if one's bosom would burst with the emotions they enkindle, and that the soul would take wing through the rent veil of flesh and soar upward to her God. . . .

With deep affection, your brother,

SAMUEL F. GREEN.

Dr. Green's father was now in his seventy-third year, and apparently in that state of indifference to his spiritual welfare, which makes one's Christian friends peculiarly anxious. The son, who had gone so far to preach the gospel to the heathen, felt constrained to pray and labor for his conversion. His letters were full of affectionate pleadings. which probably endeared him all the more The following is one of these letters.

MANEPY, *April* 7, 1849.

MY DEAR FATHER:

Not for want of inclination has it been that I have not written you often. How I should like to sit beside you, with our feet up in chairs and a basket of sweet russets between us, and tell you of all that has happened to me since I shook your hand the last time, and hear all that you might say in your humero-serious way. But it is hardly probable that I shall be permitted the joy of your company again on earth; I am the more anxious therefore to talk with you about your soul, and to point you again to Jesus Christ, the way to Heaven, that I may met you there. For, for my own part, I am determined, by God's good help, to reach that blessed place.

My dear father, your letters are pleasant to me; I am thankful to you for them; but there is one feature in them that painfully affects me,—they speak almost altogether of *this* world. They do not speak with joy of the world to come as a place of rest after your hard life is over. What theme than this more appropriate for one whose head is silvered by age, and whose cheek and form declare that he will soon be launched in that unseen eternal world. . . . Excuse me if over-earnest, and put it down to the love of your affectionate son,

SAMUEL F. GREEN.

From the beginning of his assured acceptance with God, Dr. Green held all that is revealed to our faith as unquestionable reality. His view of heaven was that of a home where everything is perfect and adapted to the highest aspirations of the soul. He believed with Paul that, "To depart and be with Christ is far better" for the Christian himself than to remain here, though he felt the importance of his instrumentality for the salvation of others. "I have often looked forward to the day of my death as a desirable point, in my existence, to be reached. All that the Christian hopes for, or the best of all, lies beyond the dark valley. After Christ by his saving influence has made one to be 'not of this world,' he becomes a mere pilgrim bound to time; with the world he has but few common sympathies, for he is dead to it; his attachments are all in heaven, for there is his 'life hid with Christ in God.'" This state of mind enabled him in all perils by land or sea to feel that even though death should befall him, he would only the sooner come to the fruition of his hope.

Considering how fully his time had been occupied, he had made great progress in the Tamil by the beginning of his third year. He wrote: "I have now got so far that I can begin to enjoy the language, and see the ludicrous usage of the uneducated natives as it differs from the pure classic speech of the refined. A vast amount of labor has been expended in polishing the language of this people. Having naturally acute minds, fond of metaphysics, and knowing no true science upon which to expend their powers, they have lavished thought and ingenuity on their vernacular tongue. It is said a man may be a diligent scholar in Tamil for fifty years, and yet meet with works in the language which he cannot read."

Dr. GREEN'S FIRST MEDICAL CLASS.

Valoopilly, alias S. Miller. Kanapathy, alias C. Mead. Adonarsalam, alias N. Parker. Padeatamby, alias J. Danforth. Poopaladasingam, alias J. H. Town. Koomadoo, alias A. C. Hall.

In February, at a meeting in a school bungalow, he made his "first set talk without an interpreter;" in March he began to conduct family worship with the servants in the vernacular; in May he preached to his patients in Tamil, and also to the congregation in Panditeripo,—using his English manuscript and translating in the pulpit. The first half of the year his health was such that he felt obliged to confine his religious work mainly to those who applied for medical aid. Even in this way he conversed with many persons from different parts of the Province. He found many who seemed to be intellectually convinced of the truth of the gospel, but few, if any, who really felt the power of it. So much were the people in the habit of assenting to the truth through complaisance that it was not easy to estimate the impressions made upon them. He rarely met with positive opposition, though that seemed preferable to the prevailing indifference.

He had now taken his Medical Class through the second year of their course of study, and was introducing them to practice in cases for which they were prepared; opportunities were always frequent, but now more than usual, on account of the cholera. Not all who have the cholera, however, will have a physician. "Some fear to take medicine lest it offend their gods; refusing medicine and taking only the juice of the leaf of the sacred tree over Genesa's temple, mixed with water." They would rather die without medicine and take their chances with their gods in the unseen world, than to recover by the use of medicine and encounter the malice of their gods in this world.

In a letter to one of his sisters there seems to be the first disclosure of that full consecration he early made of himself to the cause of Christ among the heathen. Thus far he had experienced no regret for his decision, and no doubt of its wisdom.

MANEPY, *April* 4, 1850.

MY DEAR SISTER MARY:

Without speaking from my imagination, I think I can say, that for a long time previous to my entering the missionary service directly, I considered myself as belonging to it. In my mind were only two questions: shall I stay at home and work and earn the means of supporting another, perhaps several, in the foreign missionary field, or shall I go to the heathen myself? I felt hardly fit for the latter either bodily or in my character, and settled at home; but God's providence made it evident that I should never fulfil to any great extent the former indication, and subsequent providences have shown me that I have done right in following the latter. Here I am, here I wish to be, here to live, here to die. If the question of health should ever make it expedient to leave this, I should wish to do it only for some other part of "the field"—to go to the Zulus, the Sandwich Islanders, or the Australians—wherever it might appear best, all things considered, that I should go. I am a poor stick, I know, but whatever I am, I hope I am the Lord's and never wish to leave this blessed service of making known Christ to the heathen. . . . Such were my views when leaving home, and they have become much confirmed by the fact, that as I have since got a good hold of a difficult language, and considerable missionary experience, I am more obligated (if possible) than ever to remain in the work. . . .

Your brother,

SAMUEL F. GREEN.

Later on he wrote to another sister that "the faithful servant finishes up his day's work and don't wish to quit long before the sun is down. It is very easy to receive wages; it ought to be as easy, and, more than easy, it ought to be a delight to us to serve and work hard for so good a Master as ours." He seems never to have had a doubt of his divine call to his work, and always, so long as health would permit him to labor, to have been unwilling to relinquish it for any consideration of ease or gain or pleasure or love of kindred and friends. He felt that he was not his own.

The Brahmins found him no respecter of persons; he had a quick perception of the ludicrous, and could take down their pride and conceit with unexpected drollery and facetiousness; but he would not consent, even by an external act, to any of their assumptions of superiority. If desired to feel one's pulse through silk, so as not to impart pollution, he refused. He said "one of them lay in a litter with a broken leg; I talked to him, joked him, pinched him in the ribs; and gave him the gospel in as pleasant a way as I could. I like to make free with them, and show to the people that they are in reality a little short of divine beings.

"A Brahmin wished me to examine his wife's case when there was no crowd present, and to avoid putting my fingers or any instruments in her mouth. I told him that I should not touch her more than was requisite, and he need not fear pollution, for I should wash my hands immediatety before; and she would not pollute me, as I should wash them just afterwards. This made him give a sorry laugh."

In the autumn Dr. Green wrote that he had received a letter from Mr. Dyke, the chief civil officer of the Province; "In which he intimates the willingness of the Government to give aid to the support of our medical department, and proposes to supplant the old class of medical sub-assistants throughout the Province by young men trained as Gould, Evarts, and Waittilingam have been. This proposal is the greatest encouragement I have yet met with; and if I can get a select class of six once in three years, I shall hope in the course of time, if my life is spared, to stud the Province with well educated physicians,—to be men thoroughly drilled also in the principles of Christianity." On submitting the proposal to the Mission, he was able to return Mr. Dyke a favorable answer—a willingness to receive aid without being obligated to any prescribed course of operations. Mr. Dyke was a philanthropist of a generous spirit, and a warm personal friend of Dr. Green.

CHAPTER V

1850–1852: ÆT. 28–30.

EARLY in his fourth year, Doctor Green, by vote of the Mission, removed from Manepy back to Batticotta, and into a new house. Thus far he had had an average of two thousand patients a year, who with their attendants made an average, probably, of more than five thousand persons to whom he gave religious instruction, in connection with his medical practice. Whether the spiritual results would ultimately be as great as the physical is a question which they who were walking by sight would have answered in the negative, but to which the Holy Spirit may yet give an affirmative demonstration. His spiritual efforts, however, were not in vain. "Where I see a little fruit," said he, "the produce of the soil on which the missionary labors, I am comforted with the thought that in God's service there is great reward, and trust I experience somewhat of a realization of this in my own heart."

Even his professional work he performed with a sense of dependence on God, with prayer for

His blessing upon the patient spiritually as well as physically, with the desire to regard it himself, and to have his patients and their attendants regard it, as far as possible, as religious work. His feeling in regard to this matter is illustrated in a case to which he was urgently called twenty-five miles from home. "When I arrived I found a most distressed household; all were in despair about the patient,—the Doctor and all. When I had successfully removed the difficulty, it seemed as if a most dense leaden cloud rose up and left the house, and some rays of comfort and joy beamed in. It was a moment of the sweetest professional reward to me,—better tenfold than if every second of it had been a guinea."

Some of the worst phases of heathenism are found in connection with the diseases of the people, the supposed causes of them, and the methods of treating them; and these methods are generally as senseless as the causes assigned are imaginary. They have superstitions even about the injurious and fatal effects of people seeing and talking in certain circumstances, and call these "the evil eye" and "the evil tongue." They think that, "If a man gets severely injured, and one says, 'Oh, he can't live,' that saying will have something to do with his death. "I saw a fire at the junction of two roads, for removing the effects of the evil tongue." My boy said: "Suppose one says I am a clever fellow; if within three days afterwards I am taken sick, it will be in consequence of that praise. My mother will take certain mango leaves, salt, red peppers, and the dust trodden in the track of him who praised me; the leaves she will wave thrice round my head; the salt, &c. she will rub on my body; then she will carry all thrice around the house, then away to the nearest crossing roads and burn all at eventide with one or three dry palmyra olas. Then the effect of the evil tongue will pass away and I shall get well." The following are other illustrations:

A certain man made a vow: his cow gave a "great flow of milk,—too much for his family,—but he would neither sell nor give away, fearing the evil tongue. When the cow was put out to graze, he daubed her with soot to ward off the evil eye." So it seems that the heathen are sometimes more afraid of admiration and praise than of indifference and censure; not lest they be puffed up with pride and over estimation of themselves, but lest they be injured in their persons or property.

"Akustier, a fabulous person, is the famous medical author among this people. He wrote ages ago, and they say he is now composing works on some mountain far in the West; that he is but a cubit high. They follow his prescriptions unchangingly, not knowing the effect of each ingredient, but only that of the compound."

"A Yokee—one that by a certain process of thinking, ceremonies and so forth has become holy—came to me; said he was a god and could create; that to be a physician a man should be more than a man; that he could teach me much."

"A famous practitioner in Manepy brought one of his patients. I showed him some anatomical plates. He had been in practice forty-two years, and said he had never noticed two kinds of blood, black and red; that he never saw any of the vital organs. I explained the heart and blood-vessels, and their connection with the pulse. He had the old notion that the pulse is the motion of the air within the body."

Dr. Green received a call from a young native physician "who had quite a reputation for driving off devils." This kind of practice was of course the result of the devil-worship of past generations, which had not yet wholly disappeared. "I went," said the Doctor, "to a little shed erected to Vidoveer, a real devil and feared much by the people. In this shrine is a little elevation of dried mud, about two feet high and square, made like two steps; on the upper step stands an iron trident fixed in a block of wood and about a foot and a half high; and on the lower step are placed offerings. An iron lamp hangs up on one side from the roof, and a piece of old cloth is tucked up under the thatch, ready for wicks. Fifty or sixty cock's heads are cut off annually, in the night, outside of the shed. Over the house is a margosa tree, in which this male devil is said to live, and when the sun is too hot he comes down into the booth. Many left the neighborhood of his residence for fear of him.

"A patient suggested to me that his sore finger was caused by witchcraft. A boy's friends had made many offerings to get him cured of a fever sore, supposing the gods displeased I saw three men just at the corners of the roads, one bearing a torch, one a cocoanut and knife, and another an image in mud and trimmed off with leaves, flowers, beans, etc., representing a sick grandchild of the old Tamil gentleman, chief actor in the ceremony—a sort of a scapegoat idea; by the ceremony it is hoped the sickness will leave the person and enter the image; it is conducted just at dusk and always at the cross of roads.

"In attendance on the sick the physician must mutter mysterious prayers over the patient, his remedies forsooth being a thing by the way. Mr. Minor saw several men digging where a horse had been buried; they were filling up a recipe containing no less than seventy-four ingredients, of which horse's teeth were one. Rhinoceros horn is used as medicine and generally sold in bits. Wealthy people sometimes get cups turned out of this horn, and use them for drinking vessels with the idea of their being a panacea.

"From the arm of a goldsmith, down with fever, off and on for a year, I took a charm, a gold tube with which was a sheet of lead ruled off into forty-nine squares; in this diagram were written several muntras, and under them this prayer to Siva: "Devour the ill star Devathy now in the body of Kanthar Naganiana. Save, save him and and his life, Swami, (the idol,) I invoke thee, save, save." Together with this were put sacred ashes also. The Swami, is supposed to abide specially in this mystic seat,—which is tied above the elbow on the right arm,—and to chase away all intruding devils from the body. The family seemed trusting half in this and half in medicine for the man's recovery."

The more he discovered of this sort of heathenism, the more was he impressed with the importance of his department in the Mission, and the stronger was his desire to undermine the native system of treating diseases, and to deliver the suffering people from the deceptions and cruelties of their traditions and doctors.

He had no sooner gained a good command of the language than he felt a strong desire to provide a medical literature for the Tamils. He saw the necessity of medical science in the vernacular, in order to their deliverence from the barbarous notions and practices which had been the heritage of successive generations and ages. There were similar if not greater difficulties in putting science into their language than there had been in putting the gospel into it,—the lack of words to express the ideas which were new and strange. The Mission had already done much in the way of elementary religious literature, but a medical literature had yet to be created. When he saw that what was needful was also possible and practicable, he did not hesitate because of the greatness of the undertaking. He said: "Aim at something wisely chosen, and seek to accomplish it in a hearty, thorough manner; don't merely glorify God in a general manner, live to purpose."

Accordingly he was soon hard at work on this new enterprise. "I am about starting a vocabulary, defining the English and Latin terms in Tamil. Many words already exist in the language that are good medical terms. Many may be drawn from the Sanscrit through scholars in that language, and many must be coined by giving the sound of the already existing name in Tamil letters. I wish this work as the foundation, the beginning of medical literature in Tamil. I hope to write some small pamphlets on the more important branches of medical science, perhaps accompany them with the gospel, or some good religious advice, on the reverse of every leaf, and distribute them gratuitously among the people."

This vocabulary extended over all departments of medical science,—anatomy, physiology, chemistry, botany, etc.; but of course that which was needed first was prepared first. His method was to do everything according to the best reason for doing it so, instead of otherwise. He named "the bones, with their peculiarities, from the shape, position, use, or translation, choosing the most brief, descriptive and euphonious expressions." In a similar way he went through the several branches necessary for his purpose.

He had the ability to set his students to work in ways that would greatly assist him. He arranged with those who had graduated to take each some special branch, and do the best he could with it. By comparing his own work of putting English into Tamil with their work of expressing in Tamil what they had learned in English, he secured the best test possible of the correctness of his own composition and translation into their tongue. He was at the same time doing a very wise thing for them,—improving them in the knowledge and use of both languages, increasing their knowledge of medical science, initating them into literary work for the immediate and permanent benefit of their own people.

Under date of *February*, 6, 1851, he wrote:

MY DEAR SISTER MARY:

After having in broken Tamil spoken a little to the patients, I have left Danforth to preach to them further. We have a sermon for them every day, except Sunday, at nine o'clock, giving them a brief account of the way of salvation, and combatting their most common errors. My plan is to preach the gospel as opportunity offers, to make that the great thing. . . .

I have a good class of students coming on. I hope to have my doctors stationed through the country, well-read, practical men. I hope they will feel bound to do what they can to promote medical practice on true principles. I hope to rout the superstitious practice of the native doctors; or at least to begin that rout, in the belief that ere many generations it will be completed. I want in my day to give an impulse to change for the better in all things medical in the land; to be a reformer in my department here, to practise, to write, to teach, to encourage truth in medical men and things. The Lord prospers me much and I cannot but feel grateful to Him. . . .

Your brother,

SAMUEL F. GREEN.

Though distinguished for his urbanity, Dr. Green was faithful and fearless in the discharge of his duty, no matter with whom he had to deal. On the 18th of March he made the following entry in his journal, without explanation or comment, as if he had done nothing remarkable: "Rode in with Mr. A—— to see Dr. Cowen's child; rebuked him for profanity." This appears to be the case thus related by the Rev. Dr. H. M. Scudder in his letter to a sister of Dr. Green.

"I remember an incident which will illustrate his original way of doing things. He was driving, and his companion was a young officer in the English army. The officer interspersed his remarks with frequent oaths. Dr. Green apparently took no notice of this, but soon began to interlard his sentences with the exclamation, "Hammer and tongs!" "Hammer and tongs!" The officer was troubled. He probably thought he had a lunatic by his side, and deliberated how he should act. Finally he mildly asked why Dr. Green scattered these exclamations through his speech. Dr. Green gravely replied that he thought it quite as appropriate for him to fling these "Hammer and tongs!" into the midst of his remarks, as for the officer to use his oaths in a similar way. No offence was taken. I believe the officer begged his pardon, and I presume that he never, to the day of his death, forgot the rebuke."

Early in January Dr. Green had received permission from the Prudential Committee to visit America; but so long as he could work efficiently he was not disposed to avail himself of it. About the last of June, however, he felt the need of a change and obtained leave of the Mission to visit Madras for a few weeks or even three months if he liked. At Madras he received many courtesies from missionaries, physicians, hospitals, the Medical College, and other persons and institutions. He made the most of his time there, "in the way of seeing Indo-British medical practice." He also took lessons in drawing, and making casts in plaster. After ten or eleven weeks he was back in Jaffna, "benefited both mentally and physically," in spite of seventeen day's travel in a bullock cart. From the way he occupied his time one might suppose his vacation could not have afforded him much rest; but his notion of rest was not that of doing nothing, or that of sporting; it was rather that of a change of occupation and of scene, so as to escape from an exacting routine into work at will and pleasure.

It was now about a year since Mr. Dyke had suggested the willingness of the goverment to do something towards the support of the medical department of the Mission. But the measuring of red tape is proverbially a slow process. Hope deferred, however, was unexpectedly cheered. The "Rev. B. Bailey, the Bishop's chaplain and committee who comes from Colombo to examine schools in Jaffna,—supported by Government educational grants,—gives incidentally a most eulogistic account, in his Report, of the medical educational operations 'of the medical gentleman attached to the Mission;' speaks of one of my former students (Gould), now in connection with the Government Hospital, as posessing 'acquirements quite equal to those of the majority of the young men who enter the medical profession in England,' and recommends a grant." Mr. Dyke also sent a letter suggesting to Dr. Green the propriety of sending a petition to the Government for a grant in aid of the medical department. Accordingly such a petition was sent.

It was gratifying to Dr. Green, and the Mission, that, at the beginning of his fifth year, the Colonial Secretary announced to him an annual grant of fifty pounds sterling from the Government to his department, to take effect from the 1st of January, 1852. The Mission voted him the use of the native Helper's house for a hospital, which stood about a hundred yards from his house, and had four rooms besides veradahs and kitchens.

By arrangement with Mr. Spaulding, his assistant Dr. Danforth was transferred to Oodoville to take the place of Dr. J. Evarts who was withrawn to assist Dr. Green in translation and in the study of native medicine. After finishing the naming of the bones and all their parts, they proceeded to do the same with the ligaments, then the muscles, and so on till they had made a complete glossary for Anatomy. The work was difficult, but all the more interesting and profitable to him on that account, as it advanced him in the knowledge of the language. He was beginning this Tamil Medical Dictionary just as Mr. Spaulding was publishing his Tamil and English Dictionary—of nine hundred pages—of which fifteen hundred copies were printed.

The first work he selected for translation was the "Anatomy, Physiology and Hygiene" by Dr. Calvin Cutter, of Warren, Massachusetts. He did not propose to make a literal translation; but rather to make the book the guide and basis of an elementry treatise, "put as simply as possible into the native language." He wrote Dr. Cutter, asking if he would furnish him with the illustrations, as without them the natives would find it difficult if not impossible to understand the text. He also wrote the Secretary of the Board on the subject: "Some gifts of cuts illustrative of the structure and functions of the human body would be most acceptable and useful; with them we could print illustrated books and make pleasing and intelligible to all the large reading community what without them would be a difficult and dark science because so utterly novel here." Dr. Cutter responded promptly and generously, and in due time the cuts were forwarded; thus removing the only doubt that embarrassed the undertaking, which, said he, "will be a long and hard job, but a most interesting one, I anticipate, and one that in its results will amply repay the labor expended on it. I hope to see the time when European Medical Practice shall become indigenous here, and mostly if not quite displace the native system, with the decline of which much superstition will be removed from the burdened necks of the people. I cannot but hope that European Medicine is gaining ground among the Hindus. The Jaffna Dispensary registers about three thousand patients annually, the Mission Dispensary about twenty-five hundred; adding those attended by assistants at other stations the total would exceed six thousand."

The desire and perseverance of some of the

native boys for an education is well illustrated by the following incident, related on the 5th of October. "This morning I was touched almost to tears. A nice boy, about thirteen, has been travelling from his home in Katchai, five miles distant, to the Chavagacherry English School daily and back again for four years past. He has been very persevering. The night before the examination for admission to the Seminary he was at his books from sunset to sunrise. When the failure of his case was made known to him, the poor fellow sobbed as if his heart would break.

He and his father, a poor man and head of a large family, have been anxious and struggling for his education. Out of seventy there was room for only thirty."

In his report for October he gave an account of a census of readers among his patients. "For some time I have kept a column in the Dispensary Register to show the number of readers in the community, believing that, as the applicants for aid are of all classes and ages, the results would give a pretty fair average of the number of readers per cent in the country. Perhaps in the case of females the number is higher than the average, as many of such applicants are trained under mission auspices. We find in eight thousand applicants,

Men . . . . . 5779, Readers . . . 2455
Women . . . 1671, Readers 51
Children . . 550 under seven years of age.
Those children who could read are contained in the sum of adults." If these figures may be taken as an approxinate average, in the 422,000 inhabitants of the Province there were about 132,000 readers, of whom more than 2,600 were women. As in 1816 there was but one Tamil woman in the Province who could read, and as many who had learned to read in the course of the thirty-six years must have died, the number of female readers in 1852 was prophetic of a period, not far in the future, when the education of women would be as nearly universal in the Province as it is now in Christian countries.

CHAPTER VI.

1852–1854: ÆT. 30–32.

THESE five years of missionary service had brought Dr. Green to the thirtieth anniversary of his birth, and he rejoiced "that he was so much nearer his end, which is the beginning of a brighter state." He could now preach in Tamil with a feeling of "great ease in the performance," translating his written English into the vernacular as he spoke. Daily intercourse with so many patients and with his medical students, daily study of the language with determination to master it, and translation of medical literature into it, had given him facility of expression, and enabled him to speak with confidence in the correctness of the words he used.

There was very little change in his routine of duties in his general work from year to year. So fast as his students became able to assist him in the care of patients, he gained more time for his special literary enterprise, which was undertaken and prosecuted with special reference to undermining and overthrowing some of the worst superstitions of the people and most cruel practices of the doctors, and thus disposing them to look to the Christian religion and its teachers for light also in regard to their higher need.

It was his endeavor to keep as nearly as possible abreast with his profession; but at such distance from the centres and sources of medical and surgical improvement it was almost inevitable that he should sometimes be a little behind in the treatment of some disease or in the method of some operation. Though always chagrined at his own failures, he was ever ready to rejoice in the successes of others,—thankful that any one could succeed with a patient with whom his treatment had been in vain, and glad to learn from any sourcc how to avoid a repetition of a discovered mistake. He wrote to a sister:

"In looking at Bennett, which I received a few days ago, I see that that whole department of medicine has undergone a revolution since I left America. . . . . . I find it hard to bear successes, and feel that reverses—failures—do me more good. How kind of the Lord (I have sometimes thought) to benefit my soul at the expense of physical suffering to a patient."

A sentiment expressed at the ends of his twenty-seventh and thirtieth years now reappears in a stronger utterance. "I long for deliverance from this body of death and to be in the spirit and ever with the Lord. The dreams of many are enthusiasm. The enthusiasm of the Christian is no dream, but in reality it is founded on the Word. His brighest visions, his highest hopes are all certain of fulfilment." In one so young, so free from vain imaginings and dreamy speculations, so devoted to the temporal and spiritual welfare of the heathen, so wise and enthusiastic and indefatigable in his plans and efforts for their good, it seems singular that the "desire to depart and be with Christ" should have become a spiritual habit. The explanation is found, not in any inclination to discouragement in his work, not in any lack of faith in the ultimate triumph of the gospel in his field, not in any melancholy in his religious experience, but in his consciousness of spiritual things as the most vivid and profound realities, and in the brightness of his anticipations of his future state.

In June his work on *Anatomy, Physiology and Hygiene* was ready for the press. In this achievement he felt a twofold satisfaction. "In my six months' work on this I have hit two birds—put a good thing into the vernacular, and gained much in Tamil; for I have, from the interest of the the thing, applied myself more closely than I should, had I been working at the language merely—without any specific object in view." The book was three months in going through the press, requiring his close attention, not only in reading the proof-sheets, but also in superintending the preparation of the illustrations of the bones, arteries and nerves, by three cuts executed at the Manepy press. "I did not begin to imagine the difficulty of getting out a new and strange subject in a foreign tongue; but found the process, though toilsome, no less profitable." The plates were received from Dr. Cutter too late to be bound in the earlier portion of the first edition, but were inserted in the remainder, with explanations in Tamil. In about a week a quarter of the whole edition was nearly disposed of, and he was much gratified to learn that "the native doctors were reading it eagerly."

This year there were two classes in medicine, the Junior being taught to some extent by Dr. Evarts; and as the Dispensary was cared for considerably by the Seniors, Dr. Green was able to meet the demand for more practice at the homes of patients than had been necessary during any equal period since he came to the country. Consequently he suffered more from the exposure to the sun. "The direct rays seem much less to affect the head, than the reflected rays. The feeling caused by them goes through from the eyes to the back of the head. Before coming to the tropics I fancied it would be difficult to keep cool, but experience proves the reverse, and that more attention is required to keep warm. The breathing a rarefied atmosphere constantly robs one of his accustomed tonic, oxygen, the great sustainer of bodily temperature.

Among the diseases of the people, which are not a scourge like the cholera and the small pox, the Doctor found "the itch very prevalent and of a virulent kind, but no disgrace was ever supposed to accompany it.

"Cancer of the mouth is a very common disease here, arising from the habitual use of quick-lime with the Betel quid.

"In the dewy season there is much of fever and lung affections. Even the sheep die of pneumonia in that season, so very trying is the change from the hot days to the chilly nights. So poorly clad are the people that their liability to these troubles is greatly increased. Often of a dewy morning have I—from the cold regions of the North—gone by almost chilled in flannels, while little children of the tropics stood stark naked by the roadside.

"Fever-and-ague is very common in the eastern parts of the Province, and the miserable victims of its long continued attacks are very frequently seen—with enormous bellies, shrivelled members, bloodless tongues and eyelids. The spleen becomes really prodigiously enlarged, in many cases reaching over to the right side and nearly or quite down to the hip bone.

"Many of the wealthy die of diabetes, the effect of their vegetarianism, license and luxurious indolence combined. The corpulency some of them attain is wonderful.

"The force of action in the physical system of this people is very small. I have been surprised, on feeling the pulse, to find a man, under a recent severe injury, even in the stage of re-action, icy cold." . . .

Much of their illness may be ascribed to their diet, and their ignorance of the laws of health. Even "some of the respectable people here eat field rats as well as bats and lizards. It is curious to see an old man take basket after basket of water and pour it over a child's head; although the natives may wash the body daily, they take what they call a bath only once a week (some of them at least), and then they wash and oil the head. Although a Tamil gets sick by his weekly bath of fifty or a hundred baskets of water, yet he will not lessen the quantity."

Having discovered the prevalence of secret vice among the natives, Dr. Green prepared a tract upon the subject, published it, and put it at once into circulation. This tract was not only timely, but useful enough to repay abundantly the time and expense of providing it. He also began to write out a brief Natural Philosophy to be translated for the village schools, and expected "plenty of hard work in getting it into Tamil, as the commonest ideas here must be explained and introduced by circumlocution." This he relinquished on hearing that Mr. Sargent, of Southern India, had undertaken a similar work. From Tinnevelly, in Southern India, he received an order for a hundred and thirty-four copies of his book on *Anatomy, Physiology and Hygiene*, and for seven sets of Dr. Cutter's plates; a proof that his work had not been undertaken too soon, and an occasion of joy that this study was to be introduced there also.

Though loyal to medical science as learned and taught by him, he was hospitable to every improvement or help from whatever source, whether Homoeopathy, the Water Cure, or the experience of unscientific common sense. He examined every new method in surgery, and adopted it if it commended itself to his judgment. He had many cases of disease of the eye. Having "couched two congenital cataracts successfully" within a short time, he made this comment: "I may say with thankfulness that I have by dint of practice become quite *au fait* of such operations." Though he had practised other methods, yet thus far he seems to have preferred this; still he did not like it, because it seemed barbarous. He soon tried another method; performed his "first extraction of cataract on the living eye,"—of which he said, "This is perhaps the most delicate operation in surgery; completely successful; I scarce expected aught but failure, but the Great Physician guided my hand."

He was unwilling to leave his work till compelled by a prudent regard for his health. The climate was gradually showing its ill effects upon him, and he foresaw that at the expiration of ten years of service,—the term which, as shown by experience, usually makes a long furlongh expedient,—it would be necessary for him to seek invigoration in his native land. In writing to his brother Oliver he said, "Here's my hand to meet you (D. V.) in 1857, though if before that we could both join hands in the Better Land I should still more rejoice. My heart is full to transport when I think of it. 'We are bound to the land of Canaan,' and Jesus goes before and beckons us on." In May the Mission voted him leave of absence, that he might go to the Pulney Hills for rest and recuperation,—a favor of which he gladly availed himself from June till October. While away he learned from the following letter that his friend Dr. H. M. Scudder also had been obliged to give up work for a time.

[From Dr. Scudder.]

OOTACAMUND, *June* 26, 1854.

DEAR BROTHER:

Vegetable diet is good. So we have proved and approved here. I start off on this bit of experience in the hope that you will make honorable mention of me when you get out your treatise on this important subject.

Thanks for your letter 26th December and shame to me for allowing it to be unanswered so long. I have no news to tell you but that I have got Emphysema and am here for strength. I had bronchitis with it on the plains, and so persistently that I could scarce preach for some time. Since I came here have had none. . . .

I want to revise my medical studies here, but can get but little time. It is a whirl of a place and I am tired of it. Too many people. In the woods, and on the peaks, and by the streams, and in the ferns, and in the ravines it is very fine; salutary to body and spirit also if the mind can rise above the mountain tops. . . .

I am quite worn out with watching over a German missionary . . . He is yet dangerously ill, but I have now a little hope for him. . . .

Thanks for your accounts of cases, hints, and

so forth. Please write me everything valuable, as I am delighted to learn. . . .

If my chirography is as bad and as difficult to decipher as yours, I beg you to reprove me. Love to all, even to your future wife if there be such a person.

Affectionately,

H. M. SCUDDER.

"The Hundu religion," wrote Dr. Green, "is interwoven in all the social system. Not a house must be built but the astrologer must predict the favorable day for commencing; and for a long time will a frame stand unthatched till a propitious time shall arrive for tying on the first leaf; it may then be finished at leisure.

"The custom of putting two ear-rings in each ear, when the people are able, must be observed on an auspicious day, and one part of the ceremony is to break a cocoanut to Puliar.

"In Batticotta the women will, and the men will not, kill the centipede; for once, as a woman tried to poison her husband by mixing poison in his soup, a centipede, falling into it from the roof, prevented his eating it and thus saved the man's life.

"I observed that all the patients in the bungalow headed in our direction—towards the Puliar temple. None would presume to point their feet thither. One boy, who had been educated in one of the Mission schools, disregarded the position and lay sidewise to the temple.

"The flesh of sheep and goats these people do not think of eating; nor do they kill their calves, because they firmly believe no milk can be obtained unless the calf does part of the milking.

"A barber in Araly goes to the temple, becomes siezed of the god and executes his vengeance by beating the low caste people with a rattan; this is a sign of the god's displeasure, and the people run to offer sacrifices and get rain. A man sings and prays for three days in the temple, and, if in that time rain does not come, threatens to cut off his head. For two or three nights at sunset the people drag about the 'great sinner,'—an effigy of the one who so offends Indra that he will not give rain,—and in the darkness burn it in some wilderness.

"Mootayvi is the personification of darkness, and her presence brings misfortune; and Eluchvome, her younger sister, is the personification of light, and her presence brings prosperity. If a child blows out a lamp by his mouth he is reproved for want of respect to Eluchvome; the child is taught to fan out the flame by waving his hand. The people are particular to light the lamp early in the evening, so that Eluchvome may enter; if the house be dark, Mootayvi will enter.

"When a person is dying his friends send immediately for the Brahmin, who comes running to the house with sacred grass in his hand, sprinkles with water a place on the ground beside the sick, spreads out his handkerchief and sits down upon it, calls for divers articles needed in the ceremonies; several Brahmins stand around and respond to the muntras as he repeats them. Just at the last gasp the tail of a cow, previously brought and backed up near the sick man, is put momentarily in his hand and held by some one; then the cow becomes the property of the Brahmin. The belief is, that, if the man at the last moment gives the Brahmin a cow, the Brahmin will cause the cow-goddess in the other world to come and convey the soul safe over the fiery river; and this faith seems implicit, even among educated, polished people.

"As we approached a place where dead bodies are buried we saw the ashes of a body, and the son of the deceased, with a Brahmin and another man, standing beside them. A brass pot containing money was at the head of the pile of ashes, enwrapped in a new shoulder cloth; upon it a green cocoanut, fringed below with a circle of mango leaves. This represented Puliar, or Genesa. In front of this were spread little cakes, bran of rice, rice flour, and soft boiled rice in little heaps on a large plantain leaf. Two wicks, made of rag rolled up and dipped in oil, were burning, each on a heap of the soft rice,—I understand, to to satisfy the devils. Most of the remains they were burying; but a handful the Brahmin put in a pot, to carry to the sea shore and throw into the water—in order that the ashes may float into the Ganges. The people think that if the child does not go through all these ceremonies the parent will not reach heaven.

"One does not see all that is bad in heathenism, for the people are haters of the light and carry on their orgies in the darkness. As I was returning from a prayer meeting in the pitch dark of a rainy night I saw five or six men, with bushel baskets of firewood on their heads, and a new pot, seized by the brim, in their hands, on their way to the temple to boil rice to the idol. If it foams up nicely when it begins to boil, the deity is propitious.

"What can be viler than their revered sacred books! A person could not translate faithfully Koo-rul into English without sentencing himself to perpetual infamy. When Siva is worshipped, the Dancing Girls stand by the idol, so that the first glance of the Divinity, as he comes to receive his honors, may be one of pleasure. Here you see the worst form of social corruption enshrined in the very Sanctum of the community.

"Oleanders in full flower—pink, red and white—are daily stripped of their fragrance and beauty for the temples, where they are hung upon the senseless idols.—To talk down idol worship does not require much acumen; but though one succeed in rebutting everything said in its favor, the work is not done. Behind or above the popular forms lies a network of metaphysics, fine-spun and ingenious. The most ignorant know nothing of it save that it exists, and they consider its depths of wisdom as immense. In this lies the hold of heathenism on the masses; on the enlightened its chains are worldly interest, honor, power, wealth, and peace with their relatives. The position of the Brahmins here is very much like that of him who stirred up the people to cry, 'Great is Diana.' When heathenism sinks, they will sink with it—from deities to men.

"What then do we see in India but a huge Banyan with a trunk of enormous girth, and with ten thousand branches reaching out in every direction, each with its several rooted adjuvant trunks supporting it? And this tree to fell, a few puny white boys, with plaything hatchets, are commissioned. Wait we must a century for its fall, and longer too, unless that mighty Spirit appear and make by his own divine power a short work of it in rightiousness."

The Hindu religion is perhaps unsurpassed in the absurdities of its ceremonies, in the vileness of its orgies, in the number and extent of its ramifications, in its power to blind the mind and defile the conscience, in the tenacity of its hold upon successive generations. In times of danger, especially in alarming sickness, it is often difficult for a converted Hindu to resist the temptation to go back to his heathenism; indeed it is a great triumph of his faith to trust in the Lord instead of yielding to the impulse to follow the example of his ancestors and of his friends in trusting to something which can be seen and handled,—something by which salvation is supposed to be secured as a purchase, or as a reward of merit.

Probably no missionary ever lived among the heathen long enough to discover even the greater part of their abominations; much is visible, and more is inferred from circumstances. Enough, however, is open and common to enable one in a short time to see that their condition has never been painted in too dark colors. The more it is observed and studied, the more is the need of the gospel remedy emphasized.

CHAPTER VII.

1854–1855: ÆT. 32–33.

ABOUT to enter on his eighth year of service, Dr. Green selected a Class of six medical students. He met them at noon, having prayer with them before recitation; this hour being chosen for a season on account of the unusual number of calls for his professional services at the homes of patients, for the cholera was prevailing and many needed help who could not visit him. The scourge had caused the harvest to be neglected and provisions were scarce. Pestilence and famine, however, had no more effect than health and abundance in inclining the hearts of the people towards the true source of relief. They were too blind and weak to doubt their traditions and abandon their prejudices, though they found no advantage in following them. While he prayed that these calamities might be overruled for their spiritual good, his reliance was the interposition of the Holy Spirit. "Before the rains," said he, "one might almost say there are no frogs, but no sooner fall the heavy showers than their croaking din fills the air; so when the favored time shall come it may prove that in this community now lie latent the 'seven thousand who have not bowed the knee to Baal.'"

"The people are exceedingly frightened at the cholera," he wrote, "and leave their friends to die uncared for often, themselves taking benefit of *leg bail.*" When it is prevalent, or seems likely to be prevalent, they "put margosa oil on their heads instead of sesamum oil, as the smell of it will drive off devils and prevent cholera. They firmly believe the cholera to be the sport of Ammarl, wife of Siva; they fear to offend her by resisting her will through the use of any remedy. The people at Caradive loaded a raft with boiled rice and fruits, and by enchantments got the cholera devil to board it, and then had it towed off into the mid sea, and left it to be driven to some shore or other. They think the cholera was formerly confined to the adjacent continent, but in this way it has reached this, and now they hope thus to get rid of it."

The 26th of December was observed by all the Missions in the Province as a day of fasting, humiliation, and prayer for the removal of the pestilence, and for a spiritual blessing upon the people. While five persons were recovering in a convert's house two remained very low, one of the latter being a "neighbor's wife deserted and imposed upon his already overburdened hands in this distress." In the Jaffna District alone eight thousand cases of cholera and twenty-five hundred of small pox were reported for the year. On the 9th of January, 1855, there were at the Small Pox Hospital a hundred and seventeen cases, "in all stages of the disorder, a horrid sight."

Dr. Green revised his Ticket on Cholera, and his Tract on Secret Vice; and sent a Tract on Cholera to a special committee. He directed the physicians at Manepy, Oodooville, and Tillipally in the use of the Castor Oil treatment. In every direction his helping hand was stretched out, as if the greater was the emergency the greater was his ability to meet it. The spirit in which he worked appears in his lamentation over a single neglect—probably under the temptation of pressure—to ask for divine assistance: "Undertook an operation, thought it slight, too trifling to pray over (mentally); failed in it; a lesson to show me that without Him I can do nothing."

Thus far the members of the Mission had been preserved; but on the 2d of February the Rev. Daniel Poor was attacked with cholera and gradually sank, dying at an early hour on the 3d in the triumph of that faith which he had so long preached. On the 8th Dr. Green discovered in himself a symptom "not safe in these cholera times," though it was not till the 12th that he was violently prostrated. The news quickly spread, causing intense anxiety for the result. The brethren of the Mission watched over him and cared for him with untiring devotion. Mr. Burnell kept a journal for Mr. Minor—then in the United States—noting the hour and minute of every report, and expressing distress which found relief only in acquiescence in the will of the chastening Father. "He is a useful man and is much needed, and, as you know, is very loving and lovable." On the morning of the 14th the crisis seemed to be past and all hoped he would recover. "Praise God," said he, "for this new token of His loving kindness."

Mrs. Smith wrote that same morning, "I wish I could in some appropriate way express my gratitude to God for his great mercy in hearing the prayers of your brethren and sisters, and sparing your life. Notwithstanding your great 'desire to depart and be with Christ, which indeed is far better,' for us it seemeth more needful that you abide here for a season." Invitations came for him to visit the families of the Mission and leisurely enjoy their glad hospitality. On the 17th he was able to sit up a short time, and gained daily afterwards. At the critical time he had taken, as he afterwards expressed it, "medicine enough for a horse." On the 21st he sent out the following message

TO THE MISSION.

TO ALL THE BRETHREN,—*Salaam.*

BROTHERS AND SISTERS:

For all your kindness and sympathy, your prayers and divers kindly offices, allow me most unfeignedly to thank you. "I was brought low and He helped me." May the resuscitation He has vouchsafed be a sort of resurrection to newness of life, even though on this side the river. These chastisements, though for the present not joyous but grievous, nevertheless yield indeed the peaceable fruit of righteousness to them that are exercised thereby. I should indeed be sorry to exchange the experiences of the past week for the same period of unintermitted health, though they have been bought at the expense of a good deal of trouble to others, for which, however, the Lord will duly reward them. May the Lord in mercy shine upon us and our people, and cause our hearts to rejoice in seeing the sickness temporal end in the health spiritual of this community. "Promised Spirit, grant us soon thy gracious aid."

Truly,

SAMUEL F. GREEN.

From the time of the earliest symptom, he seems to have had some apprehension of a possibly fatal termination. Though he thought that by rest and dieting he might soon be at work again, yet he took the precaution to look over his will, and to make an estimate of the property in the Dispensary, so as to have all his affairs in the best shape for his friends and the Mission in the event of his death. When his case began to look more serious, he seems to have taken no vigorous measure until two of his brethren became slightly alarmed and earnestly besought him to take powerful medicine at once. His own account to his home friends of his experience, after some details concerning the treatment, is as follows.

BATTICOTA, *Feb.* 21, 1855.

MY DEAR FRIENDS:

. . . That night and the next day I was in a wavering balance between the grave and the house. On Wednesday, the 14th, it seemed evident I should recover. The story had run all over that I was dead. I had a real longing to die,—ever since Brother Poor's departure it had been very strong,—I knew to go "was far better." However, my mind now is that so long as one *can* live (by aid of medicine if need be) he should live, and that it is wrong to die before.

Brother Lord came away over twenty miles to help me. Brother Burnell came and staid with me two days. Brother Smith watched over me at night. Brother Spaulding came over twice to stay with me; nice old gentleman, so soothing in his ways; it did me good to sleep, feeling he was along side in his chair. Brother and Sister Hastings are my next neighbors and so kind. I cannot express to you how deeply I feel the tenderness and fraternity with which E. P. Hastings did everything for me; dainty bits, fresh boquets; watching over me like an own brother, making servants keep things nice; with his own hands arranging this and that, washing me, rubbing me, changing bed, etc., etc. You know I always have had a special love and esteem for him, but if possible I love him more than ever. I have not at all felt the absence of own brothers and sisters. The whole circle have been so kind and sympathizing. All have been praying for me, and this is best of all.

Our best Friend was there too. He sat beside me and whispered, "I am with thee." O blessed Jesus, I wish to love thee more than ever. He took me down to Jordan, dipped my feet in "the swelling flood." He has brought me up again. Blessed, ever blessed be his most blessed name. I cannot speak of the past week as one of affliction, but as one of the choicest blessings of my life, a sweet precious season never to be forgotten I hope, a foretaste of the time when I may cross over the stream and be for ever with the Blessed One.

I am still quite weak, I cannot write much, and if I become interested in thinking upon any subject it occupies my mind too closely. I am at the Hastings' now during the daytime—for a little while, sleeping at home at night by preference. If you could only see how they have, with all the ingenuity of kindness, fitted up the room for me to stay in, it would just give you a glance of their most thorough and unremitting kindness to me all through. I wish I could think of some really nice valuable present to ask you to get for them and send with a note expressive of a sense of gratitude; but they are so recently from America, and have been so loaded by friends with nice things, that there seems nothing to suggest.

I think, when a little stronger, of going the round of the stations and spending a day or two with each by way of recreation. Pray excuse this scrawl. It is the best I can do just now. I would like to say much. You may well conceive my heart is full. Besides the kindness of all the circle, that of Gould and Evarts [both Tamils] and students and the good Murrays and of Mr. Davidson etc., etc., deserve mention. "My cup runneth over." "Truly, goodness and mercy follow me all the days of my life."

With much love,

Yours,

SAMUEL F. GREEN.

Some token of his gratitude and love called forth the following unique acknowledgment:

DEAR DOCTOR:

What shall I answer? I was always afraid of gifts because they are *too acceptable* and because "the gift blindeth the wise" and "destroyeth the heart." Now you know I am naturally near-sighted or rather short-sighted and need no more blindness, and as for the heart it was poor enough before. How, as a professional man, you could make up your mind to take advantage of my infirmities, even for once, is beyond my credit; and then that you should repeat the dose when one was more than enough can certainly be accounted for only by an extensive acquaintance with the profession, which I have not. So not being able to solve the mystery I may be allowed to drop it, but not without many and grateful thanks for your very beautiful and valuable present, and a sincere wish that you may always enjoy the sunny side of your work and of the world as I do that of the Doctor.

I suppose it may be in vain for these grey hairs to sigh for the youth which would make such a present practically useful, but this does not make the article less valuable, nor my feelings of gratitude less sincere.—More than ever

Yours truly,

L. SPAULDING.

OODOOVILLE, *April* 7, 1855.

NELLORE, INDIA, *May* 2, 1855.

MY DEAR DR. GREEN:

Thank you for your letter of February 7th. I hear you have had the cholera severely. You should rejoice in recovery, for there is much to be done in the great field. . . .

Did you know dear Leitch? one of the finest men who ever trod missionary shoe-leather or any other. He is gone. He departed some months ago. . . .

We have four children, not six. We should be very happy to have you come and see us. If I confess to a fancy in your favor, I hope I shall not shock your modesty.

The weather is intensely hot now. A man never knows that he has so many pores till such a fiery stratum of weather as the present sets innumerable rills in motion.

Our dear father is gone. We were daily looking for him, and then came the tidings that we should see him no more in the flesh. The older and better ones are fast going. It becomes us to gird our loins and to pray for the mantle of some holier one whose departing chariot we discern in the clouds over head.

My health is not very good, but much better than it was. . . . — Your affectionate brother,

HENRY M. SCUDDER.

Secretary Anderson and the Rev. A. C. Thompson were deputed by the American Board to visit the Missions in India and determine what changes, if any, should be made in the methods of carrying on the work. They arrived in Ceylon in April, and took time enough for a thorough discharge of their duties, following the method which they had carefully considered and determined upon beforehand, and discussing every branch of the work with the brethren of the Mission. It is not necessary here to speak of any changes but those affecting the medical department. In teaching the medical students, English was to be excluded so far and so soon as practicable,—greatly to Dr. Green's satisfaction. The grant by the Colonial Government might be retained, as the physician was not strictly a missionary and might be allowed to act the philanthropist—using funds not derived from the Board. He might prepare medical text books in Tamil, printing them with funds derived from the local government, from philanthropic physicians in America, and from any other legitimate source. Dr. Green had early discovered that the natives desired to be taught English in order to be eligible to lucrative positions under the Government; and that the only way to get them to settle down as physicians in the villages of their own people would be to educate them in the vernacular alone, at least, so far as possible; and as English was to be excluded from the Seminaries at Batticotta and Oodooville, he was greatly encouraged.

Left so largely to his own devices for raising funds, his first effort was to make his own department productive. The problem perhaps was not altogether new, and under the impulse of necessity at once took on this practical solution: He wrote:

"I am anticipating before long to make an effort to put the Dispensary on a paying basis, getting people to pay for their medicines first, and eventually for the physician's skill and trouble and surgical operations. I think of putting Reid and McIntyre into partnership, and letting them get out of the profits of the Surgery and Dispensary their salaries without any expense to the Mission; let them alternate weekly between the Surgery and Dispensary. After three years or so I hope to set off one in his own village, and associate one of the young students with the other; and then, after a while, set off this second one in his village, and bring in another young student into partnership; and thus two juniors together will carry on the business and hand it down to their successors.

"I intend to send all applicants from the regions

of these set-off practitioners to the one in their neighborhood, with prescriptions and notes of advice, and let the patients put themselves under the doctors' care. So step by step I hope to get true scientific medicine really planted in the land which being done I have no fear as to the result; but confidently expect it to displace or greatly modify the now prevailing practice.—So much for the plan, which may be more or less varied by experience and circumstances."

"My boys," he added, "are quite unsettled by the change from English to the vernacular, thinking their prospects of getting a salary from government less promising, as indeed they are, as the aim is henceforth to get doctors to settle down and live in their villages. I gave the Class a vacation of ten days to settle whether they will proceed with their studies or go to some other occupation."

Before the Deputation left, they had the satisfaction of assisting in the organization of the first native church, and in ordaining and installing the first native pastor,—the fruits of the American Ceylon Mission, in Caradive. In his account of the services, Dr. Green said, "The singing was in the Western style, much to my distaste; I wish to have a *beginning* of this kind in the national way." He had been gratified that, in an informal discussion of the question of foreign or domestic music in worship, the Deputation had favored the introduction and cultivation of the domestic. This native pastor, Cornelius, had once been a devoted Hindu.

In reply to his sister Julia's appeal that he should come home to recuperate he wrote: "I have spent too much time in getting the language, and in getting here, to run home before having really accomplished something. If I can leave behind a series of medical text-books in the vernacular I shall feel as if something permanent has been done. If I can stay out my ten years, I would prefer to do so." His reply to another sister is of like tenor.

BATTICOTTA, *July* 16, 1855.

MY DEAR SISTER MARY:

. . . . In regard to my return to America, I have thought to wait awhile, and, working as easily as I can, see how my strength rises; and, if I gradually improve, to complete my ten year's career here, and then close up all my affairs completely, so as to be able to stay thereafter in America or return to Ceylon as expediency shall dictate. Should I ever return to Ceylon I should probably need two years in America to prepare me for another ten years in this climate. . . . I have my suspicions that my conscience will never leave me easy in such a decision, for if there was a call to the work in the first place, there may be quite as much of a call to resume the work, seeing I am in some respects better fitted for it, having pretty free use of the language, a knowledge of the customs and habits of the people, of their constitution and diseases; and of their medical system, I am just beginning to get a hold so as to grapple with it, and do my best to improve in it what is good, and to combat what is decidedly bad. . . . .

Your affectionate brother,

SAMUEL F. GREEN.

The old constable of Manepy having died, Dr. Green in great sadness made the following comment: "He was years ago, I believe, a subject of the strivings of the Spirit, but has gone trusting in ashes and the grip of a cow's tail. Of course, such a trust seems ridiculous; but is it not as good and sure as the trust in one's own morality?"

A brief extract from a letter to a Corporate Member of the American Board shows how he regarded the changes effected by the Deputation:

"Our mode of operation is very much changed, but as I try it in the lock of the gospel now the key seems to fit precisely, and to turn the work smoothly as possible. We now have the sling and smooth pebbles, and when the time comes the Spirit will direct the missile, sinking it deep in the forehead of the enemy. However, I fear there is a long pull before us yet ere the Hindus convert, and sometimes fear that the way of the Lord in these parts is to be prepared by their destruction."

The Doctor's plan to make his department productive of funds was gradually put in operation. He first tried the experiment of making charges for medicines, and was glad to find it successful without much diminution of the number of applicants. Then McIntyre and Reid began their co-partnership in the Dispensary, selling their medicines and making charges for professional services. They were members of his Senior Class, and conducted the business under his directions. Implements and utensils were supplied to them on loan, and the advance on American costs for medicines was charged to them to cover expenses and risks.

As yet the students had but one text-book in the vernacular—the work on *Anatomy, Physiology and Hygiene.* Besides receiving their oral instruction in Tamil, they used their own language in taking notes of their reading in English. *A Dictionary of Tamil Medical Science*, and a work on *Medical Synonyms, English and Tamil*, were in process of preparation. The required exclusion of English, so far as possible, in teaching, made it necessary to push forward the work of preparing a full series of text-books in the vernacular. Accordingly Dr. Green wrote the Secretary of the Board that "for the execution of this work it is desirable that the Prudential Committee allow the expense of a munshi, and make a specific grant for that purpose."

CHAPTER VIII.

1855–1857: ÆT. 33–35.

BEFORE the middle of December the translation of the *Dublin Practice of Midwifery* was finished, having occupied four months, as Dr. Green had calculated when he began the work in August; and the first review and revision of it, together with the preparation of a glossary, were begun. This was at once a great help in teaching, and the use of it in this way was a help also in testing and revising it. His published book as will be seen from the following letters became the occasion of extending his usefulness in a way entirely unexpected.

I.

FROM MR. MURDOCK.*

MADRAS, *Dec.* 19, 1855.

MY DEAR SIR:

In Ceylon I was informed that you had prepared a work on Anatomy and Physiology.

*See Chapter XIV.

It occurred to me that perhaps you would kindly aid the School Book Society, with which I am connected, in the preparation of a few lessons on Physiology and Health. We are publishing a series of books for elementary schools, and deem it very important that some information should be given on such subjects. Of course the descriptions of the organs would do for any country, but the sanitary hints must be adapted to the habits of the people. The coolies in the Central Province, I know, from laziness eat raw rice; the practice is also very general to eat cold rice in the morning, in which the process of fermentation has commenced.* Then about bathing, and many other points, they require advice. . . .

It is proposed to print the regular series first in English, and afterwards in as many of the vernacular languages of India as we can manage.

There should be illustrative cuts. . . .I should feel much obliged by your informing me that you

*"In Ceylon," Dr. Green said, "The natives generally prefer cold food. The women cook about 5 P. M., when the family drink the rice water that is poured off. The rice and the curries are set by till 8 P. M. to be eaten cold as the principal meal of the day. The overplus of this cold rice is mixed, in plenty of cold water, with onions, etc., and set by till morning. At 6 A. M. this 'old rice' is eaten cold (and usually sour like swill). About noon the poor take a souplike gruel of palmyra root flour mixed in with a great variety of vegetables. The rich boil their noon rice about 10 A. M., drink the rice water, and take the rice cold at noon with cold curries. Those who can afford it eat fruit freely, sometimes a dozen mangoes at once. These are delicious and in great variety."

will kindly undertake the task.—Believe me,
Yours most sincerely,

JOHN MURDOCK.

COR. SEC'Y.

DR. S. F. GREEN.

II.

FROM MR. MURDOCK.

MADRAS, *Jan* 8, 1856.

The receipt of your kind favor of the 28th ult. afforded me much pleasure. You have undertaken a very important department in our proposed series of School Books, and I hope the good which will result may repay you in some small degree for the labor it will cost you.

I beg you will have the goodness to let me have the lessons *first* in English. We propose to print about two hundred copies of the series of Books in that language to be circulated in India and Ceylon among friends for criticism. The Third and Fourth Books will probably be printed in Tamil before the publication of the large English edition. We have on hand sufficient funds to print five thousand copies of each. If you can kindly let me have the lessons for the Third Book in April, and then the Fourth and Fifth Books a month or two afterwards it will do. Please to send the manuscript to Kandy.

I am happy to learn that you expect to get out

a large edition of your work on Physiology. The wood-cuts are lying in Mr. Hunts' office. The treatise on Midwifery is calculated to be very useful Dr. Elliott, of Colombo, published a tract on the subject; which gave me some idea of the barbarous customs of the people. They appear to be very general. I was reading lately a tract written by Mrs. Mullens in Bengal, in which she refers to them there; and in Burmah, I believe, it is still worse. . . .—Your obliged friend,

JOHN MURDOCK.

From the beginning Dr. Green had been occasionally called to attend professionally in the families of European residents, who made him valuable presents in money and other things, amounting in the course of a year, sometimes, to more than one hundred or even two hundred dollars, which according to the rule he turned over to the Mission; but since the change made by the Deputation, whereby he was to carry on his literary enterprise with funds not derived from the Board, of course he ceased to be held to that rule, and used all his professional perquisites in his own work. As an instance of their readiness to reward him, three Planters, whom he examined for Life Assurance, each gave him a guinea.

On the retirement of the missionary from Panditeripo in the summer, that station was put under Doctor Green's care, and he visited it weekly, though in his state of health he felt the burden. There seemed to be no other way to supply the vacancy. In September he noticed a symptom of pectoral weakness, if not of disease.

It was now more than a year since the Dispensary was re-organized on the plan of self-support; and during the last "six months, ten hundred and thirty-two patients had been registered—about as many as the average when all was *gratis*."

During this year his literary work was vigorously prosecuted. With the aid of his munshi, and of the Rev. Mr. Webb, of the Madura Mission, who spent a few weeks in Ceylon for rest and recuperation, he completed vocabularies for Chemistry and Natural Philosophy, besides doing much in the development of a rule by which to determine the terms required in bringing the Western sciences into Tamil. The work already published was carefully revised and improved, and an application was made to the government for aid in publishing the improved edition, which, through the kindness of Dr. Cutter, and the cooperation of the Treasurer of the Board, was to be illustrated by many cuts. The work on Obstetrics also had been twice revised and compared with the English, and at the close of the year was in process of a third revision and comparison.

Through the kindness of Dr. Stephen Tracy this work also was to be well illustrated. Much as he desired to hasten the preparation of the next text-book contemplated in the series, it is evident that he wished to have every one as correct as possible at the time of publication.

Caste is one of the great evils in the way of progress in India. It is a system of classification according to profession or occupation, and is hereditary, so that every Hindoo is born into the rank of his parents. The chief divisions are the Brahmin or Priestly, the Military, the Commercial, and the Agricultural; but these admit of subdivisions, so that there are many distinctions. The bane of it is that a higher caste cannot associate, in certain ways, with a lower without being polluted and scandalizing his own class. Dr. Green advised an assistant to seek a certain girl in marriage, who was in the Oodooville School, and whose parents were Christians; the young man objected only to her caste,—as her mother belonged to the Oil-seller caste,—but said he would not mind that, if it would not affect the disposal of his sisters in marriage. In pleasing himself he must not compromise his sisters, who, it seems, would be subject to reproach on his account.

"Caste," wrote Dr. Green, "is worth more than education or property to a Hindu, and a man, in caste would esteem its loss next to the loss of life. It is essentially a part of heathenism; it is, in its bearings, directly opposed to the spirit of the gospel. It will be considered to exist in its integrity in every individual once connected with it, who does not, by some act repugnant to the laws of caste, cut himself off from it. Professing Christians born caste men, if they would show themselves real, thorough Christians, should voluntarily and repeatedly preform that act, or those acts, which will satisfy the heathen that they decidedly reject caste as being incompatible with the teachings of the Bible. The holding of caste by church members is one of the greatest, if not absolutely the greatest, external obstacle to the progress of Christianity in India.

"We had two well-educated native preachers, Niles, who is still with us, and Martyn; the former of the Farmer caste, the latter of the Fisher caste. Niles was married, and Martyn went to his wedding, and ate; afterwards Martyn was married; Niles attended his wedding in the church, but would not go to his house and eat with him and his friends, because, though himself friendly with Martyn and long his fellow-laborer, he could not be induced to implicate his own class in associating with those of lower caste. There is no doubt as to Niles' Christian duty to a brother;

but that brother might turn upon him and say: 'Now you have eaten with me and mine and we are equal; you think yourself a great fellow, but there is no difference between us.' All his friends would, likely, throw the same in his teeth.

"Caste seems to stand like a great mountain in the path of progress; human strength can never remove it; perhaps by a long series of measures, well devised and steadily pursued and blessed of God, we may tunnel it; but, oh, that the Lord would come down, that it might flow down at His presence and become a plain."

While the Deputation were there, and they were about to ordain and install the first native pastor over a church, the Mission voted to adopt into the church covenant an article renouncing caste. "The natives consulted, and signed the 'declaration of independence'—renouncing caste *in toto*, and consenting to eat food no matter by whom prepared or offered." Within a month there were ninty-eight signatures to the anti-caste pledge.

Notwithstanding the change made the year before, this year the Medical Class numbered eight, of whom six recieved "a monthly stipend from the Government, and one from the Chundi-culy church." Lest they should too much regard themselves as pensioners, and also to give them variety of useful employment, the Doctor set them to work for the Mission. "Four spend three hours daily in the afternoon in the villages, mapping the lanes, tanks, temples and houses; reading to and talking with some of the inhabitants. These maps of the several villages, together with a general one of the whole parish, may aid in the more systematic visiting of the villages, and be a key to the doings and reports of the catechists. One of the seven acts as an accountant, one as a secular agent, and one as a writer." His influence over his students was such that whatever he wished them to do appeared to them to be not only wise but for their own improvement. He won their confidence so completely that they continued afterwards to consult him as a friend who could be trusted implicitly.

Progress in material things appears to be an inevitable result, everywhere, of preaching the gospel to the heathen. Early in his tenth year of service Dr. Green noted the fact that a man came to buy tin, of which to make labels for five hundred bandies; whereas forty years before, there was but one such carriage in the Province, or perhaps on the Island.

Two members of his Medical Class were now manifesting "interest about their own salvation—the only two yet unconnected with the visible church."

Of three persons to be received into fellowship with the church one was forcibly detained by his relatives. The Doctor went to see him, to learn his wishes, and give him such comfort as he could; but he found a great and excited crowd, and the young man's older brother sprang upon him and took his hat, when others surrounded and restrained the fellow. Their awe of him, their confidence in him, and the remembrance of what he had done professionally for them or their friends, doubtless combined to check their violence. In answer to his questions, though thus surrounded and beset, the young convert from heathenism "witnessed a good confession before them all," and within a few weeks was received into the church, seeming "determined to risk anything and everything for Christ." Then those hostile to his reformation "talked of preforming obsequies" for him and another young man who had thus become dead to them. Yet when, not long afterwards, the Doctor "went out to talk with people at their houses they were almost invariably civil," and heard him quietly and respectfully.

In December Dr. Green received an answer from the Government, declining the request he had made in September for aid in publishing an improved edition of his *Anatomy, Physiology and Hygiene*, because "the non-English policy pursued by the Mission was. in the Governor's view, disastrous and suicidal." The trouble with the policy was that it would diminish the supply of native doctors for positions the Government had to fill, by fitting them to practice in their own villages where only the vernacular was used. He was not much disappointed, however, for the poilcy and its effect were just what he desired; and, having foreseen the negative answer in the long delay, he had made arrangements to have the book brought out at Madras by Mr Hunt, the "prince of Tamil printers,"—the Southern India Christian School Book Society taking three thousand copies, and the American Ceylon Mission taking one thousand copies, thus making it inexpensive by the largeness of the edition. In January, 1857, the Corresponding Secretary at Madras announced to the public that the book would be issued by the month of August.

Meantime the work on Obstetrics was put to press in Manepy. As an indication of the value of his rule for putting the terms of Western Science into Tamil, it may be mentioned that the Doctor learned from Mr. Webb that "the Native Society in Madras had adopted to a good extent that relating to Philosophical terms, and printed it in their Annual Report *without acknowledgment.*" Mr. Murdock wrote, "I should like to consult you on some points before printing the Reading Book for Female Schools, as well as about the rendering of scientific terms. I am glad that you have devoted so much time to this subject. Its importance will be more and more felt every year."

It was Doctor Green's desire and aim to be faithful spiritually to all with whom he came in contact, whether high or low in the social scale, so far as a wise regard to circumstances would allow, though he sometimes felt a shrinking that had to be overcome with prayer and self-denial. Thus in visiting professionally "those of high position" he said he "had to pray for grace to be faithful to their souls, and the grace, according to the promise, has been given I think."

While his books were in the hands of the printers, he found the reading and correcting the proof-sheets hard work. In July the volume on Obstetrics was issued, and specimen copies sent to various persons with a view to getting it into the hands of the native doctors at the earliest moment possible, his concern being, not for pecuniary profits, but for the immediate usefulness of the book.

On the completion of these books he began to turn his attention to the proper closing up of his affairs in preparation for his return to the United States. The regret felt at his necessary departure for a season extended beyond his own Mission, and also beyond the native population upon whom he had obtained a strong hold. Something of the estimation in which he was held by European residents may be seen from the following letters—one from a civil magistrate and the other from a clergyman of the Church of England—which certainly need not have been written but for the promptings of sincere friendship and esteem.

I

FROM JUDGE MURRAY, A SCOTCH GENTLEMAN, DISTRICT JUDGE OF JAFFNA.

JAFFNA, *Sept.* 18, 1857.

MY DEAR DR. GREEN:

We shall lose, and all will miss, an excellent member of society on your departure from our shores. May an All-wise Providence conduct you safely to Fatherland; and, on the establishment there of lost health, restore you again to this dark and needy portion of the Vineyard where active, practical benevolence, such as yours, is so urgently needed.

We hope to see you before leaving. Meanwhile I may mention Mrs. Murrays wish that you should kindly accept some parting token of our regard. She writes to Mrs Hobarts, Madras (through which I believe you pass), to procure a Scotch plaid or some such article, procurable there but not here, which may minister to your personal comfort when you get into colder latitudes.—Believe me, with best wishes in which Mrs. Murray cordially joins,

Yours very sincerely,

A. MURRAY.

II.

FROM THE REV. MR. PAGITER.

A CLERGYMAN OF THE CHURCH OF ENGLAND IN JAFFNA.

JAFFNA, *Sept.* 29, 1857.

DEAR BRO. GREEN:

I regret three things: First, that you go one way and we another; Second, that I am unable to see you ere you go; Third, that I have not had more of your company.

I thank you for three things: First, your kindness to me; Second, your kindness to mine; Third, your good example.

I pray for three things: First, a pleasant and speedy voyage home; Second, a speedy restoration to health; Third, a return to your field of labor.

I wish you three things: First, a good wife; Second, a happy home; Third, a prosperous profession (should you not return).

Above all, may you have: First, the presence of your Saviour; Second, the blessings of the upper and nether spring; Third, the riches of eternity.

If no more on earth we meet, I trust: First, to rise with you in the first resurrection; Second, to stand with you at the right hand of the Saviour; Third, to be with you in the company of the blessed for ever.

What more can I say?

Adieu, and believe me

Ever

Your affectionate friend,

ROBERT PAGITER.

Mr. Percival A. Dyke, the able Government Agent of the Province, took the opportunity to give him "a special parting call."

Dr. Green had desired to show a good beginning towards the realization of his scheme for putting the science of medicine, as developed in Europe and America, into the language of the Tamils, and to leave behind him a good number of practical native representatives of the science. He had thought ten years would be required for this result of his missionary service, and had determined that nothing but the clearest indications of duty should turn him from his purpose. The ten years were now drawing to a close, and what had he accomplished? He had acquired a good knowledge of a difficult language, and such facility in the use of it that he could not only freely address the people extemporaneously, but also preach in it directly from his English manuscript. He had published several important tracts, and laid the foundation of a Tamil medical literature in the creation of a scientific vocabulary for several branches of the general science. He had published a large second edition of Cutter's *Anatomy, Phisiology and Hygiene*,—to be used in schools as well as by medical students and the native doctors,—and a smaller edition of Maunsell's *Dublin Practice of Midwifery*, both modified by such improvements as had come to his knowedge and experience since the publication of the works in English by their respective authors. He had treated, and directed the treatment of, probably more than twenty thousand patients, to whom and perhaps as many or more attendants he had also made known the way of salvation. He had instructed twenty young men in medicine and surgery till they were qualified for intelligent practice, and some of them even for instructing other young men to a considerable extent in his absence. He had been instrumental in relieving many of their sufferings, and in saving the lives of many; and it cannot be doubted that some, if not many of them will be found to ascribe to him, as the instrument, their fellow-citizenship with the saints.

Having thus completed his ten years of service, he had also come to such a condition of health as made a season of rest and a change of climate necessary to any further prosecution of his chosen work; and therefore he gladly set his face towards that circle whose centre was at Green Hill and which had remained unbroken since he left it. Much as he loved, and was loved by, every member of that circle, however, he would doubtless have preferred to continue longer in his work if he had been in full vigor; the great object of his return to his early home was that re-invigoration which would restore him again as soon as possible to the Tamils.

CHAPTER IX.

1857–1859: ÆT. 35–37.

LEAVING Ceylon on the 5th of October,—ten years to a day after he first set foot on the Island,—Dr Green arrived at Madras on the 23d, where, while waiting for a vessel, he not only met many social demands, and requests to address Sunday Schools, patients in Hospitals, and assemblies in bungalows, but also revised some of his translations, translated his little popular work which he called *The House I Live In*, and composed in English another entitled *The Mother and Child*. The latter he was obliged to leave to be translated, and prepared for the press, by the Rev. Mr. Webb of Dindigul.

Meantime he met his old friend Mr. Dixon, with whom, Dr. Paterson, and another young man,—more especially than with any others,—he enjoyed "a most soul-melting Christian interview." In a similar spiritual elevation he wrote to his sister in view of the perils of travel.

SINTADREPETTA, MADRAS, *Nov.* 20, 1857.

MY DEAR SISTER MARY:

Yours doubly welcome as unexpected, came to hand on the 17 inst., date of it 14 September. By it I was glad to learn of dear Julia and Andrew's safe termination of their western tour. Through many dangers, God's arm unseen cleared their way. No wonder Julia was timid, such fearful railway wrecks do you have in crazy headlong America; their report even away out here is terrific.

I wish we could all attain a feeling of perfect safety; it is always safe to trust in God; we can always trust he will care for us if we are in the path of duty; in short duty is safe, wholly so, always so. I hope Papa will not feel over anxious about his stray son. I feel no apprehension myself of personal danger by the Rebellion, and even though one fall it is just as near to heaven hence as from Green Hill. . . . . Dear Sister, in our prayers for those near and dear to us, are we more concerned that they daily and continually dishonor God, that they are rebels against His rule, or do we care more about their exposedness to eternal misery and death which may at any moment overtake them? We must look sharp to our motives in our prayers, or we may but pray into the air.

As to India, things yet look lowery; how long the storm may pelt both rulers and ruled none can certify; but I feel more hopeful concerning the cause here than ever; by this shaking of the tree many things noxious will fall off and it will flourish better than ever. This Rebellion is a grand epoch, I verily believe, and at this date, I doubt not, Satan's power here is receiving wounds that never shall heal. . . .

If the Lord please, I pray he may spare you each and all till I can once more see you face to face; but for this, were it left for me to decide, I should be cruel to keep any one, prepared for the Better Land, out of that blessed place and company for an hour. His will be done. At least,

"There we shall meet at Jesus' feet,
Shall meet to part no more."

Truly,

SAMUEL F. GREEN.

He sailed from Madras on the 19th of December in the *Agra*, and arrived in London via the Cape of Good Hope and St. Helena on the 1st of April, acting by official appointment as surgeon and physician to the soldiers on board and to the crew. He had the Port Watch for instruction in the Scriptures, three pupils in Latin, and three children in Tamil. On his own account he practised drawing, and continued his work of translation. His work in Jaffna, and his visits to Madras, had brought him to the notice of the Medical Missionary Society in Edinburgh, which had a Mission in Madras; and early in 1853 he had received a letter from the Secretary, inviting correspondence. This led to the mutual desire for a personal acquaintance, and, as his friends at home had offered funds for touring, he planned to visit Edinburgh, and drew up an outline of his views on Medical Missions.

On this subject he had no novel theory, but specified the duties of the medical missionary as they had been assigned to him by the Board, and extended and performed by himself, adding such others as experience and observation suggested. On putting medical science into the vernacular he said: "Mere translations are comparatively useless. It is better to devise one's own plan, and compile freely from many authors, taking their ideas only; but sometimes, as a labor-saving measure, it may be best to select a well-planned elementary treatise and use this as the basis of the vernacular issue,—which may prove to be a compilation, translation, and original work combined,—interleave it, add, erase, and transpose matter, remodel sentences, phrases and figures so as to adapt the book to the language of the people, avoiding a literal rendering and making it free and simple. Every book should be in simple, clear style, and freely illustrated by cuts,—as many ideas which, among Europeans are considered perfectly simple, are strange and nearly incomprehensible to heathens. He believed the medical missionary should investigate the native systems of medicine, know the native doctors, fraternize with them as far as possible, consult with them when desired, communicate information freely, assuming no appearance of superiority, and drawing out their views and experiences. He should also give popular lectures, and publish brief papers for gratuitous distribution on various subjects; as, "for example, on Institutions for the Insane, Deaf and Dumb, Blind, Idiots; History of Medicine and Surgery, Medical Etiquette, duties of every physician to the Profession and to the community, Evils of Secrecy; the Exposé of charms, astrology, and divers abuses; and the statement of the fundamental rational principles of medical practice."

He considered also the relations of the medical missionary to the Medical Missionary Society, to the Missionary Board with which the latter co-operates, and to the Mission in which he labors; his professional furnishings; the extension of Medical Missions; the appointment and support of Medical Missionaries; and the need of Medical Missions. On the last topic he said: "Systems of error permeate every department of the social fabric. Heathenism lurks in each land as in a many-celled cavern. While conversions to Christ should be the chief aim, systems of error should be systematically attacked and driven from their hiding places by specific endeavors. Blended with medical theory and practice we find idolatry, witchcraft, astrology, charms and incantations, philters, devil (*quasi*) possession and ejection, and divers other superstitions, absurdities and abuses;—all this affording room and crying loudly for the medical missionary's best efforts. Add to this, ignorance at large of the laws of health, the prevalence of pernicious notions and practices, and there is a claim on the philanthropist of the Profession who might disregard the higher motive."

Then follows an appeal to the Profession, and a suggestion of the various benefits which might result to the Profession in the contributions of the missionaries to various sciences and in the enlargement of the sphere of knowledge of diseases, medicine and surgery.

Obviously Dr. Green, while faithful to his commission and in perfect harmony with the Mission, was no mere employee of the American Board of Missions. He examined the field he occupied, saw what was needed, extended his sphere of labor, devised methods and means of increasing the usefulness of his department, yet all in subordination to, and promotive of, the chief aim of evangelizing and saving the people—as if he were the primary and responsible agent in it all.

Having announced his arrival in England, and his purpose to visit Scotland, he received this reply from the Secretary of the Medical Missionary Society.

FROM DR. COLDSTREAM.

EDINBURGH, *April* 29, 1858.

MY DEAR SIR:

The receipt of your kind note, enclosing Mr. Paterson's introduction, gave me great pleasure. Mr. Paterson had apprised me of your intention to visit Britain, as well as of your very friendly and much valued attentions to him. As I see the American Missionary Herald regularly, I have long been familiar with your name and your labor of love in the 'spicy isle.' I therefore anticipate with no small interest the visit which you hope to pay to this city. From what you indicate of your intended movements, I presume you are not likely to arrive in Edinburgh sooner than the end of June or in the course of July. That would be a very good season for your being here. And I may mention that towards the end of July the Annual Meeting of the British Medical Association is to be held here. On that occasion, it is likely that a number of the leading physicians and surgeons from all parts of Britain will be congregated. And it is intended to hold a special public meeting of our Society at the time, which would supply you with a most precious opportunity of doing good to our professional brethren.

But at any time that you may be able to visit us, we will be happy to arrange for a meeting of the Society. . . .

I note the addresses of some of the leading friends of Medical Missions in London. . . .

In hope of soon seeing you, I am,

My Dear Sir, sincerely yours,

JOHN COLDSTREAM.

DR. GREEN.

In London Dr. Green attended the anniversaries of various benevolent societies, especially those which had missions in Ceylon; visited hospitals, and made acquaintance with distinguished physicians. In Oxford he was the guest of Dr. Cotton, Provost of Worcester, who honored him with special attentions, and introduced him to others who extended the most cordial hospitalities. In Paris he had delightful interviews with Dr. Kissen and Frederic Monod. In London, again, he "had a word of the Canaan dialect" with an Agent of an ocean steam-ship Company, and "a long and close soul talk with the barber." Visiting Birmingham and Manchester on the way, he went to Edinburgh and had the opportunity to compare with his own the views of a Society which made medical missions a specialty, the interview resulting in the confirmation of that mutual interest and regard which brought them together. After brief visits to Glasgow and Dublin he sailed from Liverpool in the *Kangaroo* on the 7th of July and arrived in New York on the 21st. Here he had his lungs examined by Dr. Camman, who gave his opinion that there was "nothing decidedly wrong." After a week of delight in New York with his brother and sisters, several missionaries from India, many friends of his youth, and some of his medical instructors, he proceeded to Green Hill, where he found his "relatives all well," and gave "thanks to Jesus for His care of them while parted." His father had reached the middle of his eighty-second year.

He spent the winter of 1858-9 in New York, in the interest of his department of missionary service; selecting the best editions of the best works for translations, obtaining favors from publishers in the way of cuts for illustrations, conferring with theological students, securing a lecture to medical students, improving himself professionally by visiting hospitals, attending lectures on subjects of the most importance to him, and witnessing the rarest and most delicate surgical operations. There was another important matter of which he was thus reminded in a letter from Mr. Hastings: "I hope I shall be here in 1860 to greet you and Mrs. Green, as I greeted you without Mrs. Geeen in 1847." And in a letter from Mrs. Hastings: "Amidst the comforts and niceties of your home can you cast back a thought to old times? Can you make those good sisters of yours realize how you used to live so lonely and forlorn? I trust your home will never be so lonely again. I am often asked by native ladies, when you are coming back; and whenever we tell them we have heard from you, the first question is, 'Is he married yet?' So you see you must not fail to fulfil the expectation of the large circle of natives who are so interested in your movements."

He received a letter from the Rev. Alexander Paterson, a City Missionary of Edinburgh and a brother of Dr. Paterson of Madras, from which a brief extract may be quoted: "I can assure you, since the time of your kind visit to us we have frequently spoken of you, and remembered you at our family altar. David has repeatedly mentioned you in his letters, so that, had we been disposed, we could not get you forgotten. Your visit was to us a time of refreshing which we cannot forget, and a manifestation of Christian kindness towards us, of which we regret we could not adequately show our appreciation. . . . David longs for 1860 and seems to anticipate a pleasant sojourn with you in Ceylon."

From Mr. Sanders he received a request, in behalf of Mr. A. M. Ferguson, of Colombo, to purchase all the publications on Ceylon by American authors; and also an account of nineteen of his medical graduates, as well as of his fellow missionaries.

To meet expenses of books, cuts, and apparatus, he issued a circular, endorsed by leading physicians and clergymen of New York, in which he gave a brief account of what had been done, and what more it was proposed to do, the necessary means and the cost of the means to the extent of a thousand dollars, and appealed to the philanthropic and benevolent for aid to that amount. In it he said: "It is the definite aim of this enterprise to displace a false by a sound medical practice; to supersede cruel superstitions by kindly truth; to root among the ten millions speaking the Tamil language a system of physic and surgery, correct in its literature and practice, that, being self-sustained, may long endure."

Dr. Green desired that a Medical Missionary Society should be organized in New York, first for the physical and spiritual benefit of the poor and suffering in the city, and secondly for the selection, training, commission and maintenance of medical missionaries in heathen lands; and that this should be an example for other cities to follow. What he had seen and learned of such a society in Edinburgh, and of its Mission in Madras, had convinced him of the great importance of such an institution; and he believed that by making it auxiliary to a Missionary Board the medical profession might become more interested in the welfare of the heathen, and more practically appreciative of their obligations as philanthropists and Christian men. Encouraged by interviews with several Christian physicians, he drew up an outline for the organization of such a Society, and, as the summer was nigh, returned to Green Hill.

On the 22d of May he "felt more like health than in a long time before;" yet, two days later, Dr. Jeffries, of Boston, thought it doubtful if he could return to Ceylon. In regard to the judgment of his medical advisers he recorded no opinion; but his silence, and his continuance in his plans and purpose to return, seem to indicate that he had more confidence in his own views than in theirs. Certainly there was no hint of any feeling of discouragement.

In June Dr. Anderson wrote: "The Prudential Committee instruct me to say that they wish you to retain your purpose and expectation of returning to your mission, though your stay in this country should be prolonged for two or three years; and to occupy your leisure, as health shall permit, in carrying out your plans for creating the needful medical works in the Tamil language."

While Dr. Green was visiting his brothers at Chicago, the community was saddened by the loss of many lives in a railway catastrophe; which occasioned, perhaps, the peculiar hue and tone of his announcement, to his friends at home, of his contemplated return. "Our Father prospering, we hope to be at the Hill by Saturday evening, 23d July. Amid perils of journeying the consciousness of friends in Faith remembering us will cheer our way. *En route*, 'Love' may switch us off by the 'Valley' track for Zion's Hill, but this is even more pleasant than Green Hill, and so we all will say, if our meeting be thus deferred, 'God's will be done.'"

Having reached home in safety, he sent the following proposal to a professional brother in New York for his consideration and use:

"Rejoicing in the comparatively large number

of the Medical Profession in this city who are members of 'the household of faith,' and in the sympathy which that profession generally show in the promotion of Christian philanthropies, the undersigned regard it as a question deserving consideration, whether the profession be acting up fully to their opportunities in relation to Christian Missions; whether there be aught farther that can be done by them to advance the interests of the same; whether they are alive to secure increase of efficiency in their department of missions, correspondent to the widening openings for the promulgations of truth; and whether they may not improve in both the manner and the measure of their aid in this important enterprise. They cordially invite you to meet with them at——on ——day of——for prayerful deliberation on this subject, with the hope that some practical and specific plan for larger usefulness may be determined upon, and some organization effected for its systematic prosecution."

It was very welcome news that the American Ceylon Mission had voted him three hundred dollars towards the purchase of apparatus needed in his department. The correspondence which was kept up between him and his Tamil friends was mutually interesting and beneficial, and must have cost him considerable time; by their letters he learned more particularly of their condition than by those from the missionaries. He had won their confidence so completely that they wrote him freely of their occupations, reverses and successes, religious life, and even of their matrimonial affairs. Robert Breckenridge, a Tamil,—principal and teacher of the self-supporting Christian English School in Batticotta,—in acknowledging a letter written at Chicago, reveals, by implication, something of the pains-taking, friendly, and spiritual quality of the Doctor's letters, in these felicitous expressions: "I thank you for its sweet contents; it was really a delicacy to the tongue and much more to the soul." This year he had the privilege of attending the Annual Meeting of the American Board at Philadelphia, where he had a delightful interview with a party of fellow-missionaries to the Tamils, who had returned for rest and recuperation.

CHAPTER X.

1859–1861: ÆT. 37–39.

FOR some time the Secretary of the Board had been looking for a missionary physician for the Madura Mission. Dr. Nathan Ward, who had been fourteen years in the Ceylon Mission previously to the term of Dr. Green, and fourteen years absent, now offered to return. The question arose with the Prudential Committee as to the expendiency of accepting Dr. Ward's offer, and transferring Dr. Green to Madura; which of course could not be decided without having first consulted him. He replied without delay: "Were the climate of Madura as favorable as that of Jaffna, I should, on account of the larger scope and the greater demand for mission labor of all sorts, prefer that field. I fear my weak eyes would scarce endure the ophthalmia so troublesome there, and my head (even in Jaffna peculiarly sensitive to the sun and heat) would ill endure the hot dry winds and the higher temperature of Madura. I should feel willing to try it, if thought expedient, though probably I should need to be made an exceptional case, and spend always the hot season on the Hills. Though I have a strong attachment to the work in Jaffna and to many friends there, white and colored, yet I would cheerfully relinquish that for any other part of the Tamil field. Only my fear is that none other offers a climate so little trying to my constitution as that of Jaffna. I would just leave the case with the Committee—to send me, if at all, where they can turn me to the best account."

The transfer was voted on the 17th of November, and at the same time Dr. and Mrs. Ward were reappointed to the Ceylon Mission.

Not till a month later was the long silence respecting his proposal for a Medical Missionary Society in New York broken and explained.

FROM DR. HARRIS.

253 FOURTH AVENUE, *Dec.* 17, 1859.

TO SAMUEL F. GREEN, M. D.

MY DEAR DOCTOR:

On returning to my home in the city, after my summer toil and care on the Hospital Ship in the Quarantine service, I find many letters unanswered, and many duties that demand my attention.

I last evening found your friendly letter written to me in August last. I read it to my students, all of whom ought to be, and I hope will be, missionary physicians.

I wish now to co-operate with you in carrying out the plan you have proposed for a permanent organization of the friends of Medical Missions and Christian consecration to such labors.

I propose to invite some fifteen or twenty of our Christian physicians to meet you at my house any evening that you may be able to meet us, and I will also invite the more advanced of our devout medical students in the city. Please, dear doctor, to communicate to me your wishes on this subject, and very soon after New Year's I shall hope to be again at home, and ready for such personal service.

Hoping that your health is improved, and your heart encouraged by the experiences of the Summer and Autumn, I beg you to accept my hearty thanks for your faithfulness in reminding me of a duty I would have performed had I been in the city, and which now I hope to attend to if you are ready to guide the friends who may come together.

Very truly yours,

ELISHA HARRIS.

Again Dr. Green went to New York to spend the winter with his brother and sisters there, to exert his influence in behalf of missions as opportunities might occur, and to improve whatever advantages he might avail himself of at medical institutions and in the practice of eminent physicians. His experience enabled him to be of great assistance to Dr. Goodale, who was about to go to a foreign field as a medical missionary, in procuring medicines and instruments.

When it became known in the Madura Mission that he had been transferred to that field, the missionaries were very much rejoiced. Mrs. Rendall wrote: "Your kindness to me and all the little ones with me, and your daily consistent Christian conduct on board the *Agra* and in London, have caused your name to be engraved on my heart as a true and tried friend. I thank the Lord for thus richly answering our requests and supplying us with one already equipped for the work." Mr. Rendall wrote: "How glad we are all to hear of your appointment to our Mission. I received a note from Brother Hastings by which I see that he is quite inclined to demur to this arrangement. I rejoice with the Madura brethren, and, if need be, shall shed a tear or so with the Jaffna brethren. See to it that you retain a hold on some good friends at home who, without giving less to the Board, will esteem it a privilege to help you in any enterprise you may wish to carry out to increase the knowledge of the medical art among the natives. I think you will find a *wide door* open for preaching the gospel through the Dispensary in Madura. I was hoping for some good doctor who would be obliged to stammer for years; but now, behold, the Lord sends one who has the Tamil at his tongue's end."

On the 1st of March, Dr. Green, "with Dr. Harris, drew up a list of Christian physicians probably favorable to Medical Missions," called on four himself, and left others for Dr. Harris and Dr. Post to confer with. After all his efforts, however, it was deemed inexpedient to organize; those who favored the movement thought they were too few to make a beginning with any hope of success.

In the Autumn, he addressed the following letter to the Secretary of the American Board:

WORCESTER, MASS., *Nov.* 7, 1860.

REV. R. ANDERSON, D. D.,

MY DEAR SIR:

Just subsequent to the embarkation of the brethren for Ceylon, after which I consulted with Dr. Jeffries on my prospects for return to India, I looked in at your office but failed of seeing you. I wished to mention that his opinion is still decidedly adverse to my going in the spring, as is that also of an experienced and intelligent physician in this city. My head is not so fully recovered as it ought to be even for pressing business here, much less for the same in the tropics. I still wish and hope to engage again in the good work among the Tamils, but the day seems still distant. The field for a missionary physician in Madura, is exceedingly inviting and one I could enter upon with all my heart, but I must relinquish for the present my expectations in favor of some one blessed with the vigor to meet all the demands of that position. The community there is so large that perhaps two physicians could each find abundant usefulness, aud should health hereafter warrant, I should be happy to act as co-laborer with another in the same department of the Mission.

Very truly yours,

SAMUEL F. GREEN.

Dr. Anderson replied as follows:

MISSIONARY HOUSE, BOSTON, *Dec.* 1, 1860.

DR. S. F. GREEN, WORCESTER, MASS.

MY DEAR BROTHER:

Your letter of the 7th ult. was duly recieved, and the Committee authorized us to look for another physician for Madura. As there is almost no prospect of our finding the right man, I would ask how it would do for you to go, with the expectation of spending the first year or two in the Pulneys? This is a feasible plan, especially as there is now a horse road all the way up. . . .

As ever, most affectionately yours,

R. ANDERSON, Sec. A. B. C. F. M.

Affairs at Green Hill kept Doctor Green there through the Winter of 1860-61, so that he did not go to New York till near the last of March, where he employed his time very much as in previous seasons there. On the 16th of May he had his "chest auscultated and percussed by Dr. Camman, who found, on the right infra clavicular region, the respiration roughened and the expiration prolonged," but *thought* there were no tubercles and that these physical signs might be accounted for by adhesions.

He was now "gradually buying up outfit, medical and surgical, emptying pocket and filling head." On the 31st a Tamil teacher wrote: "I hope that you are quite well and you will kindly condescend to dwell among us and do good to us and *not* to Madura people. Your absence from Jaffna is felt and lamented all over *Jaffna*. I hope that you are not unconscious about it. I assure you, Sir, that your *name* is printed in our minds in capital letters and cannot be easily obliterated. Many young men desire to learn medicine, but who will teach? These young men are anticipating your arrival in Jaffna. Sir, kindly change your mind and come to Jaffna."

In company with missionaries Smith and Bates, Dr. Ward had sailed from Boston, on the 30th of October, 1860, in the *Sea King*, bound for Madras, which point they reached on the 11th of March, 1861. In due time it was learned in Boston that Dr. Ward died when about thirty days out on the voyage. On the 23d of August, Dr. Green wrote to Dr. Anderson: "My transfer to the Madura Mission was based on the appointment of Dr. Ward to Jaffna. I acquiesced in this arrangement in hope of a complete restoration to health. This expectation having been only partially realized, and Jaffna being again destitute of a missionary physician, I think it expedient to request my re-appointment to the Ceylon Mission." The Prudential Committee promptly complied with his request.

Dr. Green's father was now in his eighty-fifth year, and, on the 15th of September, with his ten children, "attended public worship at the Central church, in Worcester, Rev. Dr. Sweetser's. On the 16th, these ten sons and daughters, all assembled at Green Hill, and remained together in social converse during the day, and in the evening were joined by a circle of relatives and friends. This family reunion was the more remarkable from the widely distant places of business and residence of the family, and their long separation from the paternal mansion Their names and places of residence were as follows: Hon. William N. Green, Worcester, Mass.; Lucy M. Green, New York City; Mary R. Green, New York City; Julia E, Green, Worcester, Mass.; Dr. John P. Green Copiapo, Chili, South America; Hon. Andrew H. Green, New York City; Dr. Samuel F. Green, Batticotta, Ceylon; Lydia P. Green, Worcester; Oliver B. Green, Esq., Chicago, Illinois; Martin Green, Esq., Peshtigo, Wisconsin."

A few weeks later Dr. Green thus wrote to one of his brothers:

GREEN HILL, WORCESTER, MASS., *Oct.* 3, 1861.

MY DEAR BROTHER OLIVER:

All hail. The sun has just sprung over the old pines, and as it glows into my room I feel as if I would call some of its warm radiance and, naming it "fraternity," send it to you, my beloved brother; but as I cannot do just that, I will by ink and pen say how my heart joys over your recent visit, and how I feel full of comfort in the assurance that we are one in Christ. This is truly the *summum bonum.* What can we want beside?

"He that spared not his own Son, how shall he not also freely give us all things?" *Laus Deo.*

I have great joy in thinking of your daughters—my darling nieces—growing up under such auspices. May you be blessed to transfusing into their characters not only all of Christ there is in you, but to inciting them to seek and teaching them how they may secure more. My love to each of them and to your spouse, my youngest and much loved sister, by adoption mutual.

Affectionately, your brother,

SAMUEL F. GREEN.

17

CHAPTER XI

1861–1862: ÆT. 39–40.

UNDER re-appointment to his former position, Dr. Green now regarded the time of his return as near at hand. After three months at Green Hill he went again to New York, where he well knew how to keep himself busy, useful and improving—availing himself especially of opportunities to advance the cause of missions, and of the advantages afforded by medical institutions.

Extracts from one of his letters at this time to his sisters Julia and Lydia.

No. 1 Fifth Avenue, New York, *Jan.* 14, 1862.

My Dear Sisters:

I was much interested in hearing yours and Father's letters read last evening. Sisters two and I had a quiet time in back parlor by ourselves, . . . talking, and enjoying in silence the near presence of the beloved. . . . When in silence a number allied by blood and long association encircle an evening hearth, don't the hearts keep whispering to each other and conning *of* each other and praying for each other to God? We had a good time and you were present by epistle.

I wish to have six or eight entertaining profitable *non*-religious books for use among the Crew of the "good ship." They will serve to introduce directly religious reading into the forecastle. Will you kindly see if such can be selected from among those already well used, so that I may either buy here or take those.

. . . A Second Lieutenant's Commission is here for Nephew William. I had a good time at the New York Eye Infirmary yesterday. . . .

Truly your grateful and loving brother,

SAMUEL F. GREEN.

TO WILLIAM NELSON GREEN, JR.

NO. 1 FIFTH AVENUE, NEW YORK,

Thursday, Feb. 13, 1862.

MY DEAR NEPHEW WILLIAM:

In these days our interest for you intensifies. We have heard of the battle of Roanoke Island, and are most desirous of tidings from you. We know you will not delay intelligence as to your condition, and we shall watch eagerly for the earliest news. We will hope all is well with you.

I should indeed be delighted to see you again and to listen to some of your experiences narrated by your own lips. I shall be very glad also to see your wishes for promotion met—feeling it an advantage, not only to one very near and very dear to me, but to the cause of our Nationality—for I believe you would act conscientiously and ably, having used every endeavor to fit yourself for more responsible duty.

I am busy one way or another, addressing Juveniles, shopping on outfit, to-day send a draft to Philadelphia for a hundred and twenty-two dollars worth of Medical Books; I get forty per cent. discount by the liberality of the publishers. I am laying in a pretty good stock of Surgical instruments. . . .

I pray for you daily that God will "cover your head in the day of battle," will keep you from the pollutions of the world, and will enable you to "stand up for Jesus"—His good soldier.—With very much love and sympathy believe me,

Your affectionate uncle,

SAMUEL F. GREEN.

It was now arranged that he should sail in May, and he made his final purchases of medicines, instruments, apparatus, medical books, and whatever else was required to complete his outfit. A few lines from one of the newspapers show one of the ways in which he sought to make himself useful during his term of rest and recuperation. "His numerous friends will be glad to learn that the renewal of his health warrants him in retracing his steps to the land of his chosen labors. His numerous addresses before our Sunday-schools have been listened to with delight, and he will leave behind him thousands who will ever feel an attachment to him, and an abiding interest in his prosperity and long life in the work to which he has devoted his energies and his all."

Dr. Green returned in April to Green Hill, to make the final preparations for his departure, to make his visits to friends in the vicinity, and to give his last few weeks to his father, whom, it seemed almost certain, he was never to see again in this world. On the one subject which his friends in Ceylon had urged upon him as so important he seems to have maintained a dignified silence; not, however, a stoical or careless indifference. It soon appeared that he had chosen one to be his companion for life who was in every way worthy of himself; and on the 22d of May, at a farewell missionary meeting in the Central Church, where they both had been accustomed to worship, he was united in marriage with Miss Margaret Phelps Williams, the Rev. Dr. Sweetser performing the service. It was an occasion of special interest to the pastor and his people, manifested by a very large assemblage. They had followed with appreciation the young man whom they so gladly helped to fit out for the blessed work fifteen years before, and now they were to have a new tie to the cause of foreign missions in general and to the American Ceylon Mission in particular. Dr. Green had already received the following letter, from Dr. Anderson, Secretary of the A. B. C. F. M.

MISSIONARY HOUSE, BOSTON, *May* 19, 1862.

If the vessel sails on Monday, we must arrange for the Prudential Committee and their wives to meet the departing missionaries on Saturday evening at the house of some member, and to have the services on shipboard at 10 o'clock Monday morning. I am persuaded that you and your wife, and the friends of both of you, who shall come to Boston to see you off, will be better satisfied by a calm and deliberate attendance at both of these meetings, than by the very hurried departure, and consequent non-acquaintance with us on the part of your wife, involved in your coming from Worcester Monday morning. But having said thus much, I must leave it for you to judge what, on the whole, is best for you to do. I very much rejoice that you are to have such good company, which I doubt not you greatly need and richly deserve to have.—With affectionate regards to the lady, I am, as ever,

R. ANDERSON.

FROM THE REV. ANDREW JUKES, FORMERLY IN HULL AND NOW IN LONDON, ENGLAND; A CLERGYMAN, AND AUTHOR OF SEVERAL RELIGIOUS WORKS.

HULL, *May* 16, 1862.

MY DEAR SIR, AND BROTHER IN CHRIST:

Your kind note, enclosed in one from C. W. Knudsen and dated 29th of April last, reached me quite safely this morning; and as you tell me that very shortly you return to India I hasten to write at least a hurried line, to catch to-morrow's mail from Liverpool, which may reach you before you leave New York.

It is indeed pleasant to be reminded, by a letter like yours from a stranger who is yet a brother, of the bond which binds us so closely to all those who by grace are united to our common Lord and Saviour, who though unknown in the flesh are loved in spirit for the sake of a common life in Christ Jesus. Your letter therefore was very welcome, the more as it also brought good tidings of our not forgotten brother C. W. Knudsen. As to the little book you ask for, on the Mystery of the Kingdom, it is at present out of print, nor can I get even an old copy for you anywhere to-day; but if you could let me have your address in India, I would, please God, send one of the first copies of the new edition.

Will you tell Knudsen that we hope to write to him in the course of the next week. To-day I cannot do so, as I am fully engaged with other work, and the American mail leaves us this morning. This must also be my apology for so hurried a line to you; but I trust it will not be the end of our correspondence. I owe under God not a little to one of the first missionaries sent out by the American Board of Foreign Missions, I mean Gordon Hall, some of whose letters were once a great blessing to me, and which I reprinted years ago when I was at Cambridge. His letters quite drew me to missionary work, for which I offered myself; but God's providence kept me here.

Farewell, dear brother. Peace be multiplied to you and yours.

Yours in Christian bonds of love,

ANDREW JUKES.

The following letter was sent by the Pilot from the vessel on which Dr. and Mrs. Green sailed for India.

Star of Peace, BOSTON HARBOR,

May 26, 11:40 A. M.

MY DEAR FRIENDS:

We have just left the grouped affection out of sight (but never out of heart). The Pilot says he will take back any letters. . . . I cannot find words to fully express all the thankfulness I feel, and which is fully due to so many dear and kind and loving and faithful friends. May the Lord restore into your own hearts many fold the favors you have done. I don't know what I could have suggested that has not been done. You are all so kind. The fruits of the kindness are valuable, but the kindness and love itself are unspeakably precious. All is from the great Source of Love. To whom first be praise, and next to you each and all be thanks. . . .

With fervent affection, I am your son, brother, cousin, friend,

SAMUEL F. GREEN.

TO A BROTHER.

AT SEA, *June* 19, 1862.

As to diffidence: don't let the Devil get control of your tongue even to silence it. Encourage yourself to speak by such thoughts as, "My lips belong to Christ; my speech is owned by One who bought all with his very blood, etc." Then, for the effort, seek to *rest* in Jesus; by previous prayer acquire a repose in Him, and, ignoring self, realize you speak *for* Him, and you will speak *by* Him; He will aid you. I think I can assert this from my own experience. Seek to speak more from the *heart* than from the head, and let there be feeling manifest.

Diffidence scarce any one ever had more than I myself, and I am convinced it is pride in one of its disguises. Get out of self and into Christ, and you are ready for speaking (given the subject chosen and revolved previously). Then neither shrink from nor *willfully* seek opportunity to hold forth. But watching providence, spring with alacrity into any opening for edifying or instructing.—My dear Brother, I look for your complete triumph over this bugbear, and by anticipation rejoice already with you in it.—

SAMUEL F. GREEN.

As the time approached when the *Star of Peace* was expected at Madras, messages were sent from Ceylon to welcome Dr. and Mrs. Green to the mission.

I.

FROM THE REV. J. C. SMITH.

OODOOPITTY, *Aug.* 29, 1862.

Your welcome note in pencil brought us cheering news and took us all aback. We had given you up as a hard case and concluded that it was your fate to remain in single blessedness, notwithstanding the gloominess of it in this land. . . Perhaps the whole matter had been in a process of development *sub rosa*, communications being carried by "Electric" telegraph, and brought to a consummation at just the right time. I hear that you made provision for a double seated bandy some months before you left, which shows that you had some faith that you would be provided for in time of need.—A hearty welcome to "Sister Green."

II.

From Mrs. J. C. Smith.

We long to hear of your arrival at Madras, and more still to bid you welcome to Jaffna—not alone, as we supposed up to the last moment, for we did not understand the following sentence in one of your notes as a prophecy: "But sudden corners are sometimes turned in life's pathway, and one may confront a friend almost before he is aware." We are greatly rejoiced that this was your happy experience. "Sister Green" will recieve as cordial a welcome as any one of the company. Your native friends are greatly rejoiced by the prospect of soon seeing you again.

August 30th.

III.

From Mr. Hastings.

Manepy, *Sept.* 1, 1862.

You are perhaps passing our "Sweet Isle" just about this time, and by the time this reaches Madras, or soon after, will be at anchor in Madras Roads. Would that I had a telescope like the

Irishman's, which was of such power that it brought the moon near enough for him to hear the inhabitants "speaking with one another." If I could bring you up near enough to exchange greetings I would give you a hearty welcome. But in the absence of such a wonderful instrument I am constrained to do the next best things—send *herewith* my greetings and a hearty welcome to your double self, Brother and Sister Green.

I shall not attempt to tell you what pleasure the news of your bringing Mrs. Green gives to all—white and black. You will learn for yourself when you reach Jaffna. Since the news of your re-appointment to Jaffna many have inquired, 1st, Is Dr. Green coming back? 2d, Is he married? and when No. 2 was answered in the negative, with a look of disappointment it has been asked, "Why, Sir, doesn't he get married? Is it caste or property that stands in the way?"

We are fully prepared to give our new Sister a cordial welcome and a distinguished place in our Circle.

Dr. McIntyre, a native, wrote: "I am exceedingly happy that you are coming with a fit companion, to whom I send my humble Salaam."

V.

From the Rev. M. D. Sanders.

Batticotta, *Sept.* 3, 1862.

I am so rejoiced that you and the Howlands and *Mrs. Green* are, if the Lord will, to be with us so soon, that I hardly know how to express my feelings. It seems a long time since you were here and we had those pleasant meetings for prayer and praise. I hope that a long and useful service awaits you.

The natives begin to show their teeth in view of your near approach. I spent three weeks touring in the Wanny in June, and I found people there who knew you. At one rest house a man was complaining of his pains and quietly remarked, "If Dr. Green were here he would cure me."

I think we have a Medical Class which you will greatly value. There is real talent in it, but the boys need your presence and direction much. McIntyre (a Tamil) seems to be lame in Chemistry, and it is impossible for Rice (a Tamil) to give them all the experiments they ought to have.

VI.

From the Rev. Levi Spaulding.

Oodooville, *Sept.* 12, 1862.

I am so glad to know that you are all but with us again, and the more so as we learn that you have made vast improvements since you left us. Even a short man may become tall by "doubling his shadow." Of this we do not intend to doubt but live in the full assurance.

As for *wee* Oodoovillâns—we are just exactly as when you left us, only a little more so. We have made but few applications at your shop, though had you been really there we might have called a few times.

. . . . You will find some of us weak in body, and weak in Tamil, but on the whole most of us have made great progress in this department within a year—I say *great*, at least *visible*. Come and see and learn for yourself. Mary says: "Be sure you send my love, and hearty and warm anticipations, and what, and what not, of all good thoughts and feelings."

And now since you have enlarged your benevolent bias you will not think this is all for yourself, so please hand over a large share to others.

To his Father, Sisters and Brothers.

Star of Peace, *Sept.* 16, 1862.

Remembering you all specially on this our family anniversary, I desire to communicate to you my feelings and circumstances. We lie almost at a dead calm. We are mostly ready for going on shore; could run up to Madras in three days, and may be three weeks.

I am in very good health, I think quite as well as any of our party of six; insensibly I seem to have come to the top of the ascent back again to my usual health, which however was never very rugged. I hope this may be an earnest of permission to serve our Master among the Tamils for another decade. I begin to feel the nearness to my adopted people and desire heartily to be inclined and enabled to meet them in just the best way; for this, as for other blessings, I would "rest in the Lord."—I would offer as my sentiment to you all in view of the whole, "O magnify the Lord with me and let us exalt His name together."

While the ship was yet in the Roads, Dr. and Mrs. Green received from Rev. Dr. and Mrs. Winslow some flowers and a hearty welcome to their home.

FROM THE REV. J. RENDALL.

MADURA, *Sept.* 30, 1862.

God be praised for his great mercies to you. First of all I am disposed to thank Him for giving you a wife. Please give her my best Salaams. May you both be spared to labor many years in India.

I was greatly disappointed when I heard that you were not coming to our Mission. At first I rather thought of scolding you and Dr. Anderson. But on a second thought have concluded to forgive you. . . . You must of course come over sometime with your wife and see us. You know the value of the Pulneys. We are now building houses at Pulney the north side of the mountain, and at Mana Madura eighteen miles south of Tirupuvanam. . . . I am, as ever,

Affectionately yours,

J. RENDALL.

CHAPTER XII.

1862–1863: ÆT. 40–41.

AFTER a fortnight at Madras, and the day after the completion of the fortieth year of his age, Dr. and Mrs. Green sailed in a brig, and reached Oodoopitti, Ceylon, on the 19th of October in the evening. It was but a three hour's drive to Manepy their designated station. The joy of their arrival was not confined to the Mission, but was shared by the foreigners in the vicinity, as well as by the natives, as will be seen in the following letter from one of the native doctors.

BADULLA, *Nov.* 18, 1862.

MY DEAR SIR:

I cannot find words to express the pleasure I felt in finding your name among the late arrivals to Ceylon, but it will afford me far greater pleasure to hear from you that you have come back to the scene of your former labors in restored health and strength, and there again to devote your talents and energies for the benefit of my countrymen both in a spiritual and temporal way. Although a period of five years elapsed since you left the shores of Ceylon, speaking not only for myself but also my countrymen, I can say that your name has always lived in our memory, and we never better knew the value of your devotion for our good than when you were absent from us, and now that it has pleased Providence to restore us to you we trust that you will be spared long for us. . . . Permit me, my dear Sir, To Remain as

Yours very Respectfully,

IRA GOULD.

If there is a pleasure in knowing one's self to be missed where he has been, there may be a kindred pleasure in knowing that his absence is regretted where he was only expected. While Dr. Green received the heartiest welcome to his old field of labor, there was genuine disappointment in another, that he had not been transferred to it in fact as he had been for a time by appointment. "I every day the more regret," wrote Dr. Chester, "that your destination has been changed and that you are not coming to Madura. I think you would have had here a larger field, not alone for medical and surgical practice, but for the raising, of native medical helpers." Mr. Webb of Dindigul in replying to a short note, said, "You must not feel we have given you up because you concluded to —give us up."

His brother Andrew had felt quite unreconciled to his return to Ceylon, both because of his precarious health, and because he disliked to have him beyond easy reach and frequent correspondence. Only convictions of duty towards One whom he regarded as more than a brother constrained him to return.

MANEPY, JAFFNA, CEYLON, *Friday*, *Nov.* 28, 1862.

MY DEAR BROTHER ANDREW:

. . . . I am pressed immensely at times, and always I believe I shall have more to do than I can accomplish. So I have one more ground for sympathy with you.

If I could have you for my guest for a few days I should doubly rejoice, for besides the social enjoyment I should be sure of your reversed vote about my being here. Your wish opposing was one of the greatest trials I had to surmount in getting away from home on what there seemed, and here most emphatically proves, to be a call of duty. I should like to have you present at two or three of my hour sessions with the Medical Class, eleven in number, an intellegent set of young men most earnest to acquire the Medical Science and Art, and who hang upon me so confidingly and look to me so docilely for training;

and then to go a few times to the Dispensary and see the crowds of sick seeking relief, and to look at the Medical Department generally and see how in all its branches hard and faithful labor by a competent man is needed. Medical care of the Mission, translation of books, etc., etc., make out at least a treble and thrice loud call for one's presence here.

I acknowledge I yearn to see you, and pine to tears sometimes when I think of you. But . . . . consent to severance *for Christ's sake*, and then it will be a blessing to us both. . . .—Lovingly and gratefully and with much esteem I am

Your brother,

SAMUEL F. GREEN.

Obviously no one could have been more rejoiced at his resumption of his duties as a medical missionary than Dr. Green himself. He loved the people for whom he was laboring for Christ's sake; and it seemed to him that if any one from a Christian land could see them as he saw them his sympathy could not be withheld. When one can have every temporal want anticipated and supplied for affection's sake, it is no ordinary self-denial that forgoes the privilege, to labor for the heathen. It is surprising that one who was so recently on the list of returned invalids at home could so soon take upon himself so much as he was now doing. To carry on the work of an evangelist, of a medical teacher, of a practitioner, and of a translator and editor of medical works, would seem to require the full strength of one man in each division of labor. It was only by systematic use of his time that he could do all this. Of course he was obliged to have assistance wherever it could be used to advantage. His brief outline of the daily routine of work with the patients at his Dispensary, in the following letter, indicates the energy, industriousness, patience and zeal, without which he could not long have carried his whole burden. Of course his assistant, if not already qualified by previous experience and study, must be instructed as to the portion of Scripture to be selected and as to the proper explanation of it; and this exercise of expounding the Scripture to the patients was a means of fitting him for independent religious work, as well as of bringing the patients to a knowledge of the word of God.

Tuesday, December 9, 1862.

MY DEAR SISTER LYDIA:

. . . . Yesterday I prescribed for over fifty patients, I should judge. They assemble in a shed just south of the study, which I use as a

Dispensary and which is about four rods from our dwelling. At 9 o'clock A. M. the Assistant reads a part of the gospel and explains it to them, and gives tickets 1, 2, 3, etc. Then, in order of the number of ticket, we examine and prescribe and give medicine and send away; and then hold a meeting with the next set, that come too late for the 9 o'clock exercise, and ticket them and attend them and send them the same way. Sometimes we have a third set to attend.

Several of the Mission need Dental aid, and I am waiting for an interval of leisure, but it seems like "waiting for the river to run by," and so I intend to break away to this station and that for this purpose occasionally, leaving the Dispensary to go on by itself. . . . —Lovingly, your brother,

SAMUEL F. GREEN.

If he had not already been a firm believer in the special providences of God, he received an exemplification of the doctrine, which could hardly have failed to convince him of the truth of it; for both he and his wife had one of those narrow escapes which people generally speak of as miraculous because they cannot account for them in any other way than by divine interposition, and which no one could explain by the doctrine of chances without claiming that it was the one chance in a thousand,—which no one who had passed through such an experience would be likely to contend for, and no one who had not, but perceived the imminent danger, would be willing to risk. That one should be awakened at the critical moment, interpret a slight unusual noise as a sign of immediate danger, hasten to see about it and, in returning for a key, find himself in the only place of safety in the midst of an avalanche; and that his companion, without a change of position, should lie exactly so that the falling weight should lodge without crushing her, must be ascribed only to the special providence of God.

MANEPY, JAFFNA, CEYLON, *Monday*, *Dec.* 22, 1862.

MY DEAR SISTER LUCY:

On Friday morning last about 6 o'clock I heard, on waking, the sound of mortar shelling off and dropping from the wall, and with this occasional sounds as of snapping and cracking. I rose to look out into the south verandah, as for a long while (several years) the posts of it had stood leaning outwards, and I had apprehensions lest it should fall. The rain had been persistent for about nine days, and the heavily tiled roof was thoroughly soaked, so that the tiles were heavier than usual. I went through the east verandah, designing to go through the study to see about the south verandah. Finding the door, leading from the study to it, locked, I was about to return for the key. While in the doorway under shelter of the thick wall, the stone supporting the timber which ran along the top of the south verandah posts fell from the corner of the study wall and let the weight of the roof on to the post next it, which lurched away, and then the next, and so on. These not only carried away the verandah roof but dragged off the main roof also, in an instant uncovering entirely our bedroom and the study and half of the south verandah, and letting down upon us an avalanche of timber, tiles and mortar. For a moment I was mentally stunned by the crash, but recovering immediately I called to Margaret, who was still in bed, and was glad indeed to hear her voice, from under the wreck, sounding as calm as ever. The dragging of the posts to the southward drew the weight just past her, so that it fell without injuring her; but where I was lying a half minute previous the tiles fell in in great quantity, the heavy chunks of masonry from the roof, and the ends of the rafters, resting on what would have been the place of my mangled body. A step this way or that would have been death to either of us. A stick rested hard upon Margaret's head, which we got off (help being summoned immediately and the day having dawned and the rain having just ceased), then one which pressed on the shoulders, then one on the right leg. Not a drop of blood was lost; not a wound or a fracture. Literally she came within an inch of death, and I within a second of it.

. . . . My watch, which lay in the middle of the bed, was crushed. Our bedsteads—two single ones—stood side by side; the adjacent beams of them were broken short across, five posts were out and eight broken, a wardrobe broken at the top, four chairs, a couch at the foot of our bed, my hat-tree broken up, etc., etc.

We were just two months to a day in our adopted place and had just got well settled. But the joy of such a graciously granted complete escape of limb and life overshadows any grief at a sudden ejection from a home. "Magnify the Lord with us, and let us exalt his name together, for He has redeemed our life from destruction." I feel richer for such an experience of God's providence, and wish to realize that my exposure is constant, and my safety in Christ as continual. In Christ, safe anywhere; out of Christ, safe nowhere. . . .

Very affectionately your brother,

SAMUEL F. GREEN.

Later in the month he wrote to a friend: "I have a temple musician under treatment who is the victim of licentiousness. To care for him comes his own aunt who is his foster-mother, She is an old Dancing Girl (*alias* a prostitute by distinctly recognized profession). They belong to one of the two most famous temples of Jaffna, the Siva temple. . . .

"A Brahmin comes the distance of eight miles with carbuncle; he is very hungry and very weak, and is advised to stay a day or two (after free incisions). But he is too holy to stop anywhere about here, even in the temple rest-house close by; so he goes in his ox cart slowly home, and after duly bathing, etc., will take a meal.—Just as we were about operating, a lizard chirped, and his son anxiously reckoned whether the omen was favorable or not."

Dr. Green had long been interested in the subject of sacred music for the Tamils. He reasoned on this subject in the same way as he had on that of science and literature, believing they could never have what they needed so long as they were supplied only with Western hymns and tunes. During his former term of service he had urged the matter upon those who were able to help provide lyrics and music, and with considerable success; the result in another portion of the field is thus reported by Mr. Sanders, who had gone to the Pulney Hills:

"Providentially I had the great privilege of attending meetings in sixteen places, and at four, several in each place. In all these meetings the Lyrics have been sung, with two exceptions. The Christians all sing and seem to enjoy the music. The feeling in favor of the Lyrics is universal among the natives (so far as I can learn), and it is about the same among the missionaries. The editions of Lyrics which have been published are exhausted, and a new edition is about to be published by Murdoch and Company. May that style of church music prevail which shall be for the spiritual edification of that portion of God's people who speak the Tamil language."

The Jaffna Friend in Need Society had been in existence some years before Dr. Green's first arrival in the District, but the Hospital connected with it was not built till some years afterwards. Soon after his return he heard a rumor from the natives that the Hospital was to be put under his superintendence. As the Hospital had no connection with the American Ceylon Mission, the rumor must have started from something said, or understood to be meant, to that effect by somebody who had some relation to that institution; for subsequent movements proved that the rumor was not without foundation.

Having had some conversation with Assistant Government Agent, L. F. Liesching, Esq., about the Hospital and the desirability of connecting with it a Medical School, Dr. Green received from the Government Agent and chairman of the Hospital Committee, P. A. Dyke, Esq., a request for an expression of his views on the subject of that conversation. He complied, giving a brief outline of such a plan as occurred to him for making the Hospital more useful,—"a day-dream perhaps but somewhat of which at least a diligent and intelligent energy could make reality." This led to a call from the chairman and from the Financial Secretary, the Rev. Mr. Pagiter. This conference was soon followed by a letter from the Secretary, asking whether he would take the superintendence of the Hospital, and adding: "I shall be glad to know that you consent; for I am inclined to the opinion that your connection with the Institution would be of incalculable benefit and advantage to it. The natives have such perfect confidence in you that it would become more popular than ever."

Seeing the possible and probable advantages that might accrue to his medical students by clinical lectures, and to his department in the Mission by some additional funds, Dr. Green submitted the question to the Mission; and on receiving their approval, he consented to take the management of the Hospital for three months, to see whether two visits a week would consist with his other duties so as really to add to his usefulness. On examination he found that some important changes were needful to the best prosperity of the institution, and, at the risk of some probable unpopularity, re-organized its forces with a view to greater economy and efficiency. The connection which was begun as an experiment resulted in a continuance for several years,—the compensation being about two hundred and fifty dollars annually, besides a hundred and fifty dollars annually for traveling expenses, as the distance between Manepy and Jaffna was about five miles.

Before the middle of March Dr. Green wrote to his friends: "Our house approaches completion. I am making the roof extra strong so as tc put another fall beyond a peradventure, and so help to calm our nerves which do not yet wholly recover from the shock, but when at night similar sounds in the roof to those just preceding the crash occur we have yet a little tremor." By their calamity, others were led to examine their premises and to use such precautions as seemed prudent, thus verifying the couplet,

> Except wind stand as never it stood,
> It is an ill wind turns none to good.

Another evidence that his labor in putting medical science into Tamil had not been in vain appears in the letter which follows.

COCHIN, *May* 4, 1863.

SAMUEL F. GREEN, ESQ., JAFFNA.

SIR:

I beg to thank you for your very kind

letter and enclosure to Mr. Hunt for the illustrations I had applied for.

In publishing an Anatomy in Malayalam I hope you will have no objection to my making use of your Tamil Translation, so that the circulation and usefulness of that work may be extended to the natives of this part of Southern India. When the book is finished I shall be very happy to send you a copy.—An early answer will oblige

Yours faithfully,

P. Jos. Itteyuah.

It has been a question, perhaps, why so many Tamils are called by names familiar to Americans. The reason is that they have two names—one for the natives and one for the foreigners. The Doctor found, on his return, nine little boys named after himself. Here is a letter about the Lyrics, too good to be omitted, from two "infantile sons of one of our best catechists."

From the Masters Lee.

Naranthany, *May* 8, 1863.

Honored Sir:

We are well by the almighty power of our heavenly father. We are happy to hear your welfare from your honour. We request you very humbly to send us a book of Tamil songs. Samuel and I want it as a present. We will study ourselves and sing before the boys, cur mother will sing to the women and the girls who are coming to hear about Jesus from her, and father will use it among the people for the Lord's glory which is to be powerfully.—Your obedient and most humble children,

LEVI S[PAULDING] LEE.

SAMUEL G[REEN] LEE.

Dr. Green seems never to have been troubled with doubts or despondency, but to have always enjoyed the consciousness of knowing in whom he believed. It was his assurance in Christ that enabled him to rise above his natural diffidence.

MANEPY, JAFFNA, CEYLON, *Sat.*, *May* 30, 1863.

MY DEAR SISTER LYDIA:

. . . . It seems as if, as the years fly, the cords of affection strengthen. I am glad indeed that a strand of faith is wreathed into our family tie. It will never sever, I believe, Death shall not stretch it. We are one in Christ, and being so are joined for eternity. . . . How keenly I sympathize with you in the mental phase of a combined desire and a shrinking to speak with one directly about his soul. I know no way to surmount such a naturally impassable barrier (which may exist between even nearest relatives) but a resting in Jesus. Even in working for our Lord I think we must the while rest in him. The branch abides and bears. Well, . . . there is one comfort; if we feel unable to talk religion, we can always talk religiously—can have our conversation "always with grace." . . .—Much love to you and to all the sisters and brothers,

Yours very truly,

SAMUEL F. GREEN.

His devotion to his duties as a physician, medical instructor, and translator, seems to have always been second to his devotion as an evangelist. Notwithstanding all that was discouraging, he seems to have had strong hope of great progress in the spiritual and moral condition of the people at no very distant period. In this confidence he wrote to his sisters as follows.

MANEPY, JAFFNA, CEYLON, *Tues., June* 9, 1863.

MY DEAR SISTER JULIA:

I cannot but contemplate the field of effort around me with gratitude and hope. I desire to know nothing among this people but Jesus Christ and Him crucified. The educated already concede that God is one only; but I now crowd for the next step, namely, that Jesus Christ is that One. I substitute His name in place of the common appellation, God, in my conversations with the people . . . The people are—very many of them—pantheists, and one name serves in their view as well as another.

Affectionately,

Your brother,

SAMUEL F. GREEN.

MANEPY, JAFFNA, CEYLON, *June* 22, 1863.

MY DEAR SISTER LUCY:

I think our energies should be now largely directed to female education. . . . Though now, even, education is held by men to be but a mean to an end, and there is but little love for knowledge for its own sake, yet it has become discreditable for a boy of a respectable family anywhere in our neighborhood to be wholly unlettered. Let the same result be secured in the case of girls, and the day is ours. The influence of women, powerful anywhere, is more than ordinarily so here, as they are the property holders. As they are now the chief reliance of the Superstition of the land, so will they be, I trust, ere the close of the century, of the Truth, which shall have then the prevalence here. . . .—I am most truly,

Your brother,

SAMUEL F. GREEN.

The following letter was addressed to a distinguished physician who attended him in his childhood and with whom he was familiar in his vacations and during his short time of practice in Worcester, but who had little sympathy with him in his religious views, though he appreciated the importance and results of scientific medical practice among the heathen.,

TO JOHN GREEN, M. D.

JAFFNA, CEYLON, *July* 14, 1863.

MY DEAR COUSIN JOHN:

. . . . As I believe you will feel a special interest in the Medical Department of the missionary work, I may properly give you a sketch of my circumstances. I have as my understood duties: Medical charge of the missionaries and their families; the instruction of a Class of (eleven) youth; the oversight and general conduct of a Dispensary at my station which is Manepy five miles distant from the town of Jaffna; the superintendence (generally on Tuesdays and Fridays) of the Jaffna Friend-in-Need Society's Hospital.

. . . The Society has been long in existence but its Hospital and Dispensary only for about twelve years. . . . Percival Ackland Dyke, Esq., for twenty years or more the Government Agent for the Northern Province of Ceylon, was virtually the originator of this institution, and is its main spring at present. The Government recognize it now as established, and give annually towards its support a certain amount proportioned to the sum raised locally. . . .

The patients treated at the Hospital number about eight thousand annually,—have been up nearly to ten thousand one year. Formerly the Hospital was superintended by the Military Surgeon—living in the pretty coral stone Fort one sixth of a mile distant from it. But Mr. Dyke seems to prefer another arrangement at present. I have taken charge as a trial for three months, which time is about expired. Whether best to continue I feel hardly settled. There are two parties to be consulted in the decision. The work, in addition to other claims is pretty hard; but it gives advantages for practical anatomy very desirable to be secured for the Class, and some little surgery. The Dispensers are young men of my own training. . . .

I regret this Government connection most on the score of book-making, for which so many engagements leave me practically no time. But I hope some of the Graduates will exhibit public spirit enough to bring out each some good medical work in Tamil. I feel pretty sanguine of a Surgery thus produced—to be issued in two or three years. Able persons have promised me to bring out a work on the Practice of Physic; another at his own expense to prepare a work on Medical Jurisprudence, . . .

This people are quite intelligent. The lack with them, as looked at from a missionary standpoint, is that they know far better than they do, —which is the defect of our race. Even the most unlettered comes under this class, and the best also must confess to it as including himself.

I feel very much obliged to you for your assiduous kindness to my father in his recent illness. I like to think of your long and useful career. You have been singularly favored. We must regard the inclination and ability for usefulness as a gift and not, I am convinced, as a merit by which to secure an earned reward. Nothing, I believe, is more offensive to our Maker than self-righteousness. It contemns the righteousness He has achieved and offers for our reliance, and presumes to present as acceptable to the Omniscient scrutiny and the Infinite purity what we forsooth regard as worthy. I believe at the last grand assize men will not be condemned for this or that enormity, but for a rejection of the salvation wrought and offered us freely by Jesus Christ. So that the villain who has in contrition trusted in Christ will fare better than the purest moralist who will be beholden to none other (than himself) for his heaven.

Sivaism, in its more refined parts, is a system of morality. It inculcates alms, and the land is studded with rest-houses, road-side wells, village temples, all made as works of merit. The heathen never "found out God" but have attempted to satisfy, by gifts and tortures, Him who owns themselves and all their acquisitions, and whose demand is the obedience of the entire life, inward and outward.

But I see my letter is growing long, and I will not moralize. I only wish you may be so happy as to appreciate and enjoy the love of Christ personally for you as His penitent, grateful, adoring follower and friend. All other loves are but hints of this, as mere sparkles and twinkles compared with an unclouded meridian sun. . . . .

With best wishes, grateful memories, high esteem and sincere affection, I am,

Yours very truly,

SAMUEL F. GREEN.

Some notion of the surgical operations performed at the Hospital on the days Dr. Green visited it may be had from this record of the 7th of August: "Danforth sent me a note saying two Chank gatherers had been severely bitten by a huge shark. I saw them this morning. One has four bad, deep, large bites in his right thigh, and the other has his right thigh bitten off, leaving as stump the upper third. We sawed off a bit of the bone which projected about three inches; performed Simm's operation on an unhappy woman; and tapped a Moorman, making out a pretty good surgical clinique for the thirteen students and three doctors present."

To his nephew, in the Northern Army, Dr. Green wrote:

THURSDAY, *September* 17, 1863.

MY DEAR NEPHEW, WILLIAM N. GREEN, JR.:

Your letter of the 4th of June was most gladly welcomed. Though brief it spoke much to my heart. I would most unfeignedly thank Our Father for preserving you amidst such open and great dangers. I thank him for giving you courage and strength and success. Let us, while grateful, not alloy our thankfulness by any pride, but say, "What have we that we have not received," as an out and out gift? "Not unto us, O Lord, not unto us, but unto Thy name be the glory." I have shown the narrative of your prowess to several.

As in all things, so in daring and heroism, Jesus is still our Leader. He stands far ahead of the boldest in manly courage. Witness, His march from Galilee to Jerusalem with the infuriated mob, and the cross all in clear view and settled certainty; quiet but no blenching; no "noise of Captains and shouting" to stir his blood, but gentle as a Lamb walked He into the very face and paw of wolves —fiercest pack—designedly, determinedly, divinely met and suffered and overcame all. But let us beware of being mere admirers of our "Great Captain." Let us habitually look to Him as our only hope, our strength from hour to hour. You must have much need of His help, and constantly, for where war is abroad, vice is almost sure to be rampant. But remember it is better to stand alone than to fall with many. "Stand, therefore, having your loins girt about with truth." And may God bless you, and may you be very happy in the felt presence of the best Friend daily.

Very affectionately, your uncle and friend,

SAMUEL F. GREEN.

Dr. Green seems to have lived in close sympathy with Christ in revulsion from sin, in acquiescence in His justice and in love for His cause.

WED. 23, *Sept.* 1863.

MY DEAR SISTER JULIA:

I was thinking about you last Sunday a great deal. . . . I almost cried to think that I should offend against one so loving. Then I thought what poignancy remorse will acquire from the fact that the lost will realize at last against what wondrous excellency and love they have obdurately sinned. The rejection of Jesus surpasses in heinousness all other known crimes. We shall and cannot but join in the "Anathema" even on nearest relatives, if they at the Judgment stand against Christ. So horrible and inexcusable will rejection of the Divine love appear to us. . . .

We must not let our feelings rebel against the orderings of Providence. Nay, I would rejoice, though it be at the expense of sundering from dear esteemed and loving relatives, that I am permitted to live among the Heathen as a "Witness for the glorious Saviour. . . .

Most affectionately, your brother,

SAMUEL F. GREEN.

As this first year of his second term of missionary service was about closing Dr. Green received a letter from his friend Dr. Patterson of Madras. "I have had evidence enough," said he, "to satisfy me of this, that there is little chance of people at home doing much for Medical Missions, or enabling a man to develop satisfactorily the work which he has initiated, and I am therefore anxious if possible to take measures whereby a native staff of agents may be raised expressly to labor in the Mission field." It was natural, however, that physicians and others distant from the field, should fail to appreciate their work. But if the supply of physical wants disarms prejudice against the offered supply of spiritual wants, what relief can be a better introduction to the appeal of the gospel than the healing of the sick?

It is impossible to sum up the results of a year of Dr. Green's varied work, for spiritual results are discovered by the gradual manifestation of a renewed life. But the visible work is enough to show that a medical missionary is necessarily a busy man. To carry on the Dispensary at the station is to do the work of a merchant in buying and selling medicines, of a druggist in preparing and dealing them out, of a physician in examining and prescribing for patients, of a surgeon in cases of fracture and in those involving the use of instruments, of a teacher in superintending the work of assistants, and of an evangelist in preaching the gospel and giving spiritual counsel in individual cases. The treatment of over twelve hundred patients gave opportunity at the same time to give religious instruction to perhaps as many more of their friends and attendants.

In training a class of medical students, he not only had to give regular intructions in the several branches of medical science, but to initiate them in practice, to procure their books and instruments, to direct their work in dissections, to give them clinical lectures when it was practicable,—as it was once every week at the Hospital, —and to imbue them so far as possible with the principles and spirit of the Christian faith and life.

Add to this his preaching at stations and out-stations as occasion required, in school bungalows, and to gatherings at private houses on Sunday-afternoons, and it seems as if the amount of visible work was a good deal more than could reasonably be expected of any one. Whether the spiritual results were large or small, they were such as only God could with certainty know. But it is certain that He honors the means used by His appointment, and that the results as He sees them are as disproportionately great, as they seem to man disproportionately small, in comparison with the instrumentality.

To all this must be added his work at the Friend-in-Need-Society's Hospital,—undertaken for the opportunities of preaching Christ to the patients there, for the pecuniary benefit of his department in the Mission, and for the instruction of his students in practical anatomy,—where everything was under his direction, and where among the eight thousand patients annually treated, the worst cases, especially in surgery, were attended to by himself.

CHAPTER XIII.

1863–1864: ÆT. 41–42.

AFTER a trial of three months, Dr. Green had decided to continue to superintend the Friend-in-Need Society's Hospital. The main inducement were the opportunities for showing the way of salvation, and the advantages to his Class for the study of practical anatomy, and for witnessing his treatment of cases and learning his reasons for it. He exhibited "successfully and repeatedly Dr. Simm's famous operation—one of the most important advances in surgery of the past quarter-century."

In December, he received from Mr. and Mrs. Twynam, English residents, a gift of twelve pounds sterling, or sixty dollars. It was made in recognition of his professional services and as a testimonial of their friendly regard for him personally. But he said, "I consider it a donation to the Mission, and being now in funds I am planning for a bungalow for the accommodation of the sick in the Printing House compound southeast of the Dispensary."

The number of patients treated in 1863 at the Friend in-Need Society's Hospital and Dispensary, "although the Mission Dispensary was again opened and more than the usual number of Practitioners of Foreign medicine were engaged in the Province," was 8630; and the number treated at the Manepy Dispensary was 1217, making a total of 9847.

On the 1st of January Dr. Green wrote his father, the following letter, announcing the birth of his first child.

JAFFNA, CEYLON.

MY VERY DEAR FATHER:

Your grand daughter waves you a kiss with her own hand, and wishes you a "Happy New Year."

If the Giver spares her life, I shall teach her to love her grandfather Green, and to revere his memory. May the Savior develop this additional twig, upon the Green-family-Tree, into a bough, abundantly "fruitful in every good word and work."

Pray thus for her, and that her parents may aright train this tendril, that it draggle not in dust, but clamber on the trellis of the Cross.

Your loving son,

SAMUEL F. GREEN.

On the 4th he wrote his sister Mary: "Pray that saving grace which the Lord was pleased through your agency to bestow upon me may be perpetuated and extended in and through her to many others. I shall hope to teach her to appreciate the blessing she inherits in having so many praying relatives. . . . . I feel a new set of emotions springing into being."

In respect to native music for public and private worship, as well as a medical literature in Tamil, Dr. Green found an efficient co-laborer in the Rev. Mr. Webb of Dindigul, who collected and arranged the materials for a book. Being obliged to relinquish his work on account of failing health, Mr. Webb wrote: "You speak of the effort to introduce the Tamil music and metres into our Christian worship. *Magna est veritas et prevalebit.* It is making steady progress. I am satisfied that it has advanced as fast as could be expected; prejudice, ignorance, and ecclesiasticism are against it, but *truth* is more than these. I wish you could hear my hundred and fifty children with the adults singing with one voice and accord, and with a will too—as you could were you here. I am paid *here* for everything I have done. God will use it as a means of great blessing, and will employ it as an agent for the spread of his truth." It was not long before Dr. Green furnished fifty copies of the music book to Mr. McArthur of the Church Mission, and disposed of all he had to others and ordered more, determined to supply the community with Christian songs in their own style.

Among the numberless absurdities of the natives, which have a bearing on their social if not on their moral welfare, the following incident may be mentioned. The Doctor lost his way, and a fellow volunteered to be his guide. "We walked and talked, he long trying to find out who I was. When he learned I was the 'Padre-Physician', he very confidingly asked me to make him up a Love Potion, so he could win favor in the eyes of some one he wished to marry."

The Mission voted that Doctor Green might take a medical class of twelve in the vernacular, and employ two specified members of the advanced class to assist in instructing them; that he might get Mr. Hunt, of Madras, to print fifty sets of cuts for Natural Philosophy, and fifty for Surgery, in form suitable "to bind in with the manuscripts the boys might develop;" that he might "have printed five thousand copies of a Ticket-tract to give to registered patients at the Dispensary;" that he might get a dozen copies each of Anatomy and Obstetrics "interleaved and strongly bound for the use of the Class;" and that he might "take from the Seminary at Batticotta any unused apparatus or chemicals which would be of service in training the new Medical Class." He had twenty-six applicants from whom to select this Class.

A translation of the second part of the *Physician's Vade Mecum* was promised by Dr. J. A. Evarts (Tamil) by the close of the year. "This," said Dr. Green, "together with the Manuscript of *Druit's Surgery in Tamil*, put at my service by Dr. Danforth (Tamil), will vastly relieve the difficulty of training in the vernacular. The enterprise is an arduous one, but it seems clearly expedient to grapple with it. I hope ten years will show the best results. My reliance is on God for his blessing on hard work. I find the technical terms prepared some years ago, before I went to America, of the greatest service, coming out at this juncture like buried treasure. The highly cultivated Anglo-Tamil scholars, whose services were availed of to arrange these vocabularies, are now scattered here and there, at work on heavier pay than we can afford to offer."

In March he was two days in the District Court as a medical witness for the Defence in the case of an alleged nuisance. His description of the trial is interesting as showing progress in one direction:

"Some Englishmen, offended by the smell of

rotting cocoanut husks in the Beach mud along and opposite their residences (and our Health Bungalow on the south shore), wish to drive off the thousands whose livelihood in good part depends on this industry of getting out fibre and twisting it into rope. Young———was advocate for the Defendants, and threw himself well before the public in his maiden speech summing up the evidence. He is Doctor———'s younger brother, appeared as usual dressed in broadcloth in full European costume. He was retained, I am told, for fifteen pounds in the case, a good start for him, as the case makes a wide sensation, being a struggle between different nationalities, and is decided for the Tamils—the masses. The sight of the young man questioning the Government Agent standing under oath, a first class Englishman, interrogated by a Farmer Caste Tamilian,—to see the fellow wipe the perspiration with a large white handkerchief, occasionally indulging in a pinch from his snuff-box,—all together shows a progress of some sort, somewhat an advance in civilization if not in Christianity. There was a crowd of a hundred or so about the Court, and I was impressed by the fact of seeing only two to five foreheads bearing Sivite marks. A Madras heathen would almost think we had a nominally Christian community here, I think."

To a considerable extent the natives were accustomed to dispense with physicians and rely upon themselves. "Hitherto," said Dr. Green, "medicine among the Tamils has been a family thing. This and that secret passed down from generation to generation. When we have many educated on one basis in a common general system of medicine, we may hope for this pervading quackery to decline somewhat."

To his sister he wrote:

MANEPY, JAFFNA, *March* 18, 1864.

MY DEAR SISTER LYDIA:

. . . . I rejoice much in assurance that you enjoy much, and that you receive trials and joys both in faith. It is the chiefest value of life—this living by faith and so from year to year broadening our basis for the eternal growth in bliss. My heart does not sink nor quail, but it almost trembles in tenderness to think of Death waiting for you and for me and for each of the dear inner band. The mails between us fly to and fro, and we must expect some letters to bear news of bereavement. Who lingers last will bear the most of this trial, and who go the first, the least. Let us take this all into our calculations habitually, not in gloominess but in quiet resignation, nay, preference for God's plan in it all. Death is enumerated in the category of the "all things are yours." We will appropriate it and profit by it even beforehand, letting it also "work together" with all else "for good."

With the greatest esteem and affection, I am

Your brother,

SAMUEL F. GREEN.

Saturday, March 26, 1864.

MY DEAR FATHER:

How often I think of you and pray for you. When I feel my affection so drawn out toward my little child I realize as never before how much my father loved me. When through sleeping hours waking you carried me "far enough to go from Green Hill to the Ohio," I can see that love prompted the patience shown towards a fretful babe. I see the little girl is a great teacher, and the relation established in providence between her and me, gives much light on many words of Scripture, where the figure of Father and child, is used to convey to us an idea of the relation existing between God and us.

Mr. Joseph S. Kendall once remarked how much my ways resembled yours, and so I cannot but feel that my parental emotions are not only in the general but in particular like yours. I hope all will make me love you still more tenderly and gratefully, and help me to love my Heavenly Father with all my heart, as I delight to have my little girl love me.

How it does set my bosom aglow to have the darling gaze fondly in my eyes and smile her love so unmistakably. Does an earthly father so value the love of his child, and is our Father in Heaven less loving than we? "God is love." Let us, dear Father, love Him as He discloses Himself to us in Jesus Christ, growingly, fully, perfectly. It is due. What a shame that we love so little, so inconstantly, Him who always and infinitely loves us.

31st.—My dear Father, I have to thank you for your two kind notes received on the 29th. Dates to 1st ultimo. Your expressions of affection and interest are duly appreciated, I assure you. I am glad to learn of your entrance upon your eighty-eighth year. May your long evening be precursor of a glorious day. Among all the tender emotions concerning you, one rises paramount—the desire to be assured of your hearty humble acceptance of Christ as your Sovereign and Saviour.—With much love I remain most respectfully and affectionately

Your son,

SAMUEL F. GREEN.

Saturday, *April* 2, 1864.

MY DEAR SISTER MARY:

. . . . I enjoy much rest in God. I understand it to be His gift, and know my reliance for the supply of faith all along must be solely on Him who at first conferred it. No earthly treasure is to be compared with it. It appears as if the whole tendency, the main design of Jesus in this providence, is to fix our trust in Himself fully, solely. I know this comfort is not from self, for naturally none is more distrusting than I. It will continue as long as He perpetuates it. It will cease the moment He ceases to sustain it. He is the author and finisher of our faith. But what a finisher. He does not finish by putting an end to it, but by bringing it to the highest state of finish, by perfecting it.

I have to thank God for the influence of dear Mr. Knudsen. He strongly bent me to "trust all in God." This phrase, often on his lips and always in his life, he seems quietly to have impressed on my inner life. He has been, under God's hand, the signet of great peace to me. I know any hour the peace may be dissipated, but I know equally that if lost, God can fully restore, and He can so guard and cherish it that the inward rest shall never cease save as it merges and blends into the rest of heaven.—With very much love I remain

Your brother,

SAMUEL F. GREEN.

The parental heart will appreciate the domestic tenderness of Dr. Green in the following extracts from letters to the sister whose name he gave his child:

JAFFNA, *April* 13, 1864.

MY DEAR SISTER JULIA:

I should greatly delight to see our little Julia in her namesake-aunty's arms. She shows much affection and intelligence already. O dear Sister Julia, to see her speaking eyes beam out from her face all lighted with smiles makes me about as happy for the moment as I can hold. I know you will pray for her; ask her early regeneration. For all else in comparison I care little.

July 20th.—I should like you to see baby. I think she is pretty and very active and bright. If I put on another coat she observes it. She says Papa now very distinctly. I have so many things to tell you about her, but when I come to the penning all seems to fail. However, you understand about babies and can imagine it all. Suffice it to say, she is a "well-spring of pleasure," a charming teacher, a choicest treasure.

July 29th.—Yester-afternoon I went home after part of two days absence. The little thing gave me such a hearty welcome back,—seemed so glad to be in my arms again,—dear little precious, I felt it worth a long journey to get such a greeting.

August 6th.—Little J. has to-day taken up the

word Mamma; so, with the word Papa, she calls each of us distinctly.

Believe me most affectionately,

Your brother,

SAMUEL F. GREEN.

Here is an incident suggestive of untold misery resulting from the senseless customs and prejudices of heathenism. "A wealthy Moorman," wrote Dr. Green, "called to consult about his wife who has apparently a mammary abscess. I suggested that he take Latimer (a Tamil) and let him examine, and if needful use the lancet. He could not consent. No one could be allowed to see his wife. I proposed that she be seated behind a curtain through which the Doctor could do the needful. But he would not agree."

Dr. Green not only urged his former students to assist him, but made them feel under obligation to do so,—as is evident from this letter from his first Tamil graduate.

BADULLA, *May* 6, 1864.

MY DEAR SIR:

I received your kind note a few days ago, and was hesitating how to answer it because I have often promised undertakings of a like nature and have as often failed—of which I feel thoroughly ashamed. I have, however, made up my mind to make an attempt, and to carry it out I require help to a great extent.

What work will you recommend for the translation? The edition of Taylor, which I have at present, is an old edition—1852. During the last twelve years great advancement has been made in Physiology and Pathology, which throws great light on Medical Jurisprudence. It is therefore very desirable that I should translate the latest edition of the work. Could you spare me a copy?

Yours, most dutiful,

IRA GOULD.

The two Classes of Medical Students, eleven and twelve, assembled with the servants in the Doctor's sitting room at 8 o'clock A. M. for prayers. Of the Seniors seven were Christians, and of the Juniors five.

In the course of the summer he "finished finding, coining, and adopting names for all the ligaments of the body—work very interesting and proportionally exhausting; a long vista of it in the rest of Anatomy, to say nothing of Chemistry and other branches beyond." He also "completed the examination of a Manuscript Dictionary left in 1857, and secured the transfer of the desired words from it to a more recent and larger manuscript work."

Dr. Green received a letter from a Tamil enclosing money for his brother, which furnished occasion for the explanation of so many Tamils having English names. "The youngest of the three," he said, "is known in the Class by the name of Levi Spaulding; but in the letter he is called Sinnatambi,—which means little-younger-brother. It is not a heathen name, but the case is a sample of many occurrent, of using a name to suit foreigners and another to suit the villagers. Dr. Evarts' (a Tamil) little boys are named for the foreigner, Henry, James, and Alfred; for the village, Periyatambi, Sinnatambi, and Iliyatambi, meaning respectively, Great-, Little-, and Younger-younger brother. All this is less objectionable than the usage in some professedly Christian families where there is for each child some European name and a name of some Hindu idol."

The news of the death of his nephew, Lieutenant Colonel William N. Green, Jr., at New Orleans, from a wound received in the battle of Pleasant Hill, called forth the following letter.

UDUPITTI, JAFFNA, CEYLON, *July* 28, 1864.

MY DEAR BROTHER OLIVER:

. . . . . . Your welcome note of 10th

May I have in hand. Soon after it was penned our noble and beloved nephew passed into the immediate presence of his Judge and ours. It comes very near to us—this affliction. May it do us good as it doth the upright in heart. We have but to exercise faith to secure this, and faith is the gift of God who gives liberally. We shall have all that we will use.

Who knows whether this maelstrom will suck away any other near and dear? whether the Draft will crowd off from home and friends any other one of our loved band? We can scarce expect to be exempt. Perhaps we should not even over-anxiously wish it, seeing our Country is in such sad case and her only way out seems to be through blood.

Worcester has given largely. The Christian, be he soldier or citizen, may rest all on Christ, assured that He is Lord of lords, be they Presidents, Generals, or Dictators, and that all shall, *nolens volens*, fulfill His purposes. I cannot but feel that when the clouds, now so murky and dark over our dear Land, shall have dispersed, we shall see the Sun of Righteousness nearer noon than ever he stood before.

Here I have re-read your letter. It does me good to see your interest in the good cause look out incidentally here and there. I don't think it restricted to exertion and success among the heathen nor among the unconverted anywhere. There is Christian growth, individual and collective, to be encouraged. There is the advance of nominally Christian countries to real Christianity.

The work of the Devil is going on all the world over; but the counter-work of Christ is also going on, and growingly so, while the other must steadily decline. Here and there the struggle waxes intense; everywhere it is in progress. In politics, in socials, in all sections of the race's life, tyrannies must down, freedom will rise. While I feel in the dark about our Country as to the immediate future, I feel all clear as to the Great Future. I think those principles that cropped out in the Reformation, in Puritanism, in Democracy are in the aggregate the "Stone" spoken of by Daniel, which became as the mountain that is to fill the whole earth. It is to "dash in pieces." It is at work in the old world and in the new. Though great events are transpiring, still greater, one is impressed, must be near. You there and in your way, I here and in mine, are under the same Master and at work for the same great end. May He keep us faithful to the end, and vouchsafe us visible successes as we can bear them. . . . —Most affectionately, Your brother,

SAMUEL F. GREEN.

In a letter of the same date to his friends at Green Hill, occur the following sentences:

"We all loved our dear William, we admired his spirit, watched with interest his rise into maturity. Our Heavenly Father has seen it best his sun should go down early. What His might performs,

His mercy plans, His love decrees. I feel the blank, but I would say, 'Thy will be done.' I pray the event may be blessed to each of us as individuals, as a family, as citizens concerned for our Country. May it deepen our sympathy for the many distressed. We are brought more into fellowship now with the children of sorrow. Dear boy, I will hope to meet him in happiness at last. I thank you for the copies of those touching notes of the loved one. How excruciating his agony, and prolonged. We must praise God in all. It may be seen that all this was for his soul—that he had a month to adjust himself to meet his Maker, instead of being dashed into His presence in an instant as were many of his fellows. The Lord does all things well."

To his family at home he wrote:

JAFFNA, CEYLON, FRIDAY, 16 *Sept.* 1864.

TO MY DEAR FATHER, MY DEAR SISTERS FOUR, AND MY DEAR BROTHERS FIVE:—*Greeting*:

Allow me, as bound and privileged, to report myself on this our Family anniversary,—I am favored with fair health, with every comfort I can reasonably ask. My work enlists my lively interest and all my available energy. I see it promising for the future, pleasant to day.

The funds of the Med. Dept. tho' limited according to the million scale are abundant for all current expense and allow of judicious plans for expansion.

The assistants are intelligent and tractable—the students progressing hopefully. So much in brief about self and circumstances. In spirituals I enjoy much and expect to much more. I have the germs of bliss and confidently anticipate the full fruition—be there never so many trials between.

My desire for each of you is a firm and a growing faith in Jesus, for I am sure there is no other basis of happiness but this one only. May we all meet in glory, to part never again.

With very much love your son and brother,

SAMUEL F. GREEN.

Dr. Green was very careful not to encourage the natives in mistaking civilization for Christianity; but he found occasion to say: "I begin to think that the change here will be from a waist-cloth to pants, from a scarf to a coat, from a turban to a hat, from vegetarianism to carnivorism, from a hut to a house and so on till many while yet unchristianized may be denationalized. I would rather here see Christian Hindus than Hindus Europeanized."

He had an exalted conception of the missionary work, but not to the disparagement of Christian work of any kind or in any place; he said:

"I consider this work of establishing the kingdom of Christ in hearts at home and abroad as the leading enterprise of every age. I regard all movements among the nations to have their chief importance in their bearing on the advance of the cause of the Redeemer.

"Happy is each in being permitted in his place and calling to live for this. This object elevates the lowest and ennobles the most servile. The fact that not where nor what, but *how* we perform 'the common task' makes us co-workers together with Christ, may well encourage us to patient continuance in well-doing. '*In* the service'—the discipline, the successes are 'great reward.' *For* the service, 'glory, honor, immortality' superadded, double the recompense. Who would not work for Jesus?"

As to the condition of his field he said: "Light has so increased in Jaffna that the very head place of Sivaism is seen to be a den of infamy, and some of the heathen, for very shame I believe, are calling for reforms. One of the leading priests is a votary of the Sakti system, and is now a patient with a bad fracture, consequent I believe on his drunkenness. All the Brahmins about this shrine are reported licentious, and the temple is but the partner of the brothel. When equal light shall permeate India, Brahminism will have become a thing of the past."

CHAPTER XIV.

1864–1865: ÆT. 42–43.

ONE of the results of missionary labor, and especially of foreign civilized society, among the heathen, is the adoption by the latter to some extent of the habits of the foreigners; and this within certain limits is encouraging. But Dr. Green deprecated the pride and self-importance consequent upon the adoption of such habits, so far as it tended to destroy the usefulness of the educated natives among their own people. "I hope," said he, "by going into vernacular education, to get some doctors who will in native dress start off afoot in reponse to calls, and not demand a horse and carriage to be sent and a heavy fee also in addition. This aping European habits is very well in moderation, but young Jaffna overdoes it."

Again he said, "I am passing through a juncture which lies on the higher side of a promising future of my work. Once I succeed in bringing the science of medicine into the vernacular by the graduation of a Class taught in it, I shall have, D. V., in notes, glossaries and manuscripts, the basis on which to conduct future Classes so easily that I can simultaneously have Classes in English and in Tamil, and thus be doubled in one section of my usefulness."

Early in January, he received a letter from Mr. Murdock of Madras, speaking of having seen in Calcutta "a very handsome Medical Book in Hindustani with colored plates," of there being "a committee formed at Madras to attend to the forming of technicals for the introduction of the Western Sciences into Tamil," also speaking of "Dr. Smith, a very pious man, head of the Madras Medical College." According to his intention, Dr. Green probably wrote to the Secretary of the committee to see what he could learn in the way of forming scientific terms, and to Dr. Smith to see if he could get any aid in "printing and publishing Medical Books." "In fact," said he, "Mr. Murdock's note is a streak of light from the west, but my dependence is upon that from the very Zenith."

Within a few weeks, Dr. Green wrote: "Dr. George Smith, Principal of the Madras Medical College, thinks to teach medicine scientifically in the vernacular would be a half-century retrograde." He also wrote: "Dr. Paterson, of the Free Scotch Church, Madras, is about to open a medical training school to raise medical helpers for missions,—vernacular. He has a scheme to raise two thousand pounds for buildings, etc.; most of it is raised already in Scotland. I have tried to put myself in communication with him, so that we can mutually aid and strengthen each other."

Of the birth of his second child he thus wrote:

MY DEAR FATHER:

Here's another grandchild for you. I wish I could reach her over to you that you might place your hand upon her head and pronounce adoption. Lacking this, she claims her place upon the Family tree, and will, I hope, grow, not only worthy of this, but of a place also on the True Vine, and abide therein and bring forth much fruit of the Spirit. . . .

I hope, dear Father, you are comfortable and happy. I long that you have a well founded hope of eternal bliss to cheer and sustain. A hope badly founded may cheer, but it deludes and will destroy. . . .

Your affectionate son,

SAMUEL F. GREEN.

He wrote to his family at Green Hill:

March 21, 1865.

MY DEAR FRIENDS:

I think I have almost unconsciously for years been oppressed with an apprehension of changes in our loved circle. It is a mistake; in Christ it is our privilege to anticipate rather than apprehend. Who of us, with a true worthy hope for the hereafter, would consent to an immutable fixity of our present condition, individual or associated? How far better than even the full cup of temporal good we quaff, the things eye hath not seen nor ear heard—prepared for those who love God. How thoroughly we change when we pass from self to Christ. Thenceforth we pass on from all we might deprecate to all we can desire. The night is behind, the dawn is before us. God not only gives us in Christ many things the world knows not of, but in those many things common to all we enjoy their richest quality through this relation."

Dr. Green recorded this sample of his employment of a Sunday afternoon:

"I called on the thousand-cocoanut-breaking blacksmith and talked with him about his diabetes of which he is dying, and closed with another oft-repeated offer of the gospel. Then went to a house where was a group of hardened degraded Sivite women, with whom we had a seemingly profitless talk. Then to a Palm-root-bed by which some women were scolding and quarrelling about a three-quarter penny piece which one of them had lost and charged the other with stealing, challenging her to go to the temple and swear she did not take it. Then to an educated man who was building his house, asking if he approved of a weekly rest-day, and reminding him to spread its benefits by his example. Then to the temple opposite where a young Brahmin was rather irritated and rude, closing up with a promise to send him a Gospel, which he promised to read impartially."

A little rift in the cloud of stolidity which had so long hung over the people is thus described:

"The Sivites in Vannooponny, the native centre of the Province, have lectures every Sunday evening in support of their system and against Christianity. On the following Tuesday evening the Christians have their lecture. A reporter tells what points were taken up in the Sivite meeting, and the Christians rebut what is said. Some two hundred or three hundred attend these meetings, and the circumstances are very encouraging. I hope and pray the movement may rouse many from apathy, and that many may seek and find the truth."

The work of creating a scientific nomenclature in Tamil was so difficult and yet so extremely important that Dr. Green was always glad to get the critical opinions of scholars in that language. "I received," he said, "a letter from Mr. Tracy, of Madura, expressing himself and the best translator of their Mission pleased with the Rules devised by Brother Webb and myself several years ago, and somewhat in detail giving approval of my procedures in the construction of Terms. This is very timely, as I hope soon to discuss and determine about this matter with Dr. Paterson who is, I trust, touring towards us."

On the subject of the war in the United States, which then was about being brought to a close, he wrote:

MANEPY, *May* 8, 1865.

MY BELOVED AND REVERED FATHER:

.... I congratulate you on being spared to see the close of a terrible war—wicked, inexcusable, savage on the part of the malcontents. May the Lord give them repentance and a better mind. I think I see all this wrath of man made to praise God, caused to subserve the advance of that kingdom which is Liberty, Peace and Love. My dear Father, let us be sure, trying ourselves prayerfully by the word, that we are in this kingdom. Then for time or for eternity we shall be blessed. . . .

With much affection, your son,

SAMUEL F. GREEN.

Saturday, May 20, 1865.

My Dear Sister Mary:

It is in my heart to repay you fully in kind for your most acceptable communications. They help me spiritually and I prize them highly. Our highest employ, so far as I know, seems to be adoration of Immanuel. In this there appear to be two grades—one for his goodness to us, the other for his essential goodness and glory. How condescending to receive our praise, so low and feeble is it even to our own apprehension. . . .

The recent news from our native Land stirs one's thanksgiving. I desire not to be elated by it, nor to be depressed by any reverse. The worldling resting on Earth's fluctuations naturally tosses up and down. One can be no steadier than his foundation. The child of God mounts higher into the serene above all human perturbations. . . .

I feel I am much favored as to my health. I am pressing on an amount of work which I did not imagine I should do on my return. But the Lord is very gracious, and has arranged things so that I am saved all needless harassment, and gives strength according to the task imposed. I wish self eliminated, and Christ incorporated in all I do: Then it will be to purpose, and He will establish the work of my hands upon me. . . .

Very affectionately your brother,

Samuel F. Green.

The following letter from John Murdock, LL.D., agent of the Christian Vernacular Education Society, shows his sympathy with Dr. Green's views of Medical Education.

NELLORE, *June* 24, 1865.

MY DEAR DR. GREEN:

. . . . I have your paper on the rendering of scientific terms, and the other lists, etc. It will give me much pleasure to discuss the various points with the parties named, and let you know their opinions. Some weeks must elapse before I can reach Madras and see Dr. Paterson and Mr. Percival, but you may be assured that the matter will not be forgotten.

So far as I have been able to judge from my brief visit, (to Jaffna) my most sanguine hopes with regard to native Medical education promise to be realized. I have been greatly encouraged by what I have seen. I rejoice at it especially because it leads me to hope that *eventually* on the continent similar results may be secured. . . .

With kindest regards to Mrs. Green,

Yours affectionately,

J. MURDOCK.

Obviously the coining of Scientific terms must precede translation. "The plan is, D. V.," wrote

Dr. Green, "to give 1864—1867 to Class and Terms-making; then 1867—1870 to Class and book-making. After securing a set of vernacular Medical Text-books, I wish to publish a number of popular sanitary Tracts.

"In Tamildom," continued he, "are six Protestant Medical Missionaries; viz., Lowe of Travancore, Lord and Chester of Madura, Scudder (Silas) of Arcot, Paterson of Madras, Green of Jaffna, the last the senior of all (except perhaps Dr. Lord). My old friend John Murdock, Esq., LL. D., Agent of the Christian Vernacular Education Society, travels about India from Lahore to Ceylon, Madras, Calcutta, Bombay. He is a shrewd investigator, a close observer, a laborious, devoted, simple-hearted, cheerful Christian. I value his opinion on medico-missionary matters in Jaffna. Members from the three missions in the Province met him at Nellore, Jaffna. We canvassed the question of Tamil style: concluded there had been a hue and cry unwarranted by facts, and that good Jaffna Tamil and good coast Tamil were identical, and that books could be spread from there here and from here there as might be desired. His Society occupies an important place as a link between different Mission bodies. I hope he will unite the six Medical Missionaries to act in concert, and so we may achieve the more."

FROM DR. MURDOCK.

MADRAS, *July* 31, 1865.

MY DEAR DR. GREEN:

. . . . I have showed the list of books, and rules for translating technical terms. Messrs. Lord and Lowe took copies of the latter. Mr. Chester seemed to think that, as changes are taking place so rapidly in medical science, students must know English to keep up with the times, vernacular books soon becoming obsolete. I think he exaggerates the progress. However, *I* should feel well satisfied if the native doctors in India were only quarter of a century behind Europe and America. . . .

Although a few Europeans who do not know Tamil may throw cold water on your plan of getting out a series of text-books, I hope you will persevere. I am persuaded that in time the people will appreciate them. . . .

If spared to meet Dr. Paterson, I shall be able to encourage him by an account of what I saw in Jaffna. . .

Yours affectionately,

J. MURDOCK.

FROM DR. LOWE.

NAGOOR, NEAR NAGERCOIL, SOUTH TRAVANCORE,

Aug. 23, 1865.

MY DEAR DR. GREEN:

. . . Though we are not personally known to each other, both before I left England and since, I have heard a good deal about you and your interesting work, and feel assured that it would be a great advantage to me, in carrying on my work, to enjoy the benefit of your experience and advice. . . . I rejoice in your success, and trust that ere long, as the result of your efforts, the Senior Medical Class in Trevandrum and my Class in connection with our Medical Mission here will be provided with good practical Text-books in the Vernacular. If we are to train Natives to be efficient assistants and fellow-laborers in the medical department of Mission work, the publication of such works. . . . is of such importance that, if necessary, I should consider that what funds we could spare (and I am thankful to say our Medical Mission is very liberally supported) would be well spent in aiding you. . . . Friends in Scotland are deeply interested in this experiment, and have helped me much. . . .

The Medical Missionary Circular, published monthly by the Hon. Mrs. MacKenzie, of Edinburgh, I wrote to be sent to you from the commencement and to continue regularly. I hope you will receive them. . . .

Yours very sincerely,

JOHN LOWE.

FROM DR. LOWE.

NEGOOR NEAR NAGERCOIL, *Sept.* 16, 1865.

MY DEAR DR. GREEN:

I received your kind welcome letter of September 1st. . . . I shall most gladly render assistance and co-operate with you in the literary work in which you are engaged, and having as my colleague at this station one who has for many years been engaged in such work, and. . . . had fully six years training in a Chemist's shop and received a partial medical education, . . . I think, in the way of revising your manuscripts and to some extent testing their adaptation, Mr. Baylis and I may be able to render some help. I think your idea of first using the manuscript with a Class or two a *very* good one. In no way would there be more likelihood of securing a thorough and satisfactory revision before going to press. . . . If the manuscripts were gone over systematically, I don't think the delay would be great. At intervals of a month or six weeks, the sections we have gone over should be forwarded to you with our corrections, alterations or suggestions for *your* consideration and decision. In this way, . . . by the time we had finished it, you could have it ready, or nearly so, for the press.—I shall be most happy to receive a copy of your manuscript of Druitt's Surgery as soon as you can send it; I shall feel much obliged too for a copy of your set of Terms for Anatomy.—I am glad to learn that, so far as funds are concerned, you are so very well off. . . .

In cases of suspected poisoning . . . our Judges in Criminal Courts know nothing whatever about Medical Jurisprudence, and justice is often frustrated through such ignorance. The Dewan suggested the preparation of a simple treatise on the subject, suited to the capacity of men who had not received a medical education. . . .

Yours very sincerely,

JOHN LOWE.

"In changing from English to vernacular Medical Instruction," wrote Dr. Green, "the course seems to be to select intelligent young men and train them by the book and by actual practice. The former is being attempted by putting the best Text Book in each branch into the hands of a Teacher, and furnishing him with equivalents for all the Technicals, either selecting or constructing these as the case may require. The Teacher precedes the Class in writing out a translation which he communicates in daily dictations to the Class, who write it and the next day pass it in review at an examination. The Teacher is enjoined to avoid as far as possible the use of Technicals, and to give the instruction in common language.—The latter is being done by showing occasional cases in the Dispensary at the Station, and by a weekly Clinique at the Hospital in Town.

"It is contemplated to develop these Teachers' Translations into books to be printed, and to append to each book its Glossary, which will be an expansion of the Vocabulary used by the Teacher in his instruction of the Class.

"The series of Books proposed is to comprise a volume each on Anatomy, Chemistry, Physiology, Materia Medica, Practice of Medicine, Surgery, Obstetrics, and Medical Jurisprudence. To these it is desirable to add eventually a volume each on Diseases of Children, Diseases of Women, Pharmacy and Botany.

"The present state of this work may be thus described: A volume on Obstetrics was printed in 1857. A Translation of Druitt's Surgery, with additions from Erichsen and experience, is about completed by Dr. Danforth of the Friend-in-Need Society's Hospital.

"Vocabularies for Natural Philosophy, Chemistry, Anatomy, Physiology and Materia Medica have been prepared, that for Anatomy only, as yet, in both its direct and reverse forms (i. e. English and Tamil, and in Tamil and English forms). All should be thus completed in both forms. Ultimately all the Glossaries should be brought into one Tamil-English Medical Dictionary."

On the day of the Family Anniversary at Green Hill he wrote:

MANEPY, JAFFNA, CEYLON, *Sat.*, 16 *Sept.*, 1865.

MY DEAR FATHER:

MY DEAR SISTERS LUCY, MARY, JULIA, AND LYDIA:

MY DEAR BROTHERS WILLIAM, JOHN, ANDREW, OLIVER AND MARTIN:

With gratitude to our Common Father, with undiminished affection for you each, with intense interest in your weal severally, I would, on this our Family Anniversary, address you a few words of greeting. It is four years since we met.

Goodness and Mercy have still followed us. I would in spirit join with you in ascription of praise to the Author of all our blessings, and supplicate, through the prevalent Mediator, the continuance of that kindness which has hitherto been so abundant and unintermitting.

I consider it my duty to report my place and occupation, and my condition this day to you; looking for an account of your state, from some kind pen among you. I am in comfortable health, am supplied with everything needed for my comfort and for the prosecution of my enterprise, am very much encouraged in my work. Circumstances have been kindly adjusted, for my working to the most advantage, with ease and comfort, with prosperity and effect.

My domestic affairs are flourishing and joyous. The little ones are in good health, are intelligent and well inclined. The wife is quiet, true, devoted, a Help in every way, in my temporal and in my spiritual estate.

My cup overflows with benefits received, and my desire is, as I have "freely received, to learn so freely to give." I would have my heart not like a cistern, but as a spring, constantly receiving and as constantly yielding. We are happy in so far as we make others happy, and in this Divine trait of our being, we may see the highest quality with which we are endowed.

May the Spirit of Grace stir up each of us to "seek first the Kingdom of God and His righteousness," to "follow after peace and holiness, without which we can never see God."

With grateful recollections, growing affection, and sincere esteem, I remain,

Your son and brother,

SAMUEL F. GREEN.

On the 25th of September Dr. Green learned that his father had died "in the Lord," on the 27th of July, in the eighty-ninth year of his age. The same day he wrote a general reply to his sisters and brothers.

Sept. 25, 1865.

My Dear Friends:

. . . . When I saw three letters for me, and one of them in brother Andrew's hand, I surmised some special tidings. I opened brother Andrew's letter first and at once learned of our beloved father's removal. After the first burst of grief is over, I have much peace and happiness in thinking of the departed. My mind is much occupied when at leisure in reviewing his history, and in recounting the goodness of the Lord shown to him, and through him to us all. I will rest in the hope that he has passed into glory. I believe he is happy, and "washed in the blood of the Lamb." I think "Our Father," overruled his Universalist entanglement to keep us stirred up about his salvation, to constrain us to importunate and long continued prayer. I believe God has heard prayer, and that our kind, excellent, lovable father is among the redeemed and is glorified. I feel deeply the kindness of the Lord in lenghtening out his life so long, in giving him at last but brief suffering, in affording many ameliorations of that suffering and our grief. I am glad that more than half his large family were permitted to speak with him and to stand by him in the closing scene. "The Lord gave, the Lord hath taken away; blessed be the name of the Lord." I feel his withdrawal markedly. The head of the list in my daily intercessions has gone. I kissed the two bairns, and spoke to them, though not understood, of their grandfather. I fondly hope to teach them to cherish his memory, to love their father's father for his own sake.

I took my large Bible, and with Margaret looked at the only unfilled space in grandfather's flock; I filled in the date and place, and the record of that whole large family is ended. Between us and the grave now stands no antecedent generation. We are advanced to the front. "The graves are ready for us." May we be ready for them and the bliss beyond. . . . . .

I feel very deeply your call of affection, very gratefully your offers so liberal. I thank my Heavenly Father for your love so enduring, so strong. Could I see it duty, I would with delight respond by a prompt return. But I think my health is every whit as good as when I landed three years ago; and Margaret's health is also as good as when she left America, and that of both the darlings is good.

As to our enterprise, all is prospering up to our highest expectations, and the programme that has naturally formed, and which invites our continued and best energies, cannot be completed without a somewhat protracted stay yet. Left prematurely, what seems so promising would go to wreck. Any abrupt change would appear disastrous. The Lord seems just to be bringing to our aid Doctors Lowe and Paterson. They are juniors to me in this Medico-Missionary Vernacular Educational work. I may in all humility perhaps say with Nehemiah, "Should such a man as I flee?"

If the Lord permit us to carry out our original plan, we have accomplished one-fourth of our stay; nine years will soon roll away, and then perhaps, with our work done fully and well, we may seek your presence and thenceforth abide with you, with no misgivings to disturb us, no far off call unheeded pursuing us.

Should the Lord allow our health to fail, we should see the way toward you open, and your most attractive beckoning would wing us to your society again. We speak this prayerfully. We yearn to dwell with you; but we cannot, unless God-bidden, withdraw our family tithe from the Foreign Missionary work.

Margaret joins me heartily in every expression of sympathy with you in our sorrow, and in much love to you each and all.

Your affectionate brother,

SAMUEL F. GREEN.

To his sister he wrote:

MANEPY, *Sept.* 27, 1865.

MY DEAR SISTER MARY:

I received your sorrowing letter on the 25th. Our dear loved father is gone. But I can but hope to the happiness of heaven. He knew salvation's pathway well. He has long prayed. He fully confessed his sin. He avouched Jesus and Him only to be his Saviour. God can call effectually at any hour, and the Holy Spirit's diversity of operation is as great as the character and the circumstances of the subjects of his gracious influences. I rejoice in the Providence that secured us the comfort of a burial service by one of His own children. . . .

What you say about my return affects me strongly. I feel very grateful for the affection that prompts the urgent counsel to go and dwell with my kindred. I am confident that were you with me for a month, looking into our work, seeing the critical condition of its various details, you would say remain. I apprehend that Mr. Sanders may have given too dark a picture of our health. I did not come out at all as a strong man. God is very good to me, and though I am favored to accomplish a good deal, it is so arranged that I manage to go along with comfort, and I have so many aiding me that I can do still more indirectly, far more than in person. I see no one to whom to commit the work. The week I left, it would mostly stop, and soon wholly cease. I shall keep in mind your united fraternal call, and aim to so hand over things (perhaps to Doctors Lowe, Lord, and Paterson) that, in case I am constrained to leave by ill health or otherwise, there shall be the least possible detriment to the work. My work is most encouraging; it seems expanding in its reach. Thank the Lord on my behalf, and pray that I may be faithful and may be kept to my work till it is done.

Much love to Mr. Knudsen and yourself.

Your affectionate brother,

SAMUEL F. GREEN.

MANEPY, *Sept* 27, 1865.

MY DEAR SISTER JULIA:

Your very sad letter speaking of dear father's departure came to hand on the 25th inst. You and sister Lydia being habitual co-occupants of the Home with the beloved one, must feel his withdrawal even more than the others occasionally only at home. I know you have learned long since the only and effective Source of comfort, and to Jesus I commend you, and may He with comfort mingle what is of more importance still—His sanctifying grace. By it vouchsafed, we shall each be the better for this affliction.

What you narrate of father's last expressions gives me great comfort and hope that he is with Christ in paradise. . . .

How very timely dear brother Andrew's arrival, to have three days of quiet enjoyment with dear father before the attack of serious illness. I hope sister Mary was in season to have some converse with the dear one before he became insensible. . . .

How constantly kind and indulgent he was. His memory is very, very dear. How much his character mingles in and pervades ours, whether we have warped or woven in his excellences. Dear father, I hope I may do as well by your grandchildren entrusted to my charge.

Believe me, dear sister Julia, as ever,

Your affectionate brother,

SAMUEL F. GREEN.

A few days later Dr. Green made this reference to the peculiar relation of his brother Andrew to their father: "By the roadside about one and one-half miles from us on the way to Batticotta, stands a Banyan. The parent trunk, bulky and decayed, has long parted from the soil and is lifted up in mid air, borne up by a staunch secondary stem. It reminds me of the venerated sire and the noble son who so liberally and tenderly has cared for him these many years."

CHAPTER XV.

1865–1867: ÆT. 43–45.

AFTER the many appeals made to his father, and the years of daily intercession for his self-surrender to Christ; and after the comforting evidences that such surrender was finally made, Dr. Green's chastening was less grevous than joyous, and his joy overflowed to his kindred. The lateness of the following letter may, perhaps, have been owing to want of time to answer all his friends in season for the last ocean mail.

MANEPY, *Nov.* 4, 1865.

MY DEAR SISTER LYDIA:

. . . . I feel heartily like joining you in expressing thanks to our heavenly Father for all his goodness to our honored and beloved sire, especially for the hope He has allowed us for the eternity of happiness upon which the loved parent has entered. I miss the dear one much, even at this remove; how most of all of us must sister Julia and you miss him. The house for a time will seem desolate, but other influences, other forms and faces will mingle in the scene, and gradually the current of daily life will flow as usual till another is taken; then a halt, a sigh, recurrent memories for a time, and the passed from earth will be passed from mind. However rooted here, even by the growth of four score years, how completely, how utterly is one severed from earth by death,—no lingering, no gradation, but a stroke, a cut-off clean and final.

Many thanks to you, dear sister, for the full report of dear father's sayings—his utterances concerning his soul and his Saviour. Thanks for carefully gathering his messages to us and transcribing them for our perusal. . . .

With great affection,

Your brother,

SAMUEL F. GREEN.

By the 22d of December, Dr. Green had sent to Dr. Lowe, of Travancore, four parcels of his Manuscript Surgery, but had yet to send many more. "I feel much interest," said he, "in awaiting the result of my Terms and Vocabularies—to see how Medical Missionaries to the Tamils will receive them. If all can agree to use and spread the same vocables I should be encouraged and rejoice."

As a result of teaching a Class in the Vernacular, the full notes taken by each of the eleven students were bound in sheep and labelled in gilt, so that there were now eleven volumes of Materia Medica in the language and each student had the beginning of a library of his own make. Having received from Madras thirty copies of the *Tamil Lyrics*, he put them in circulation, believing that "as the sweet plaintive tunes took the fancy of the people, the singing of these Christian songs far and wide would displace, at least to some extent, the vile songs which so abounded even in the mouths of children."

As Dr. Danforth, one of Dr. Green's early Tamil students, had completed his translation of a large work on Surgery, Dr. Green, early in 1866, sent an application to the College of Physicians and Surgeons, of New York, for a diploma conferring on him the honorary degree of Doctor of Medicine. He wrote he did not "intend to apply for those unworthy, nor for those who would not *earn* it by doing a *bona fide* service in the cause of Tamilizing Western Medicine. Their service must be gratuitous and valuable, and they must stand repeated examinations at the hands of educated Foreign Physicians, and show Certificates for their proficiency and ability aside from any he could give." One object of the application was that the success of it might stimulate others to engage with earnestness in the enterprise he was prosecuting for a Tamil Medical literature.

In February, Dr. Green wrote: "The Madura Mission have voted Brother Lord fifty pounds a year for a Medical Class. He inclines to conduct it in the vernacular. As I have one and a half year's start in this line I respond offering to put copies of all our available Manuscript at his disposal. Dr. Lowe has sent five pages foolscap of criticisms on the Manuscript of Surgery. On the whole this translation promises well. Dr. Lowe, after going over the Manuscript with his Class, is to send it on to Dr. Paterson, of Madras, to scan with his students; and all the suggestions I hope to have together, and decide, and finally prepare for the press.—A young man lies here with his left arm mortified to the shoulder in consequence of maltreatment,—a proof of the need of Medical teaching here."

Dr. Lord wrote in March: "Your long letter, with curriculum and suggestions as to Medical Class, I prize more than I can tell, and it decides to drive the Class in Tamil only. . . . The Vocabularies would be almost a necessity, as you have so far the start, that I think your Terms, etc., must take the lead in Tamil works." Dr. Green was much gratified at this, and hoped for another ally in his enterprise in Dr. Lord.

In April Dr. Green received Mr. Murdock's *Classified Catalogue of Tamil Printed Books, with introductory Notices.* Dr. Green was pleased to be able to write: "I see he gives in it, the set of rules devised by Mr. Webb and myself for the production of Terms for bringing Western Sciences into Tamil."

To keep his Classes advancing, to forestall changes of teachers, and to supply his associates in Southern India with Manuscript for use with their Classes, kept Dr. Green at work to about the utmost of his strength. He found it necessary to engage four persons in copying, besides employing a munshi, a Sanskrit munshi twice a week, and two teachers who also translated and wrote out their work.

MANEPY, *June* 6, 1866.

MY DEAR SISTER MARY:

. . . . The "Dictation of Boards" may hamper somewhat in some particulars. But a responsible agency to receive and distribute the "alms of the people" is most needful. It happens sometimes that the most excellent men are the worst pecuniary managers. "The Cause" is, in its machinery, no exception to the old adage, "Money makes the mare go;" and some kind-hearted yielding men would allow the treasury of this or that Mission to become such a resort for pretenders, paupers, etc., that "the mare" would surely go to the bottom. We (praise God for the gift of economy) live comfortably, give our tithe—which of all our outgoes is the sweetest—and at least keep square, if not forehanded. . . .

Death is but an incident in our way Home. "The hour we first believed," it was entered on the list of those "all things ours," and is counted "precious in the sight of the Lord." Shall we be averse from what is the Bearer to all we can hope for and more than we can conceive?

Affectionately your brother,

SAMUEL F. GREEN.

On the public works in Ceylon from three hundred to five hundred Kulis (laborers) were employed in a Division, and as the Divisions were widely scattered a physician was necessary for each one. The Principal Civil Medical officer, Dr. Charsley, of Colombo, having asked and received of Dr. Green several of his graduates, thanked him "very sincerely for the material aid afforded in obtaining the services of the several young men," and testified concerning them: "I am pleased with the appearance of them all, particularly Mr. McIntyre (a Tamil) whom you last sent me."

To His Sisters and Brothers.

Manepy, *June* 18, 1866.

. . . . I am impressed by glimpses of the rush for gain and fame in America, as elsewhere, in fact everywhere. It seems such blind infatuation to chase butterflies on the run towards the precipice. So foolish to exclude or omit from our plans that *to* which we are going and *in* which we must be forever, and only be concerned about that *from* which or through which we are passing. May the Lord open our eyes to see aright, to scan wisely. Without a right hope in Christ, what is the princely manor, the social exaltation? The merest vanity—the merest nothing. *Nolens volens* we cannot *stay*, we are ever on the *move* to the Judgment. Our plans must take the wider sweep and include that also, or we shall awake to remorse and cry out upon ourselves as self-befooled.

July 24.— . . . . A man of wealth, apparently, came to the Hospital, being twenty-one days from Trincomalee, expressly to have me see his grandson, the only boy progeny among his grandchildren. The lad had a decayed front tooth of the first set; the fang of it pricked through the gum and gouged the lip. A momentary touch of the forceps set all right, and the party was informed they could at once go home again. A Yankee would at once have applied nippers at home and saved twenty to thirty days time and travel. . . .

I never expect to repay you adequately at all, and so take refuge in a sort of bankrupt act for the benefit of favored but hopeless correspondents.—

SAMUEL F. GREEN.

On a recurrence of the Family Anniversary he wrote:

MANEPY, JAFFNA, CEYLON, 16 *September*, 1866.

MY DEAR SISTERS LUCY, MARY, JULIA, AND LYDIA, AND MY DEAR BROTHERS WILLIAM, JOHN, ANDREW, OLIVER AND MARTIN:

Allow me in due form and with the utmost cordiality to salute you on this fifth recurrence of our anniversary. I would join you in praising Our Father in Heaven for all His goodness to us severally and collectively. May that goodness constrain us each to a grateful devotion of our all to His service and may he keep us faithful, "enduring to the end."

I report myself and my dear ones three, well and prospering. Exemption from distress, a full supply for every need, encouragement in our enterprise, constitute the leading marks of our state. An intense desire to meet you again ere long in our own land, and still stronger in that land where we shall never part, rules my breast.

With fervent affection,

Your brother,

SAMUEL F. GREEN.

The remaining work of this missionary year was so similar to what has been described as not to need special mention. In his Report for the 1st of October he said:

"The business is now wholly in the Tamil language; the names of medicines and diseases, the Register and Books of account, the Prescriptions and Labels having been brought into the vernacular. The change has been effected with some endeavor; but its aid in the practical training of future Classes in the mother tongue of the land will abundantly reward this.—The present Dispenser is a Christian . . . . and is instructed to read to the patients assembled a synopsis of the Christian religion, followed by the reading and explanation of a Scripture portion, according to a table of Bible selections for every day in the month. . . .—The printing of the Surgery is already commenced."

Definiteness of plan, and system in pursuing it, enabled Dr. Green to calculate his progress with approximate accuracy, to forecast special needs and provide for them in season. After Druitt's Surgery should be issued, Gray's Anatomy would be put to press. He wrote to Messrs. Lea and Blanchard of Philadelphia, acknowledging their liberality in respect to cuts for the Surgery, and soliciting their further aid in respect to cuts for the Anatomy. He wrote his brother missionary, Mr. Sanders, then in the United States, asking his influence to the same end. He sent his request to the Prudential Committee to appropriate so much of his own salary from the Friend-in-Need Society as might be requisite for the purchase of the cuts in Dr. Smith's Anatomical Atlas, published by Messrs. Lea and Blanchard, enforcing it with these considerations:

"I regard a volume of this kind as most distinctively aggressive on Hinduism. There is a radical antagonism between the truths it will spread and the prevalent ideas here concerning the body. It should be shown that the body is the Lord's wondrous mechanism, and not the lodgement of divers gods, nor its various parts controlled by the constellations. With plenty and good illustrations the book will be doubly useful. It will be as different from a non-illustrated volume as daylight from dawn. These will advance one item at least of missionary work far towards that desired state in which 'the light of the sun shall be as the light of seven days.'"

In due time the Doctor learned that the Prudential Committee promptly granted his request to the extent of four hundred dollars.

In November he wrote in regard to his health: "I spat a few drops of blood. I feel the ail about the larynx progressing slowly. I had it ten years ago more or less. Now, sometimes in reading aloud, a little pledget of pus rises and suddenly clogs the vocal cords; no tickling or pain. The sentence of death in "our members" is written for us each, yet cannot we tell its precise style though we know its sum."

To his eldest sister he wrote:

MANEPY, *Dec.* 8, 1866.

MY DEAR SISTER LUCY:

. . . . I imagine you engrossed in School cares again and am glad to learn that a prosperous opening has been vouchsafed. How much more elevated your lot than that of a mere luxurious fashionable Time Waster. Many will rise up and call you blessed. . . . I feel much interested in the question of the School—its continuance, its change of situation, etc. As the indications rise shall, I trust, learn how you are guided and on what determine. Was it in 1840 that the present term began? A long career. Prosperous pecuniarily, and successful in respects far higher than worldly good. . . .

Counting in my five years in America, I shall next year have been twenty years a missionary:—one of the veterans. I never saw my enterprise more hopeful. I feel I have already been permitted, since return, to accomplish enough to repay the out and return voyage and the years of withdrawal from those dear as life. All praise to the Saviour.

Affectionately, your brother,

SAMUEL F. GREEN.

To his brother in South America he wrote:

December 17, 1866.

MY DEAR BROTHER JOHN:

My wife and my two daughters and myself are all well although the season is very sickly—much cholera throughout the district. I was reading yesterday in the Report of the British and Foreign Bible Society for 1865, among other lands, about Chili. I felt a hope and wish that my dear brother there would do all he could by tongue and pen and prayer to encourage Bible distribution in that country. If an agent or colporteur should visit your immediate locality, do cordially espouse his endeavors and express all you can in words and acts to aid and comfort a spreader of God's word.

I hear of you occasionally through the sisters. I think of you daily. I hope I enjoy alike frequent thought with you. Let our remembrance be ever with "the prayer of faith." How do you get along pecuniarily? How as to health? How as to spirituals? Do you meet encouragement in the "fight of faith?" I find the worst adversary of my own heart to be impatience, irritability. I pray against it and try against it, but still it occasionally floors me. Let us not be discouraged in the struggle, for the Saviour will bring us off conquerors and more than conquerors if we seek and rely on His strength and fight it out to the end.

With very much love from us all and best wishes for your prosperity, I am as ever

Your affectionate brother,

SAMUEL F. GREEN.

In January occurred a great native holiday when "heathenism was out in gala style" notwithstanding the raging of the pestilence. A thousand handbills were printed for the Government Agent "to issue with cholera medicine;" and a thousand more, in a modified form, were printed for the American Mission. The exigency was such that Dr. Green found it necessary to take these methods to meet it. He was of course not alone in this responsibility, other Foreign physicians co-operating in their own circuits. He sent his tract on Cholera to Dr. Chester, of

Dindigul, who had it translated, and proposed to his Mission the printing of two thousand copies.

The demands for Dr. Green's professional services, for counsel and direction to his assistants and students, necessarily interfered with his literary enterprise; yet in March he had four different works in the hands of his graduates for translation.

MANEPY, *April* 9, 1867.

MY DEAR SISTER LUCY:

. . . . I often think of the old Hill clock that has sung out the hours for three generations and is speaking now to the fourth. After the third and fourth are all gone it may still ting, ting to some stranger, who will regard it chiefly as an antique.

The somerset in the English Papers was one of the most remarkable phenomena I ever beheld in periodical literature. I am thankful to hope the clouds that threatened a re-opening of civil war lift from our land. . . .

May the Lord guide in all your plans for your great establishment. If Providence so favors, it would seem better to transplant the tree, as Mrs. Smith did, rather than fell it. . . .

I still regret, however, that eyes and time and strength are so limited that whatever is given to correspondence is just so much taken from my stent.

With much affection I remain,

Your brother,

SAMUEL F. GREEN.

From one of his translators Dr. Green received a manuscript of nearly two thousand pages in June, when he was also through with the work which had occupied him a good deal for three or four years on vocabularies.

MANEPY, JAFFNA, *July* 10, 1867.

MY DEAR BROTHER ANDREW:

. . . . I am glad to learn your views on the affairs of our distressed Land. Let us rejoice that our punishment did not come later and so heavier. The Negro has had two centuries of such pupilage as has resulted in his degradation. Emancipation gives at least an opportunity to try something else for him. Perhaps after two centuries we can better tell whether servitude or freedom most benefit and befit him.

It would be very nice for brothers to dwell together. I, as keenly as any one, love home and kindred. But we must be cosmopolitan and cherish the Brotherhood of man. I hope the work I am engaged in will lessen the sufferings of thousands now and in generations to come. But higher than this it rises in my hopes, and will result in their liberation from superstition. Hinduism deprives of much that a Christian people enjoy, and imposes sufferings a Christian people never experience.

It is a very great comfort to me to feel that Christ overrules our Land and will make all that transpires result in good. While we may do all we can to oppose the rush of villainy, we should never be disheartened, but calmly rest all on Him. . . . . .

I argue from myself, the possibility of the Lord's changing the views and practices of many of the people, though I need not, for the promise is sure; "I will give thee the heathen for thine inheritance;" and multitudes of other promises there are. But one clear one is enough, one unmistakable command sufficient. May our love to Christ and our interest in His cause steadily increase.

Affectionately, your brother,

SAMUEL F. GREEN.

This missionary year closed with a personal affliction to Dr. Green—the death of Percival Ackland Dyke, Esq., who for forty years had efficiently conducted the affairs of the Northern Province. At the funeral, "numerously attended by all classes," Dr. Green was assigned the place of "second mourner," "thankful to have had the confidential friendship of the first man in Ceylon."

CHAPTER XI

1861–1862: ÆT. 39–40.

UNDER re-appointment to his former position, Dr. Green now regarded the time of his return as near at hand. After three months at Green Hill he went again to New York, where he well knew how to keep himself busy, useful and improving—availing himself especially of opportunities to advance the cause of missions, and of the advantages afforded by medical institutions.

Extracts from one of his letters at this time to his sisters Julia and Lydia.

No. 1 Fifth Avenue, New York, *Jan.* 14, 1862.

My Dear Sisters:

I was much interested in hearing yours and Father's letters read last evening. Sisters two and I had a quiet time in back parlor by ourselves, . . . talking, and enjoying in silence the near presence of the beloved. . . . When in silence a number allied by blood and long association encircle an evening hearth, don't the hearts a new Class of twelve medical students. His example was already followed to some extent in Southern India. There was a class gathered in Trevandum to be taught in the vernacular. There was another in Arcot, gathered and instructed by Dr. Silas D. Scudder, who sent to Dr. Green for several copies of his Surgery and of his Obstetrics for their use.

To a brother then resident in Michigan:

MANEPY, *December* 17, 1867.

MY DEAR BROTHER:

Am I right in fearing for your health bodily and spiritual? Don't you crowd too hard? He that makes haste to be rich is not innocent, the Lord tells us. There is more enjoyment in quiet living as we go, than in luxury and its concomitant invalidism. Settle it now, on the experience detailed in Ecclesiastes (which is on a greater scale than anyof us can try for himself), that the pursuit of wealth is sheer delusion. If you will to make money for Christ and His cause I would not object, for then not money but the Lord's glory is the aim, and a blessing may crown the end.

I hope you will be very jealous of intrusion upon your God-granted weekly rest. Don't let the same person make free with your Sabbath repose more than once. Recéive politely, entertain kindly, and part decidedly on that point. Else one immersed in business is very liable to the disastrous squandering of hours indispensable to spiritual converse and culture. *Guard the Sabbath* If the outworks must go, keep this, the citadel as you would keep your soul for the Sabbath unending.

Affectionately, your brother,

SAMUEL F. GREEN.

MANEPY, *February* 3, 1868.

MY DEAR BROTHER WILLIAM:

I am concerned to hear such accounts of your health. I fondly hope you may weather the damps and chills of the coming spring and enjoy greatly the summer and autumn months. I feel much for you in your weakness and in your bereavement. I daily commend you to the Comforter. My prayer is that He will sanctify to you your trials and that He will abundantly console you.

Let me urge you to read the Gospels much and to muse upon the truth with prayer. Thus become acquainted with Christ. Learn to regard Him as near you, concerned for you, loving you, willing and ready to do all needful for you. Trust in Him only; in Him *per se*; in Him apart from all that men massed, or man-individual, have, since His life on earth, been wrapping around Him. "Jesus here and now" is the formula for comfort and salvation. Held to in filial love; this is enough —"the all-sufficiency of Christ sufficient for all." That you may fully know "the joy of this salvation," and may be in all your way "upheld by His free Spirit," is my yearning desire.—Much love to dear sister Sarah and to dear Timothy. Ever and most affectionately,

Your brother,

SAMUEL F. GREEN.

In the Spring Dr. Green received permission to visit the Pulney Hills at his discretion, but he used his discretion to keep on at his work. He relinquished public speaking, on account of his health, and instead of visiting from house to house on Sundays had a Class in the Sunday-school, and held a meeting with the servants.

MANEPY, *March* 30, 1868.

MY DEAR SISTER LUCY:

I feel great interest in the near future before you. I wait to see what path you will take in following the guidance of an unerring Friend. May your way be made very plain. You are happy in having both a useful retrospect and a glorious prospect. May your happiness rise till it lands you in the abode of the ever and wholly blessed.—I imagine the environs of No. 1 may have so changed as to weaken your attachment to that spot where you have done and borne and enjoyed so much. So it comes to pass also with the very body we dwell in. Infirmities gradually so encompass it, changes about it so multiply, that we are at last glad to withdraw and begin anew elsewhere. How favored we are that our change is not problematical, that it is assured and glorious. While others would fain dwell here, the child of God would not even lag but gladly hasten to a better and an enduring inheritance.—I sometimes yearn for the society of my near relatives, but one need not be impatient; for while we yet speak of it we run express to the meeting of all the good and the lovable, arrive and stay. . . . Ever affectionately,

Your brother,

SAMUEL F. GREEN.

MANEPY, *March* 30, 1868.

MY DEAR SISTER MARY:

. . . . When one for years stoutly resists conviction and will not believe what he ought, may it not be a judgment upon him to be left to believe what he ought not? . . . . . All that is distinctively Romish is anti-Christian. All that is Christian in that body is to be found in purer communions. Why leap into dogmatism to find rest, which is delusive, when it can really be found only in Christ? The Romish priesthood seem to me a set of politicians. Romanism is by far the most efficient opponent to the spread of the gospel. . . . Robed in emblems purloined from the Bible, the Sorceress bewitches in every land multitudes who wish to be saved yet not in the Saviour's way. . . .

Truly,

SAMUEL F. GREEN.

MANEPY, *March* 30, 1868.

MY DEAR SISTER LYDIA:

. . . . Through the tie of affection we "rejoice with those that do rejoice," and so multiply our own joys and share them too with others. When a noble worthy love pervades the race, knitting all in one and tying all to the Lord of love and light, how happy a state it will be. The Master is bound on inducing just such a condition, and He will neither fail nor be discouraged till He accomplish it. In so far as we succeed in cultivating, and habitually bear within, a worthy love, in so far do we possess a little heaven here and prepare for the great heaven hereafter. In this divine enterprise may the Lord vouchsafe us a steadily growing prosperity.

Much love from us all.

Most affectionately,

SAMUEL F. GREEN.

MANEPY, *June* 8, 1868.

MY DEAR BROTHER WILLIAM:

. . . . I also sympathize with you sincerely in the withdrawal from steady business. It must be some satisfaction to you to have held the office so long as it existed. Considering the mutations in politics you held the post wonderfully long. You can be thankful for the past, and now wait and see what a kind Providence will open before you instead of this door just closed.

I feel a deep and most hearty sympathy with you in your sicknesses, your bereavements and your trials as to business. It is a consolation to remember that nothing happens at random, that One infinitely wise and equally good controls all that affects us and, further, will, if we but love Him, make all that transpires concerning us to work for our good. Try, dear brother, to receive all as from our Father in heaven patiently, gratefully and humbly.

I feel that we all, and especially perhaps you and I, stand on the very confines of eternity. This is no bad thing if we are by faith joined to Christ. To those in Him, Death has no sting, yea, rather is but the Bearer of the soul to glory.

I feel that I read the Bible too little, and I wish that both of us might be much with it. I am ashamed to detect myself ready to catch up a newspaper to while away a little time, but reluctant to give that odd fragment of time to the perusal of God's word. Let me suggest to you to read and dwell upon the word. If it don't relish, keep at it and pray over it till the Spirit who gave it shall give appetite and enjoyment of it. Thus your soul will grow into harmony with the Author of revealed truth, and the truth shall make you free.

With very much love to your dear self, to dear sister Sarah and my beloved nephew Timothy, I remain

Yours ever most affectionately,

SAMUEL F GREEN.

MANEPY, *June* 26, 1868.

MY DEAR SISTER LYDIA:

I enjoy the perusal of the copied note of dear brother Martin. It is a matter of thankfulness to see the tender love still within as it was in boyhood when we were a happy group together in the old hive. Alas that he or any of us should consent to live overtoilsomely—to live in a constant pressure and hurry. We can live but once on earth, and a quiet life with "a heart at leisure from itself to soothe and sympathize" would no doubt most gratify our Master. . . . . .

I wish brother Martin would arrange to live on the Hill. It seems unwise that he should spoil his days by harrassments and shorten his earthly term. Were I not in the most important yet most neglected enterprise of missions, I would be glad to close up and go and dwell with my sisters. But only a tithe of those the American church should send are yet out among the heathen, and we should only as a last necessity do aught to diminish the far too scanty force. Pray, all of you, that "more laborers may be sent into the harvest." I hope all my children will be missionaries to the heathen.

Your affectionate brother,

SAMUEL F. GREEN.

MANEPY, *July* 9, 1868.

MY DEAR SISTER LUCY:

. . . . The Celtic element pervades New England, and the Puritan element pervades the West. The country is to be homogeneous though a mixture. I look for a still more rapid growth after the Pacific Rail lines are completed. I think it would be better for the country and unspeakably better for other lands if some thousands of the cultivated young men and women of Christian principle would spread and dwell here and there out among the heathen and degraded nations of the earth. . . . One of the main results to be wished from all the revivals said to be occurring in America is the augmentation of the missionary force, the spreading of it into lands hitherto unreached.

I must thank you deeply for your very liberal offer of funds for the issue of Tamil medical books. I shall not hesitate to accept the offer if there should arise a need for the funds.

As to return home, I am more in favor of that than any of you can be, for it is no easier for one to be away from several than for several to spare the one. I hope the way will be opened by the completion of work here to return and spend the evening of life with you all. Should I be with you by the time I am fifty-six, I might perhaps hope for many days of enjoyment with you. We are so blessed by being in Christ, that the fact stands, as to any plan we may form, that "it is either this or something better."

With much love from us all,

Your affectionate brother,

SAMUEL F. GREEN.

MANEPY, JAFFNA, CEYLON, *July* 18, 1868.

EDWARD DELAFIELD, ESQ., M. D.

President College of Physicians and Surgeons.

DEAR SIR:

Permit me through you to express to the Trustees of the College of Physicians and Surgeons my gratitude for the favor they have extended me in conferring upon Mr. J. Danforth the honorary Degree of Doctor of Medicine, and my conviction that he will reflect credit on his adopting Mother. I believe this recognition of merit will have a happy influence upon the many Practitioners trained in Medicine by the American Mission.

I doubt not, on the receipt of his Diploma, Mr. Danforth will speak for himself his high appreciation of the honor the College has done him.

Pray accept my hearty thanks for your very kind action in this matter, and believe me to be, dear Sir,

Yours respectfully,

SAMUEL F. GREEN.

In the summer he summed up results of labor since his return in the autumn of 1862 partially as follows. Having found a Class already one third of the way through their course of medical study in English, he had led them through the remainder, graduating eight physicians. He had carried eight others through their whole course in the vernacular. He had trained three dispensers wholly in Tamil,—the first ever so trained,—and three others partially. He had made out six vocabularies, and completed four others which were partially prepared before his visit to America; carried one large volume through the press, and prepared another; secured three volumes in manuscript soon to be ready for printing, and five more in a crude initiatory stage only; work, said he, "which would else be undone, which most urgently needed to be done, and needs to be prosecuted till the enterprize as a whole shall flourish here as an acclimatized transplanted Western vine—the outgrowth of a true religion there the aid to the spread of true religion here—for the greater part done by others under my direction,—what I have caused to be done.

"My action is not single," he continued, "but combined with that of others. There are perhaps two hundred missionaries to the Tamils; of these perhaps five are medical missionaries. Did I feel that I worked alone, I should consider myself bound to engage in the direct proclamation of the gospel. I stand, however, adjuvant to those who proclaim it, and I wish to live it and to make my profession subserve the success of the Truth among this people. I feel comfort in the conviction that I am *where* the Lord would have me, and some good degree of comfort and assurance that I am doing what He would have me do."

Mr. Murdock wrote: "Whatever a few men unacquainted with Tamil may themselves think, there cannot be a doubt but that you are on the right track, and accomplishing a great work. It is perfectly true that native medical men are required with a thorough knowledge of English, but it is also as certain that a much larger number is required of a humbler class. If your work is not sufficiently appreciated at present, you have only to 'bide your time.' Succeeding generations will reap the benefit of the attention you have given to the subject, including the dry but very important question of the renderings of scientific terms."

Before the close of this missionary year, Dr. Green resigned the Superintendency of the Friend-in-Need Society's Hospital, recommending Dr. Danforth for the position, and asking the continuance of these privileges: The advantages of practical anatomy to his students; the arrangement by which the Society's Dispensary and that of the American Mission could accommodate each other with supplies at seventy five per cent. on London cost; and sending the pauper sick to the Hospital. His resignition was accepted with great regret, and because it was final. The committee expressed the wish that "it were possible by any offer or by any concession" to retain his services which had brought the institution "to its present high state of efficiency." The official said: "Should it at any time suit your convenience, or again become compatible with your missionary duties, to resume the charge of the Hospital, the Committee would hail with the greatest satisfaction your return to an office which must otherwise long remain vacant for want of a successor who will be worthy of you." They adopted his recommendation, however, and granted his requests.—His term of service, begun as an experiment, continued five years and five months.

At each recurrence of the day observed at Green Hill as the anniversary of the last meeting of all the members of the family, he was accustomed to write a letter for the occasion.

MANEPY, *September* 16, 1868.

DEAR SISTERS AND BROTHERS:

. . . . Seven years ago to-day we gathered a happy ten about our beloved sire. Since, he has gone before us (we trust to the Better Land) and we remain disunited from him and our bond to each other in him dissevered, but all knit indissolubly in heart by that "brotherly love" which he exemplified and fostered in us. The Lord forbid we should be sundered in the unseen world. If all are joined by faith in Christ we shall be in the best and most enduring manner compacted in one Ethnological family.

A great number of things most potent the apostle recounts as unable to separate us from the love of God which is in Christ Jesus our Lord. There is only one thing that can break up our family; that is unbelief. All manner of sin may be remitted and we left whole, but unbelief defiantly keeps off remission. May the Lord save us each from unbelief; in so doing He saves us wholly. May "peace in believing" be the uniform experience of us each to the end. . . . .

Your brother,

SAMUEL F. GREEN.

MANEPY, *October* 3, 1868.

MY DEAR SISTER MARY:

I brought up the matter of illustrative cuts for a Chemistry at our Business Meeting on Thursday last. The Mission instructed me to write to Mr. Murdock, inquiring whether any one else in Tamildom is preparing a work on Chemistry; whether his Society will print such a work if the Manuscript be furnished; whether his Society would procure and own the requisite cuts. I wrote Mr. Murdock pursuant to these instructions yesterday, mailing to Madras. I added that I contemplated a work adapted for the highest classes in Seminaries and for medical students; that I had the offer of the cuts in Wells' Chemistry at a moderate charge each, naming it fully; that Mr. Wells' book had been recommended to me as the best one for my purpose; that I had all the Terms prepared, and also had a Manuscript translation of Porter's Chemistry in hand but not revised. I now wait to hear from Mr. Murdock, and expect to report his answer to the Mission.

I send you Dr. Wood's letter to me. Pray that the Lord will raise up Friends and Funds for this work, and that it may be early and well done, that this swift witness against Superstition may be abroad on its mission among these millions.

I trust ere this reaches you, you will have joyfully welcomed back from their tour husband and brother.* With very much love to yourself and to them both, I remain,

Your grateful and affectionate brother,

SAMUEL F. GREEN.

*They had been traveling in Europe.

CHAPTER XVII.

1868–1870: ÆT. 46–48.

WITHIN a fortnight from his relinquishment of service at the Hospital, Dr. Green noted an improvement in his health, apparently owing to out-door exercise in the cool of the day instead of in the heat as before. By his gain of two days in a week, the rate of literary work was greatly increased, his hours being now from seven o'clock to nine, from half past ten to twelve, from one to two, and from three to five, though he was often interrupted by the Dispensary, the Class, correspondence and social claims.

Full manuscript translations of *Churchill on Diseases of Women* and of *West on Diseases of Children*, were soon in hand, but yet to be "verified in teaching them to the Class, and then to be passed to Dr. Green in fair free copy for final revision for the press."

MANEPY, *October* 24, 1868.

MY DEAR BROTHER ANDREW:

Thanks for your most pleasant note from Lon'on town. I have enjoyed also the perusal of some of your notes from Erin. The program of your tour onwards from Killarney round to Gotham again is most attractive. I hope you may return recruited, and so accomplish all the more in your philanthropic efforts.

I desire first for yourself and myself and our brothers, that we succeed in the art of living deliberately, the art of habitual diligence, having the while "a heart at leisure from itself to soothe and sympathize." I wish you would arrange for more leisure, if even at the sacrifice of a share of present income. "A man's life consisteth not in the abundance of the things which he possesseth." It is not what comes into one's pocket but what comes into one's mind that is really worthy. By constant pressure we diminish present enjoyment both for ourselves and for others around us; we also damage our development for the lasting joys of the future. I hope you will contract the sphere of your engagements to snug limits, and take time for social and scientific amenities. Our real life is however within. Never was word more lucid poured on our nature than "The kingdom of God is within you." There is the root of our troubles; there must be set and tended the roots of our happiness. "I am the true vine," says Christ, "and my Father is the husbandman." Admit and cherish the abiding of these soul friends; so clusters of joy and wine of gladness shall refresh us ever.

I long to be with you. I yearn for your company. I rejoice, however, that the Lord Jesus can and will make you perfectly happy and keep you so. Consent to him. Love to you from us all. Ever and most affectionately,

Your brother,

SAMUEL F. GREEN.

MANEPY, *January* 7, 1869.

TO HIS SISTERS AND BROTHERS:

. . . . The world allures one way and Christ the other. The world enwraps us and we can only get away from it to Christ by a sustained effort of the will. It is essential to the soul's weal that we keep renewedly conversant with the Saviour. There is no substitute for the daily reading about Him in the history He has written for us. We need habitually to contemplate His character, and in the light of His example to see the worthlessness of our best works. Without this daily reference to the Standard we easily lower our view to the prevailing grade and come to think well of ourselves. Thus self-righteousness is as natural and common as the true righteousness, the vicarious righteousness, is essential and rare. "The wicked flattereth himself in his own eyes, till his iniquity be found to be hateful." No more dangerous snare than this. Whatever else we may omit, let us never omit to read leisurely a portion of God's book daily. The more our pressure, the more our need of this steadying, elevating influence. We neglect it at our peril. . . .

SAMUEL F. GREEN.

At the meeting of the Jaffna Auxiliary Bible and Tract Society, Dr. Green was put upon the Publishing and Revision Committees. He sent thirty copies of his Surgery to Madras, twelve to Madura and twelve to Nagerkoil. Having called on the new recruits just settled at Batticotta, he said, "I for the first time look upon juveniles, feeling myself a veteran."

MANEPY, *Thursday, January* 7, 1869.

MY DEAR SISTER MARY:

I desire to express my deep sense of obligation to yourself and to Mr. Knudsen for your great kindness in the matter of books and cuts. You have spared neither pains nor expense. I hope by the blessing of God you may one day see a nice volume on Chemistry in Tamil, and so be gratified by ocular proof that your exertions have resulted in substantial good to a great people. . . .

Affectionately, your brother,

SAMUEL F. GREEN.

MANEPY, *July* 17, 1869.

MY DEAR SISTER LYDIA:

I am deeply moved by the account of your health by last mail. I feel no anxiety about you, for I know you rest in Jesus. I can do nothing for you, because many friends surround you devotedly. Could I be of essential service to you, I should deem it duty to go to you as soon as possible. I use my privilege to pray for you frequently. I feel called upon to praise the Lord also for all the abounding goodness shown you, the crowning mercy of which is "a heart to taste His gifts with joy." The Lord will strengthen you on the bed of languishing. He will make all your bed in your sickness. Goodness and mercy will surely follow you to the end, and you will go and dwell in the glory of the Lord forever. I rejoice over you in Christ, and confidently anticipate the happiest meeting with you above.

Love from us all.

Affectionately,

SAMUEL F. GREEN.

Mr. Murdock wrote Dr. Green, suggesting the preservation of his works by presenting copies to the Museum and the Medical College Libraries in Madras, to the American Oriental Society, to the British Museum Library, and to the Royal Asiatic

Society's Library,—where "the copies would be carefully preserved and the titles printed in the catalogues."

Mr. Capron, of Mana Madura, wrote him: "His Excellency the Governor has been visiting Arcot, and praising and helping Dr. Scudder. Here is one sentence, half of which belongs to you; 'In conclusion, I beg to call the attention of Government to the good service which the American Mission is rendering to humanity, and enlightenment, by the education of native Medical Students and by the translation of Medical Works into the vernacular of the country.' All *American*, and no time to distinguish; but His Excellency refers to page 6, of the report where you are catalogued."

In September Dr. Green received "a letter from Dr. Smith, President of the Madras Medical College, asking suggestions towards a scheme to popularize Medical Science" among the "55,000 villages of the Madras Presidency;" to which he wrote six pages in reply.

On the 30th he was agreeably surprised by a call from the Class, asking permission to write from the teacher's dictation the study they had just begun, and which he had directed the teacher to communicate orally, "not wishing to tax them with too much labor." On this evidence of interest he granted the permission.

Mr. Russell, who succeeded Mr. Dyke, as Government Agent of the Northern Province, became so much interested in Dr. Green and his work that afterwards, when Government Agent of the Central Province and a member of the Legislative Council, he initiated, without solicitation, a movement in his favor, which greeted him with an agreeable surprise.

FROM MR. RUSSELL.

KANDY, *Oct.* 12, 1869.

MY DEAR SIR:

You have probably learned from the local press that the establishment of a Medical School at Colombo is contemplated by Government. At the discussion of the subject in Sub-Committee, I mentioned the utility and high character of your Medical School, and from the reception with which my remarks met, I am inclined to think that if the case of your institution were properly brought before the Legislative Council, it might be possible to obtain a grant of Government funds in aid of your School. I shall be happy to do what I can to further so desirable an object, if I know that you are willing to accept a grant. Will you kindly let me know this by return of post, and at the same time give me any details which you think it is expedient to communicate with reference to the present condition, the scope and the future prospects of the Medical School at Manepy. Believe me, my dear Sir,

Yours very truly,

H. S. O. RUSSELL.

DR. S. F. GREEN.

Dr. Green replied at once, that "The Mission would be very glad of some additional help from the Government in their endeavors to promote Medical Education, and to develop a Medical Literature, in Tamil;" giving an account of the enterprise, the Class, and the expenses, and saying that "two hundred pounds a year would be most gratefully received and strictly applied."

MANEPY, *November* 8, 1869.

MY DEAR BROTHER:

. . . . I have two things much on my mind concerning you spiritually. One is my fear that you may be entrapped by self-righteousness. By the Lord's favor you are enabled to walk honestly, uprightly, purely as compared with many around you in the same social grade as yourself. There is danger that the suggestion will be often made to you that you are better than others, etc., all which may be quite true; but the hint, that we have nothing good but what we have received, will be withheld, and you be encouraged to rest in self-complacency—in self-righteousness—and so be ruined. Now I beg to warn you on this point, and entreat you to seek familiarity with the character of our Lord Jesus, and to contrast yourself with Him frequently, not in externals but in inner character; with Him as Comptroller of the Central Park; with Him, as in your place and times. Thus keeping or own inner selves alongside the great Standard Character is the only way to a truthful view of ourselves; to an abiding conviction that "all our righteousnesses are as filthy rags." Resolve, dear Brother, to begin, or if begun to continue this scrutiny of self daily. There is no other way to true humility, to salvation. I earnestly entreat you to this converse with Christ often and statedly; commune with Him over His word in solitude. We grow like our company. We must company with Christ, would we grow like Him. We bar ourselves from heaven by neglect to cultivate this likeness.

The second thing is, I fear you may yet be confounding death and a preparation for death. We can't be dying all the time. We must act in the living present. But we can and should live in a state of readiness to die; not of willingness, necessarily, but of preparedness. This state of preparedness consists in reconciliation with God by faith in Jesus Christ. This abiding faith must be the substratum of character. It will not interfere with energetic devotion to business, but will be a vast help to work effectively and comfortably. It will raise the grade of our toil from that of the selfish to that done for the Saviour; from the moral to the spiritual. ' Don't, dear brother, stave off this matter, half unconsciously determining to attend to death when you come to die. But secure readiness *now*, by settling with the Father of mercies through our surety Jesus. Attend to it at once, whether you live longer or shorter. The Lord grant you comfortable life till seventy or eighty; but certainly it will be none the less comfortable should you bear all the while the Policy of Heaven's Life Assurance on your heart.

Think of these two things and, if not already done, set right now the dearest brother that ever was.

Yours ever and affectionately,

SAMUEL F. GREEN.

After finishing this letter, Dr. Green learned that his youngest sister, to whom he last wrote on the 17th of July, had died on the 7th of September. The way the tidings affected him, and the way he desired the chastening might be endured by his sisters and brothers, appear in the following letters written the next day.

TO HIS SISTERS AND BROTHERS.

MANEPY, *November* 9, 1869.

. . . . We must rejoice for her. But who shall fill the void? Assuredly Jesus. He is our Elder Brother. "A brother is born for adversity." In sorrrow's night the promises, as stars, glisten. I feel anguish, but, more still, thanksgiving. Thanksgiving for the preciousness of Christ. Now the heart more fully appreciates His work. . . We are constrained to give thanks for our Father's goodness, for all the way of dear Lydia's beautiful life and for such an appropriate ending. Blessed be God for upwards of forty years together, an unbroken band, and for the hope of an eternity in glory. God grant none of us may "despise the chastening," but all so use it that it shall "yield the peaceable fruits of righteousness." My heart's desire and prayer for the circle is, that each may be saved, that none may be so mistaken as to neglect the great salvation. If deferred, ages of remorse may never reach it. Lord, seal on our hearts this verity, "*Now* is the day of salvation."

I should much rejoice to be with you in these days of sorrow. In providence, however, we are sundered; but we can by faith meet at the throne of grace and aid each other by our prayers through the all-prevalent Name. Be assured I should most gladly close up here and go to be with you. But I know you would say to me, "Stay," could you on the spot look over the work we have in hand. While all may be in the Lord's work here or there, the force detailed by so large a family is but a fragment. We could not expect the Master's blessing to rest on any arrangement in which His cause was put second. "First the kingdom," afterwards our convenience. . . . Surely Missionary interest should be as dear as any social or pecuniary interest. Dearest spot of earth though it be, yet Green Hill had better be relinquished than our mite in the Foreign Missionary work be withdrawn. This work will interest us long after the dearest scenes of earth have lost their hold on our affections. It is, I feel, self-denial to remain apart; but let us but once settle it as expedient for Christ's sake, and His love will make us happier, though afar from each other, than could daily and familiar intercourse held in preference to His call.

Even should health be spared, it would be wise in one here from U. S. A. to return after, say, twelve years, or at the most fifteen years, to recruit mentally at least. God willing, I hope to be with you, should we all be spared, in five or eight years from this time. I suspect five years, and perhaps three, may be the limit of health for us here. Don't pray for us that we may stay nor that we come home, but that we may live to God's glory, and prosper in His work. That is the desideratum for each of us. . . .

SAMUEL F. GREEN.

MANEPY, *November* 9, 1869.

MY DEAR SISTER MARY:

. . . . We have now begun to pass over the river, the brink of which we have as an unbroken band been long nearing. The youngest sister first; who of us next? Some one must be the last, the one to say Good Bye to nine. . . . Happier they who earlier go. Best for each the Lord's appointed time. I rejoice over our beloved one as now with "the just made perfect." Our Father graciously grant that none be called unready. . . . Her memory is blessed. Thanks be to God for Jesus Christ. Such an affliction emphasizes His value. Ever precious Saviour, most precious in sorrow. Victor over Death. . . . May the Comforter Himself daily solace you. . . . It seems easier to go now; the better land seems nearer. Oh that all the dear "ten circle" may meet there and dwell there together and with Christ forever.

Affectionately,

SAMUEL F. GREEN.

The last week in December, Dr. Green learned from Dr. Charsley, of Colombo, "that an additional hundred pounds" would be granted by the Government the coming year in aid of the Medical Department of the American Ceylon Mission. At first the grant-in aid was fifty pounds and this was the second time it had been doubled. It was certainly an encouraging appreciation of the public benefit of his labors, that the Government should voluntarily appropriate a thousand dollars annually to his use in vernacular work, while it was about starting a Medical School to be taught in English.

Mr. Murdock wrote that he was going to England and would do what he could there to assist him. To obtain the best books, permission to translate them, cuts to illustrate them, and funds to publish them, involved a great deal of correspondence; the voluntary agency of friends of his enterprise was therefore very grateful. Dr. Lowe had written, before he left India for Great Britain, that he would not rest till he obtained assistance for him; and how well he succeeded will appear in a letter published in the Medical Missionary Journal of February, 1870.

DR. LOWE TO DR. THOMSON.

"PORTOBELLO, *Feb.* 11, 1870.

"MY DEAR BURNS THOMSON:

. . . "All this ought to call forth praise and thanksgiving to God. It shows us that the experiment we attempted in much fear and trembling has, with God's blessing, proved a success.

"The great business of the European Medical Missionary is to train up a native agency. These native medical evangelists, when well selected and trained, are the men who can do the work. They know the people, their social habits, their peculiar weaknesses, their prejudices better than the cleverest European ever can; they multiply the power and influence of the European medical missionary, and they, by and by, will be able to fill his place.

. . . "How hopefully and prayerfully should we watch these young men, and the devoted band of students, who have lately and so successfully finished their course of study under our dear friend, Dr. Paterson, of Madras. Dr. Scudder, of Arcot, and Dr. Green, of Jaffna, both medical missionaries connected with the American Missionary Society, have likewise a number of young men in course of training; but Dr. Green, in view of this important department, has done, and is at present engaged in sending to all, a most valuable, special benefit.

"The native youths we have trained, or may yet train, for medical missionary service require for their proper equipment our standard practical medical and surgical works translated for them and published in the vernacular. Dr. Green has set himself to this task; and without the aid of the manuscripts of his translators of *Gray's Anatomy* and *Druitt's Surgery*, which he kindly lent me for the use of my students, I question if the experiment of training my native youths would have turned out so successfully. . . . With aid from the American Missionary Society, and other sources, Dr. Green has prepared a series of medical and surgical works in the vernacular. Works on Anatomy, Surgery, Midwifery, and Physiology are already published, and Manuscripts on Practice of Physic, Materia Medica, etc., etc., are ready for the press. The work on Practice of Physic is a translation of the last edition (1865) of *Hooper's Physicians' Vade Mecum;* the translation is completed and is ready for the printer. . . . These illustrations, useful in English, *are absolutely necessary in a translation.* . . . I wrote to the editor at once, and to-day received the following reply:

"'Mr. Renshaw, the chief proprietor and virtual publisher of *Hooper's Vade Mecum*, has himself no objection to the proposed translation, nor does he apprehend any on the part of his partners. But before applying to them he says that the arrangement for the wood cuts must be definitely made. He authorizes me to say that electrotypes, properly mounted on wood, will be furnished for 5s. apiece. I need not add that I have no feeling in the matter beyond a wish that my work on Hooper's Vade Mecum should become as extensively useful as possible.'

"Now, dear friend, the cuts must be secured. Dr. Green's service is entirely a labor of love, in which, as medical missionaries and as friends of medical missions, we ought to feel the deepest interest; it is a service more directly perhaps benefitting us medical missionaries than any merely missionary society. . . . Shall I write to him, on behalf of yourself and your many generous friends, that electrotypes of the cuts are ordered, and will be sent out free of all expense? This would indeed strengthen hands and the encourage the heart of our dear hard-working American brother, Dr. Green. One hundred and three electrotypes at

5s. each is £25, 15s. . . . Will you just add a postscript to this to let your constituents know what you have recommended.

"Ever yours affectionately,

JOHN LOWE.

"(Believing as I do in the importance of the object, it was impossible to resist Dr. Lowe's urgent appeal, and so he carried with him instructions to order plates.

W. B. THOMSON.)"

Dr. Lowe sent a periodical, containing an announcement of his success, which reached Dr. Green on the 28th of March, but was not read till about a week later; so that the latter said, "This answer to prayer was several days under hand before I knew it."

This year "the Colonial Surgeon for the Province, highly reputed as a botanist, kindly gave the Class weekly teaching on indigenous herbs." Besides his other work, Dr. Green found an average of three pages a day in the work of translation was enough for his strength. He sent home for electrotypes of the two cuts needed to illustrate Spectrum Analysis and Bessemer's Steel

Process, saying, "Every ray of light one can command should be brought to bear in introducing these matters to the Tamils."

Dr. Green had now three daughters. In various letters he afforded glimpses of his way with them, in such remarks as these to his brother Oliver:

"I hope in 1877, if not before, to see the two groups, yours and mine, brought acquainted with each other. May we be enabled to imitate our sire in fostering in them union and liberality. I have only recently, aided by the *Witness*, grasped the whole of that text which, so comfortingly to a Christian parent, includes his children: 'Believe on the Lord Jesus Christ and thou shalt be saved and thy house.' The Lord increase our faith, and make it daily tell directly upon the salvation of our children. . . . The children are developing hopefully. We don't urge them to study, only guide. We drive out with them almost every evening a little before sunset. Occasionally, having reached a retired spot, I alight with them to wander about for shells or flowers. I take a short canter in the saddle each morning, and on return let each of the three take a turn round the yard.—Cement the branches of the Green family all you can together. I deprecate my children growing up estranged from those of my beloved brothers.—I would rather my children knew 'the three R's' well, with sound bodies, than that they were accomplished in literature with feeble frames. Allow each child to develop on its own peculiar plan. Each character is one *per se;* there should be no arbitrary standard, and no rules laid down before they are found necessary. Study a child and see first what needs repression, what encouragement, then with light the rules can be adopted.

Praised be the Lord for the union that has ever prevailed among the dear 'ten circle,' and for putting it into the heart of our beloved sire to so frequently advise us, 'Children be united.' My love for the dear 'ten circle' knows no wane. Our love should strengthen as we near the ocean of eternity, as rivers' mouths broaden and deepen in nearing the sea."

JAFFNA, CEYLON, *June* 4, 1870.

MY DEAR BROTHER WILLIAM:

I have to-day received the nice spectacles you so kindly sent me. They seem to be exactly what I shall first need to wear. . . . I thank you very much for such a valuable article, and for the fraternal love that prompted the gift.

I am much concerned to learn of your poor health. I pray that the lengthening of your days may prove to be for the eternal tranquility of your soul. I yearn that you should believe that "All Scripture is given by inspiration of God," and that you should daily use it and find it "profitable, for instruction in righteousness." May the blessing of the Spirit so rest upon your prayerful study of the Wōrd, that you shall indeed become a "man of God, perfect and furnished to good works." Rest, my dear brother, all your cares, all your concerns, temporal and eternal, on the infallible Jesus, the "Friend above all others."

It would be a great gratification to me to see you frequently, and to do aught I might personally for your comfort and happiness. But you need not me. Earthly friends cluster around you, and the best Friend watches over you. Believe with all your heart on the Lord Jesus Christ and be saved; and when you leave, it will be with assurance of a glorious awakening, and we shall all have comfort regarding you, and hope to meet again. The old original arrangement, "Do and live," broke down. It is now, "Believe and live." Nothing keeps us from meeting this condition but rebellion. We must submit, must meet the Lord on his own terms.

. . . Love from all to you and yours,

Ever and affectionately, your brother,

SAMUEL F. GREEN.

Dr. Lowe spoke of the *Vade Mecum* as ready for the printer. He may have said this from what he knew of Dr. Green's calculations and expectations; but probably he mistook the readiness of it for the printer to begin upon for the readiness of the whole translation.

Though Dr. Green engaged his graduates and students in the work of translation, he was profited less by their work than they were; they were embarrassed by insufficient knowledge of English to get always the author's meaning, and by too little experience in translating to Tamilize always well what they did correctly apprehend of the English. As translators and copyists, however, they were of great use to him. His revision of a single work will show how largely their translations became his own before they were ready for the press.

By the 12th of April, 1869, if not earlier, Dr. Green had begun the revision of the Physician's Vade Mecum—a close printed duodecimo of 791 pages. On the 24th he said, "The translation requires so much alteration that it amounts to ploughing one's way, rather than a walk of survey over the field." On the 3d of August he said, "It is the hardest revision I have yet grappled; the translation is bad and the subject obstinate, but I am well into the second chapter, and hope by prayer and pains to gradually work through. I can only hope to go on with it by availing of the best helps attainable. I am having multiplied by a copyist a little paper on the Tamilizing of English words. I wish to send it to some ten or dozen individuals, in hope to influence aright this matter, which assumes importance now the push is great to put the Western sciences into this magnificent language." In January, 1870, he wrote: "My disappointment as to Evarts' aid is relieved by the fact that the case demonstrates that NO *Tamil man* can do this work. Dr. Evarts' translation is generally the English words in grammatical Tamil. What is wanted is the idea in idiomatic Tamil. Through his translation one can see the Englishman; one should see only the Tamilian." In April he said, "The only path to the real accomplishment of our series is that of persistent personal endeavor. Experience demonstrates that both languages must be represented, each by its native, in order to a satisfactory result; and that my expectation that Western ideas can be transplanted in their integrity by even the most accomplished Tamilian is illusory. I have to do over about nine tenths of all the translation prepared for my revision by the employees." Not till September, 1870, was he able to say, "I am feeling quite relieved by the completion of the version (or rather re-translation, very few sentences have escaped re-translation) of the Physician's Vade Mecum." Thus the revision of this book consumed about fifteen months. In the midst of the work he had a long test paragraph translated by Dr. Evarts, and also by Mr. Nevins, the Munshi, "two of the best educated and endowed men" in the community; also by Dr. Paul; and with Tamil help he translated it himself. These four versions he sent numbered, but without the names of the translators, to several good scholars for their preference. Mr. Howland gave his decided preference to that marked "2," for "accuracy and simplicity;" so did Mr. Anketell, who "could have no clue" to Mr. Howland's preference; which was the number of his own translation wrought out with Tamil help. "These four versions," said he, "I keep to show in proof of the necessity, in the work of translating Western science, of having the English and the Tamil represented in the process, by each its own native-born worker."

MANEPY, *Friday*, 16 *September*, 1870.

MY DEAR SISTERS AND BROTHERS:

I am glad, on this ninth anniversary of our reunion, to be permitted to report myself and mine to you, as all well and prospering.

Two of the happy eleven, gathered under our common roof-tree, have since that reunion been promoted to the undying world; leaving us a good hope that they are blessed.

This is a bright cool morning at Manepy. The parrots and the squirrels make music—one seems to live in a Zoölogical Garden. A pleasant saddle ride of a mile out and back, was followed by a turn about the grounds, on Browny, with M. R. G. in front of me; immediately on her dismouting, J. E. G. and L. M. G. took each her ordinary ride, the hostler, Aiyan, leading the old pony. Since that they have been over to the office, to see Papa, bringing each, some little gift of flowers picked by the way.

They brought a number of the scarlet rain spiders, which I advised them to give to their mother for preservation, to send to friends in America.

If health and life be spared, I hope in about four years, to be with you again; before that having completed the foundation of a correct medical system, for the enlightenment of the darkened and degraded millions.

Let us continue daily prayer for each other, that each may steadily grow in usefulness and in meetness "for the inheritance of the saints in light."

With esteem and affection, tender and true. I remain as ever,

Your brother,

Samuel F. Green.

CHAPTER XVIII.

1870–1873: ÆT. 48–51.

MORE than twelve years had now passed since Dr. Green prepared some vernacular lessons on Physiology and Hygiene for the School-books published by the Christian School-book Society of Southern India. The usefulness of those lessons may be inferred from a published extract, in which, however, he is not mentioned. "Dr. Murdock, who, like Dr. Watts' sun, 'never tires nor stops to rest, as round the world he goes,' has branch Societies all over the Continent, which he vivifies by his appearance every year, and every year makes some fresh inroad on native ignorance and European indifference. An incarnation of modesty, he seems never to estimate the immense value of the work he is doing; but every Missionary in India cherishes a name with which his efforts on behalf of vernacular literature have made the Goverments of Ceylon and India very familiar." He seems to have put the highest estimate on the efforts of Dr. Green to introduce Christianity and Western science into the hearts and minds of the Tamils. Soon after the beginning of this ninth year of Dr. Green's second term, Dr. Murdock wrote: "The little popular account in Tamil of *The House I Live In* is nearly out of print. Are there any changes you would recommend in a second edition? As you are aware, the general complaint against the Jaffna Tamil is that it is too high. I have not heard this complaint made of your little work, but if time permit you might glance over it to see whether any word might be simplified."

To several of his brother missionaries on a furlough, Dr. Green wrote in January: "At a dark hour in the Medical Department three rays of cheer. Dr. Ramapillai, the head of regular indigenous practice in the Province, wishes his son to enter the Medical Class. The nephew of Dr. Layambar (and cousin of his successor), the first practitioner in the old line for women's ailments, wishes to join the Class; paying down three pounds to meet the outfit for himself at the close of the course. Mr. Morris, Government Agent of the Eastern Province, writes asking about Medical books in Tamil, with the view of asking Government to purchase for distribution among the people at a low rate." The "dark hour" was the temptation on the part of the best educated natives to go to the new medical school at Colombo, where they could pursue their course of study in English, and thus have a better prospect of lucrative positions under Government after graduation.

The new Class, which began the 1st of February, numbered ten, of whom none were yet professing Christians, though two were inclined to make profession. There had been professing Christians in every previous Class, and one religious exercise with them daily in the afternoon. With this Class, however, the teachers had a Bible exercise at the opening of both the morning and the afternoon session. In the course of the year one of them was received into the church.

With reference to his oldest brother, Dr. Green wrote: "To bring one to the Saviour by sickness and weakness would be a more valuable answer to prayer, than to recover such an one to bodily vigor to pursue a course of worldliness;" and when he heard of his brother's death, he rejoiced greatly that he was "one reconciled to the Heavenly Father through the great Mediator."

This new bereavement seems to have emphasized the desire of his brothers and sisters, that he should return and dwell with them. To one he answered: "Your very kind offer of a home for me and mine touches my heart. It reminds me of the kindness of our Great Elder Brother who has gone 'to prepare a place for us.'" To another he replied: "The more I see the impossibility of a pure literature for this people, without Western aid, the more it grows upon me that so long as I can work, whether now or after recruiting, I must work for the Tamils."

Notwithstanding the slowness of the press, and the partial efficiency of his assistants, Dr. Green persevered, subjecting every portion of manuscript to retranslation where needed, to criticism, to comparison, to inspection of copy, before passing it to the printer. A little work for the benefit of mothers was prepared in Tamil this year and put to press. The Doctor restricted his attendance at the Dispensary to twice a day, except when cases were urgent; but the Dispensary was kept open every day in the week and every hour of the day and night, serving the three-fold object of religious instruction, prescription and medicine, and the practical training of the graduates in charge,—each of those selected holding his place for a year.

FROM DR. MURDOCK.

MADRAS, *June*, 29, 1871.

DEAR DR. GREEN:

. . . When passing through Madura and Dindigul I tried to ascertain the feeling with regard to Medical Text Books in the vernacular. Dr. Palmer seemed to object chiefly to adopting terms from the Sanskrit. He wished them transferred, if there are no vernacular words. Mr. Chester went farther, so far as I can judge. He thought that such works should be studied only in English; that those who mastered them in the vernacular would be ten years behind those who knew English. I replied that they would be at least a thousand years in advance of the native doctors. Mr. Chester has an idea that Dr. Balfour—now acting, I believe, for Dr. Smith—takes the same view, and discourages the vernacular. As a set-off look at Bengal and North India, where there have been vernacular Classes for many years. However, Mr. Chester spoke highly of *The Mother and Child.* He thought such popular works might be very useful.

Yours affectionately,

J. MURDOCK.

Sec'y. Chris. Ver. Ed. Society.

Dr. Green wrote: "In regard to popularizing medicine, I have written and put into Tamil three little pamphlets for the Christian Vernacular Society; *The Soul's Abode*, *The Mother and Child*,—a tract which is now being struck off in an edition of three thousand, and which will comfort myriads, I hope,— and *Domestic Medicine.*

"My main work has been on books strictly scientific and largely technical. This is pioneer work and most important work and will tell towards the death of superstition."

In both the lighter and the heavier line of work, Dr. Green had already exerted a wide influence. He was regarded as a leader in the creation of science in the Tamil language. He was consulted by the Professor of Vernacular Literature in the Presidency College of Madras for his views upon the introduction of Science into Tamil. Recent documents, printed at Calcutta, on the subject of Terms, were sent to him for perusal.

PRESIDENCY COLLEGE, MADRAS, *Oct.* 22, 1871.

SIR:

The accompanying papers are sent to me by the Director of Public Instruction, Madras, asking for my opinion regarding the rules to be adopted for the rendering of technical and scientific terms on a uniform system.

He also leaves me the option of consulting any friend whom I may consider qualified to pass an opinion on the matter.

Though a stranger, I have heard from various quarters of your professional and scientific skill, and I firmly believe that you are an authority upon philosophical and scientific questions of this nature; and therefore I have ventured to ask your valuable opinion on the subject, which will be forwarded in original to the Director.

I take this opportunity also to make your acquaintance, of which I shall ever be *proud.*

I beg to remain, Sir, yours ever faithfully,

D. SASHILUGAR,

Professor of Vernacular Literature.

TO S. F. GREEN, ESQUIRE, M. D., etc , etc., etc.,

JAFFNA.

Communications from men of experience were of such a nature as to make Dr. Green feel confirmed in the wisdom of his course and the value of his productions. He rejoiced that the subjects upon which he had been so earnest, had excited interest in Calcutta and in Madras, and regarded this as an aid in arresting the attention of Educators generally.

Having been nine years of his second term in the field, and having come to a condition which would soon require a change of climate, he began to plan for his return to America. The narrative may be gathered from his own pen, in letters to brothers and sisters.

Nov. 4.—I am busy in fastening the loose ends of the various strings I have been pulling, or spinning, these few years back. I am drawing off full directions as to the completion of the several volumes, in hand, but (through the extreme dilatoriness of a press which has a virtual monopoly) still unfinished. The heaviest task remaining is the translation of two hundred pages or so of the Chemistry. I have just finished the prefaces of the *Physician's Vade Mecum*, the *Anatomy*, the *Physiology*, (cuts etc.), and the *Chemistry* in diglot. I have composed a prayer to put in at the end of each, should space allow; each specifically fitted to the subject matter of the volume. These I have to translate. They are to sound the name of Jesus out among the brazen crew of imps and idols thrust in by Satan to catch the worship of this people.

Dec. 18.—If S. F. G. is to be the *last* American physician here, he may have to stay on yet awhile longer; for I seriously doubt whether, if willing and able to return, the A. B. C. F. M. would send him. The powers seem to think the Medical work of the A. C. M. ought to be about finished by this time. I wait with much interest to hear from Dr. Murdock; to learn from him whether the Madras Government may be expected to take up the work of providing Vernacular Medical Text Books.

Jan. 13, 1872.—I have called Vaittilingam, now named Chapman, from Government service to the Mission. I await a reply from Dr. Charsley, releasing him for my sake. When Chapman shall be settled with me, I hope to carry forward the work steadily. I wish to take up nothing new, but only to compact and complete what is in actual process.

Jan. 30.—Circumstances are now unmistakably the voice of the Master, bidding us tarry yet awhile. This interest is too important to be ignored.

Feb. 19.—Dr. Chapman has reached Manepy, and is now helping me. I wish, so far as he proves worthy, to work him into my place before I leave.

May 13.—It seems as if physicians should be among the most grateful of God's beneficiaries; for none more than they can realize how closely and constantly we border upon agony, and how none but a hand as strong as the creative can ward off the harms to which we are ever exposed.

July 4.—To-day's *Morning Star* has on its English page a long and fulsome article on Dr. Charsley, and another on Dr. Green. I regret to see this little paper, which could be and ought to be so useful, abused as a means of flattery and personality.

July 5.—You will rejoice with me in the completion to-day of the *Chemistry*. The son of

Vettivelu, the leading indigenous surgeon of the Province, comes this morning and applies to study medicine.

July 24.—The longer I stay the clearer I see the wisdom of so doing. With occasional exceptions I am able to do an effective day's work daily, besides keeping a hand on the helm of the Medical Department.

Aug. 24.—The *Anatomy* (8 vo. pp. 838), which has been on hand for some eight years, is at last through the press and in the hands of the binders.

Oct. 7.—The new Medical Class is in progress. Twenty good fellows. There weie over fifty applicants. I hear of a Goverment call for seventy-five doctors.

Oct. 8.—It is very encouraging to see eagerness for the study of medicine, although instruction is given in Tamil, and the Class is to proceed with little if any foreign guidance. The working force in the Medical Department of the Mission is just now: One Supervisor, a member of the last English Class; two Teachers, graduates of the Training School, and, since, of the Medical School; one Dispenser, graduate, of the first Medical Class in the Vernacular; and one Writer, member of the third Vernacular Medical Class. My hope is that these, with slight Missionary oversight, may carry on the School and the Dispensary with a good degree of efficiency.

Nov. 5.—It is a trial next to death to leave thus one's chosen work; but the indications are unmistakable; and we can do this, or can die even happily, for the promise is of grace according to the day.

Nov. 7.—All things in the Medical Department seem shaping advantageously; so that it may run well, I hope, for some years—till some hand shall reach from America or elsewhere to hold the tiller. Perhaps the young Tamil in charge may grow to it; I trust he will. The Lord has prospered me to produce nearly if not quite three thousand octavo pages in Tamil, which will effectually graft Western science, in several of its branches, upon this sturdy Tamil language. One very great want in translation is a pure literature, idiomatic, simple, instructive. For half the work of producing this, at least, the Foreigner must inevitably be responsible.

Eleventh Anniversary.

MANEPY, *Monday* 16, *Sept.*, 1872.

MY DEAR SISTERS AND BROTHERS:

The goodness of the Lord permits me to report myself and mine to you this day, as every way prospering. I am in the midst of the last of three Vocabularies, which I hope to publish in one group as the close of my medical book work.

Margaret is to have Miss Agnew to spend the day; which she has never done yet, as we are so near to her station, Oodooville. The children are abroad about the grounds this cool overcast morning. Julia I left riding the old pony; Lucy, gathering up palm nuts for planting to sprout, for arrowroot; Mary has just led Nathan to the office, to call on me here and give me a peacock flower.

Letters received from friends, recently passed through England, stir in them a good deal of anticipation, as to the wonders of art they may ere long see.

I would fain magnify the Lord with you, for all his wonderful goodness to us individually and collectively.

Eleven years hence, several of us yet on earth, may be privileged to mingle this strain of the family choir, in the "new song" before the throne. May the Holy Spirit possess each one of us and thoroughly dispossess us of worldliness, self-righteousness and every evil disposition; making us "meet for the inheritance of the saints in light."

With growing affection,

Your brother,

SAMUEL F. GREEN.

Jan. 16, 1873.—At our business meeting last Tuesday the Medical Department and the Mission Post Office were transferred from Green to Hastings. For two or three days I have been looking over, and largely filling the waste basket with documents connected with the Medical Department for the two decades during which I have been privileged to have charge of it. I am impressed in the process by the evidences of the loving-kindness of my Master in vouchsafing me so much consideration and kindness from rulers and people.*. . . . I have vocabulary all closed up for the mail in five parcels. The parcel No. 1 I sent this morning to Nagarkovil, and send one parcel a day till all is off. When I hear of the safe receipt of the entire manuscripts my work here is done.

Jan. 31.—Ninety-six years ago to-day was born in a lowly home a little boy, whom fond parents named William [E. Green], who has passed through all the ages of human life and been garnered 'as a shock of corn fully ripe.' Still there are years lacking to fill out a century, and a century is but a tithe of one of our Lord's years. Our little earth has all this while sped but a little arc of her sweep about Alcyone. If these few years have turned for us each with so much happiness and enjoyment, what may we not look for 'in Jesus' for the 'ages to come.' Thanks be to God for boundless progress ever from what is good to what is better, and from what is better to what is better still.

* It is to be regretted, that Dr. Green, prior to leaving for America, destroyed an immense number of letters and documents received from divers sources.

March 6.—I have thought I would like all our property, and whatever may have been willed to us, given in whole or in part to found a Medical Professorship in Jaffna College (provided such a disposal commends itself to the judgment of my sisters and brothers,) in case we should all pass from earth while on our way to you.

March 7.—We expect to leave Manepy, immediately after dinner, for the *Serendib*, and to weigh anchor early to-morrow morning,—sleeping on board to-night.—I showed some twenty-seven Medicos over the cabins and the engines, furnishing them with food for thought for months to come.

COLOMBO, *March* 12.—I had my first letter from Jaffna this morning, sent by my assistant Chapman—very thankful for the exhibition of the *Serendib.*

March 14.—I have written to the brethren of the A. C. M. once round, and now commence the second time in a letter to Dr. Spaulding.

The following letter from Dr. Loos, Colonial Surgeon at Colombo, indicates his estimate of Dr. Green's work.

COLOMBO, *March* 27, 1873.

MY DEAR DR. GREEN:

. . . I am grieved that sickness has prevented me from seeing you. I should have been happy to take you round our hospital and show you the work we are carrying on—a work in which we are humbly imitating you. Medical education in Ceylon is deeply indebted to you and your predecessors. You have loosened the foundations of quackery, and I trust it may please God to bless us also in our efforts to place the medical practice among the natives of this Island on a more rational and scientific basis. Your Tamil works on Medicine will remain a memorial of you after you are gone, and you will not soon be forgotten. We, as natives of this Island, are much indebted to the American Mission for their efforts in the cause of Christianity, civilization and science, although these have been confined to a part of the Island. . . . I feel that "it is good for me that I have been afflicted." I trust I have advanced in faith and patience, and wait God's own time to give me health.

I cannot hope to meet you in this life; but I cordially echo the hope that we may meet where there will be no pain or sickness. May God grant you and your family a safe and pleasant voyage, and a happy re-union with those you left behind.

Yours respectfully and sincerely,

JAMES LOOS.

Before Dr. Green went to Ceylon, seven or eight young men had been educated in medicine by the Mission. During his two terms of service, sixty-two were educated much more extensively and thoroughly, and thirty-three of them in the Vernacular; besides these, a class of twenty were well started in medicine before he left. On graduation they received each a copy of every text-book he had mastered, if already in print; otherwise they had written out their books, which were well bound for them, and included such illustrations as could be provided at the time. Besides small and popular treatises, he had produced eight volumes, either already printed or in process of printing, and four volumes in manuscript yet to be revised for the press. His graduates, now living, were in the employ of foreigners and of Government, or engaged in private practice. His hope of studding the Province with well educated practitioners had begun to be realized. The people had lost confidence in their native doctors to an encouraging extent; and the Friend-in-Need Hospital, now manned by his graduates, had more patients than all the hospitals in the other provinces.

After spending a week at Kandy and a fortnight at Colombo, in the enjoyment of most cordial courtesies and hospitalities, Dr. and Mrs. Green with their four children embarked on the *Good Hope*, sailing from Colombo on the 29th of March, touching at Aden, Port Said and Malta, and landing in London the 19th of May. Leaving London the 9th of July, they visited Reading, Oxford, Bakewell in Derbyshire, Durham, Edinburgh, Melrose, and Liverpool, sailing thence on the *Canada* the 13th of August and reaching New York on the 26th. On the 13th of September they went to Worcester; and as they wound up the long and charming lane to Green Hill and approached the mansion, they were greeted with "mottoes in large moss letters on white"—*Welcome, Home of our Childhood, Welcome Home*,—by the road side and at the entrance of the house, while "Home, Sweet Home" and "Auld Lang Syne" rang out from "a Band of music concealed in the shrubbery." The old mansion had expanded and towered, and taken on architectural forms,—the extensive country-seat of the Hon. Andrew H. Green, of New York; and providing separate and ample apartments for the brothers and sisters and their families, who assembled three times a day around the hospitable table, and as often as they pleased in the library. A feast of delicacies was in readiness, and "a Home furnished lovingly with every requisite" for the Doctor and his family. The grateful record runs thus:

"*For bringing us safely and comfortably through manifold perils, and granting us to meet in health and happiness our beloved and esteemed relatives, the Lord be pleased, through Jesus, to accept our unfeigned thanksgiving.*—S. F. G.—M. W. G."

CHAPTER XIX.

1873–1876: ÆT. 51–54.

HAVING returned to the home of his childhood, where he had so long been desired and to which he had so long looked forward as a place of rest after his utmost had been done in his foreign field, Dr. Green was for a time unable to engage in any labor that was not itself recreation. He found the home changed very much both internally and externally. His father and youngest sister as members of the household, and his oldest brother as a near neighbor and familiar visitor, were missed almost as for the first time, notwithstanding he had become somewhat accustomed to think of them as departed. His brother Andrew had added so much to the farm and to the mansion, and made so many alterations on the place, that memory had to supply much that was once familiar to sight. He had expressed the wish in his boyhood that this brother might become proprietor of the homestead; and now his wish was realized far beyond what his youthful imagination had ventured to think possible. It was, however, the same free home he had ever known, where all who survived were ever welcome, and where he and his might take no thought for the morrow as to what they should eat or wherewith they should be clothed.

The changes already made, however, were only the beginning of a long series either already contemplated or increasing with new suggestions as the seasons marked the progress towards the ideal rural home on the confines of an ever-encroaching city. It was therefore easy for Dr. Green to make himself useful, even while strolling about the premises or driving about town for recreation and pleasure. It was his delight to keep his brother informed of all that took place, his pen never wearying in expressions of affection, obligation and interest.

With ample separate apartments for all the household, Dr. Green could live in as much retirement as he pleased, but he never allowed himself to be forgetful of proprieties. From his childhood it had seemed to be almost a necessity of his own nature to be helpful to others. The most generous provisions for his own comfort never weakened his love of order and economy. As the household gathered thrice a day in the dining-room, he was promptly at his place at the table, having his family with him, so as never to lose time himself, or to be the occasion of the loss of it by others,—thus avoiding annoyance to any portion of the household, and contributing by his example to the ease and efficiency of the household service.

GREEN HILL, *February*, 1874.

MY DEAR BROTHER ANDREW:

. . . I contemplate the expenditure here with some degree of composure, trusting it does not intrench in the least on investments, but I fear I have not much complacency in it. I anticipate, however, the developement of this feeling when yourself shall be in the enjoyment of what is steadily shaping for elegance and comfort. . . .

I am enjoying a little resumption of work again. I hope I may gradually settle into efficient labor once more. There is great enjoyment in useful occupation. To do nothing is the hardest work. I sometimes think such work will be the lot of the lost. A "fast man" they say. Yes, fast rushing from intense activity to blank monotony; no flitting from scene to scene, but one glum dusky loneliness, and no one to blame for it—all recoiling and weighing on self. . . .

Affectionately, your brother,

SAMUEL F. GREEN.

GREEN HILL, *March* 28, 1874.

MY DEAR SISTER LUCY:

. . . . Should the month of August find your finances prospering so as to warrant it, I shall rejoice to avail of your permission to add a thousand dollars to the little sum already gained in Jaffna as a donation toward the endowment of the *Green Professorship of Medicine and the Natural Sciences* in the Jaffna College. . . . It will be necessary to make such conditions, restrictions and limitations as shall prevent any perversion of the funds. . . .

Affectionately your brother,

SAMUEL F. GREEN.

In due time, by his sister's permission, the gift suggested was made. The doctor's "resumption of work" thus extended beyond his books, even to an immediate and permanent blessing to the people for whose welfare he had devoted so many years of labor and so much prayer.

GREEN HILL, *April* 13, 1874.

MY DEAR BROTHER ANDREW:

. . . I thank you for your offers of remedial and hygienic means. I have already all that heart can wish. Every need is met, every comfort supplied, and it is an additional joy that a good Providence affords all, not through the hard strife of business; less through the cold hand of charity; but through the warm hearts of those beloved and esteemed. The lines fall to me in a pleasant place, and I have but the one want and wish—to receive all more gratefully and use all more gracefully. . . .

21.—It seems that the Secretary of the Board very properly wrote, sounding the Mission as to the desirability of our return. They discussed the matter fully, and voted unanimously for our return if possible and as soon as practicable. This is gratifying, for we "like to be missed at home." I am informed of the completion of another volume, and of considerable progress on the printing of still another. Also I am at last encouraged to expect an instalment of manuscript translation. . .

Ever and affectionately,

SAMUEL F. GREEN.

Medical Missions had become a subject of great interest to Dr. Green. A brief but condensed summary of his views was published in 1874 in the May number of the *Quarterly Paper of the Edinburgh Missionary Society*, and followed immediately by the comment of the editor: "The foregoing contribution has been sent us by our esteemed friend and fellow-laborer while in India, Dr. Green, of Ceylon, than whom no living Medical Missionary has had such lengthened experience, nor done so much to extend the benefits of European skill, by translating and publishing a comprehensive Medical and Surgical Literature in the South Indian vernacular, and by training native medical evangelists."

High as is the editorial commendation, no man acquainted with the facts, especially no medical missionary, could justly detract from it by a word.

Dr. Green still regarded himself a missionary, so far as it was possible in his poor health and absence from his field. He had made arrangements by which he hoped to have his contemplated series of medical works in Tamil completed. His translator was to send him from Ceylon from time to time a portion of the work in hand, which he was to revise and return, until the translation of the whole work should be ready for the press. The possibility of loss by mail made it necessary to keep a copy of the corrections made, or to take the risk of having to make them again. This revising by instalments gave him interesting employment and kept him in frequent communication with the Medical Department and in close sympathy with the Mission. His heart was largely with the people for whom he had labored, and nothing but inability or necessity would deter him from laboring for them still. He persevered, revising parcel after parcel of translation, till a volume was finally completed; and then he began on another.

The young Tamil physician whom he left in charge of the Medical Department sent his first instalment of his translation of Dalton's Physiology so that Dr. Green received it in May. Some notion of the nature and amount of the work he had to do in revision, and in keeping Tamil friends up to their duty, may be gained from the following letter.

To Dr. Vaittilingam.

Green Hill, Worcester, Mass., U. S. A.,

June 25, 1874.

My Dear Chapman:

Herewith you will receive the nine small pages of notes on your instalment No. 1 of sixteen large pages. Allow me to express my gratification at the excellence of your translation. I hope that with growing experience and pains ,your style and accuracy may still further improve. As we have repeatedly talked, simplicity is the chief characteristic of a good style. In works of science we want as little technicality as possible, but should not prefer circumlocution to the use of a technical.

In all the rest of our series let us rather prefer the usage of the *Physician's Vade Mecum* to that in the Anatomy; and put in plenty of aids in the way of English Captions, catchwords and emphasized Tamil words. Please see page 4 of my remarks about references I have made. . . . . Mr. Jones writes me that he has despatched the remaining forms of the *Physician's Vade Mecum* to me by Book Post; so I daily expect their appearance here. Please remember us all kindly to your wife and sister; to Messrs. Moody, Strong and Asbury; to our common medical friends and to any inquiring acquaintances. How many dissections have you had at the Hospital the past year?

Your friend,

SAMUEL F. GREEN.

On the 26th of August Dr. Green wrote: "To-day ends a year for us in America. I can never forget, nor can duly recompense for, the favors of this year. My heart melts in recalling the meeting at the ship, the tender care at the New York home and at Norwalk, and the joyous welcome at the Hill."

His watchfulness over his own heart, and his readiness to extend to others the benefit of his own self-administered corrections and rebukes, are alike beautifully exhibited in this extract from a letter to the one who might possibly have shared with him the objectionable feeling. "I felt much your so sudden withdrawal. I was conscious of a feeling of elation in driving about in the carriage (just after leaving you) behind a fine pair of horses. Then the thought crossed my mind, how heinous a sin pride is, that it thrusts in its head where gratitude should show itself."

GREEN HILL, *Feb.* 26, 1875.

MY DEAR BROTHER ANDREW:

. . . Your note bears three facts that call out our earnest solicitude and sympathy: The greater fierceness, the increased number of foes, and the lessened number of friends and helpers. Look up for guidance, and foward with as much hope as you may. . . . It can scarcely be your duty to sacrifice your health or your property or peace of your relatives. There is a satisfaction in the successful resistance of wrong.*. . . Perseverance is a virtue; its extreme is persistency; its excess is pertinacity. All the virtues exist *within* the circle of Love; each is a sturdy spoke in the wheel of life. If any one juts beyond the tire, its vicious length jars and jounces along to discomfort and danger. . . . In a fight one should

*Andrew H. Green was occupying at this critical time the office of Comptroller of New York.

not only look at the foe in front, but should give a look right and left, that his blows harm not those he counts his friends. . . . Don't let the vehemence of indignation force you a step further than Wisdom will sanction. . . .

Ever and affectionately,

Your brother,

SAMUEL F. GREEN.

GREEN HILL, *March* 24, 1875.

MY DEAR BROTHER ANDREW:

I have Dr. Draper's book* in hand. It is written in a charming style. It is most captivating. It seems to me for contemplation like a glittering iceberg. It chills one while it charms. I do not see that it touches, much less solves the problem of sin and suffering. Crimes—political, social, domestic—abound around us. Will science stop a little from her soarings toward the tenuous ether to suggest a remedy? The taint of sin attaches to the inner self of every human being. To rid himself of it, which branch of Science had the Philosopher best pursue. Professor Webster followed out Chemistry faithfully, and murdered Dr. Parkman. "Light has come into the world."

*History of the conflict between Religion and Science, by John William Draper, M. D., L. L. D.

The desideratum is holiness. Shall Science with her torch lead us to it, or shall we follow the Greater Light. It is to be wished that Dr. Draper would discriminate between the Pope and the Lord Jesus, between interpretations of Scripture and Scripture itself. . . .

April 7.— . . . It strikes me as remarkable that a man so astute in many things should perpetrate the error of estimating the relative values of spirit and matter by bulk. If a soul is immortal and endlessly progressive, it far transcends in importance the largest sun ever gauged by astronomers. . . .

April 17.—I have carefully read Dr. Draper's book through; some of it twice. It is charming in style, entertaining and instructive in items, bad in logic, because mistaken in its premises and its conclusions. It has inconsistencies. I am glad to have read it, am obliged to you for placing it before me. I would like to go over it again. . . .

Affectionately,

SAMUEL F. GREEN.

In reply to a sister's inquiry as to the wants in the family, he wrote, "I have referred your inquiry as to our needs to Margaret. It seems that by the goodness of God through the kindness of our friends we are brought in to such difficulty that we feel unable to name any unsupplied want."

To the American Ceylon Mission.

September 30, 1875.

Dear Brethren:

I have for years purposed to prepare some simple rules for the general guidance of those resorting to our Dispensary. I send herewith a draft of these for improval and for translation. I would like a copy of the translation for revisal. I suggest that when ready it be printed with an appropriate heading. Every patient receives a ticket on which is a synopsis of the Christian religion. On this is written his number according to the register. To Christians and to those obviously *conversant with Christianity* these rules may be given instead of the old ticket. The patient's number can be equally well put upon it. To intelligent heathens both may be given. It may properly be charged to the Government Medical Grant.

If approved by the Mission, will they please have it copied, and the verified copy translated as simple as practicable, and a copy of the translation sent to me, and so much oblige,

Dear Brethren,

Yours respectfully,

Samuel F. Green.

GREEN HILL, *Tues.*, 12 *Oct.*, 1875.

MY DEAR BROTHER ANDREW:

Mr. John N. Flagg, of Bennington, N. H., called to-day, to look at Green Hill, for old acquaintance's sake. He used to live here, from 1810 to 1813. He was a lad of eight years, and contemporary here with Miss Bethesda Rugg.

He recalls our aunt Mary, as a very lovely woman, who nursed him kindly when he had cut his foot deeply at the woodpile. He remembers grandmother, and her burial in the Old South Church glebe. He used to dig worms, for some of father's law-acquaintances, to fish with in the pond: (of about 30 acres.)

His fishing there was so facile that it spoiled, ever afterwards, the attempt at the sport elsewhere. He accumulated in perquisites, by the visitors, a sum of five dollars, which he lent to one Taft, a man who worked here, but who enlisted afterwards in the army and never returned, with either principal or interest.

He says father was always very pleasant with him. "Never gave him a cross word." He would say, "Johnny, ah you're a rogue." Aunt Mary once sent him to Millstone Hill to call the woodchoppers to dinner, from which errand he returned abashed, through failure to find them.

He has a recollection of the Licorice in the garden: of the English Walnut tree: of the row of Mulberries and of the great profusion and variety of peaches, cherries and pears.

He remembers father's marriage with Julia Plimpton.

He says father had a Chinese sow, almost black, which he kept till she was nearly twenty years of age. His recollection of the house dog then is not very clear, but he thinks it was a shaggy yellowish one. He remembers brother William, about two years younger than himself, also a little girl about: probably sister Lucy. He was pre-engaged for dinner, so he could not stop with us. He entered his name in the Green Hill book.

He seems sedate, intelligent and sterling. We had a real treat of reminiscences, and should have enjoyed it still more, could all of you, now at No. 1, have been present.

Affectionately your brother,

SAMUEL F. GREEN.

Dr. Green was remarkable for two traits of character which do not often go together or appear equally developed: the absence of all pride against being a beneficiary, and the constant presence of the sense of gratitude for the favors received. Perhaps this was owing first to his consecration to Christ, and then to the fact that he regarded every gift of man to him as belonging to the Lord, whether in the hands of a benefactor or in those of a beneficiary.

To Mrs. and Mr. Knudsen.

Green Hill, *November* 9, 1875.

My Dear Sister and Brother:

. . . Shall I try to balance your generosity by my gratitude? The sick fox lies by the pathway and sees the tracks of bounty-laden lions, elephants, etc., all pointing one way. Mr. Rand* used to say "It is easier to condescend than to be condescended to;" but your favors all come with so much of fraternity enwrapping them, that I do not experience the difficulty. May the happiness of the giver be with you each large interest on each benefaction.

With love for all four,

Ever and affectionately yours,

Samuel F. Green.

To His Daughter.

New York, *Monday Evening*, 6 *Dec.*, '75.

My Lovely Lucy Darling:

. . . It seems a very long week since I bade you all good bye in the lobby at the loved Homestead. The sounds and sights and scenes

*John Rand, an eminent artist, long resident in England, and an able and scholarly gentleman.

have made many and varied and strong impressions on my mind; and life is more truly measured by mental emotions and actions, than by the calendar.

I was rejoiced to receive a letter from your sister Julia, and shortly thereafter one from you also. I feel gratified by the correctness and neatness of your productions; as well as by the facility and range of expression. And now to-day comes in a very pleasing note from your sister Mary, the third in the children's series; I responded to dear Julia's last week, now to yours, and perhaps next week to dear Mary's. I hope also to write to your little brother—and my little son—in due course. Then, I fear, I shall have to deny myself; as I see I shall have to work pretty hard to overtake all the items of business that I have planned to execute before turning homeward.

Oh, if I only had you just now by my side and could prattle a few phrases with you and nip the finger tips, to and fro, once or twice! I will hope soon again, to have that five minutes which flees so apace, just before the iron hand so inexorably warns the beloved trio to bed.

I hope my lovely walks closely along with the Blessed Jesus through the hours of each day. I trust she is the quiet peacemaker and her mother's cheer. Realize that our Lord was once just of your age and that he passed through childhood and through his teens and knows exactly all the trials and temptations, all the wants and wishes, of my dear lassie. Neither pen nor tongue can tell all that is in my heart, of yearning for my Lucy's weal. We conclude in saying that but "one thing is needful," and I wish daily my darlings shall ask that for papa, as he for them. May the adorable Saviour aid both you and your sister to adorn your profession of loyalty to Him, to "adorn the doctrine of God our Saviour in all things."

Tossing you and all four a kiss, I close, as the late hour commands me to retire.

Ever and most lovingly,

Your father,

SAMUEL F. GREEN.

It fell to Dr. Green to conduct an immense correspondence. His kindred were numerous, and have preserved many letters, generally very brief, however, because of the constant pressure of the work he was doing, and of the constant necessity of favoring himself. To his friends he wrote hurriedly, as well as briefly, but always out of the fulness of his heart, spontaneously suiting every letter to the individuality of its recipient. He was so strong in his affections, so spiritual in the temper and habit of his mind, so practical in his views, so desirous of the consecration of every one to Christ, that the transitions from news and from business into sentences and paragraphs of sentiment seem to have been as easy and natural as the beating of the pulse. His habit of brevity, formed by necessity while abroad, seemed to be a matter of course after his return so that scarcely a day passed, except Sunday, without one or more letters. It was his method of intercourse with the absent, his substitute for their visible and audible presence. No apology need be offered for the insertion of a few of his letters in chronological order with the narrative, whether they relate to the subject of the context, or have no other relation to it than that of the order of time. They are valuable as revealing his own mind and heart; his love for his kindred and friends, his desire for the salvation of all, his consecration to Christ, his willing self-denial for His cause, his unworldly spirit, his entire freedom from doubt concerning the reality of the things revealed and the genuineness and certainty of his own renewal by the Spirit, and of his own heirship to the full fruition of the divine promises. He realized in himself that "godliness with contentment which is great gain." All things were his because they were Christ's, and to him there was nothing worth living for except the preparation of the world for which Christ died for the glorious inheritance which He had purchased and promised to share with his followers.

To his Daughter.

New York, 27 *January*, 1876.

My Precious Julia:

Perhaps you know how very much Papa wishes to see you. I got an unexpected look at your picture the other day, and was delighted. I could scarce help laughing out, for gladness. How happy it is to look forward to the spirit-world and think that matter will not there have place to darken with its shadows; to hide us, one from the other. How beautiful to have all supple and clarified; to see into each other's hearts and through each other's being; to "know, even as we are known." Till all gross and unholy is eliminated, "God (in mercy) hides from all beings but Himself, ... the human heart."

How, dear daughter, could we possibly reach this hallowed state, when opposed by the treachery of a "heart deceitful and desperately wicked;" by an alluring world all in rebellion; by an adversary, malicious, experienced, incessant; did not the Blessed Jesus seek us, stand by us, uphold us and clear the way before us.

What shall we render to Him for all He is to us; for all He has earned for us; for all He prepares us. Let our "mouth be filled with His praise and His honor all the day long."

I like to think of you, placed so eligibly; sequestered at a beautiful homestead; surrounded by loving and faithful friends; senior, and so leader, of a group whom you daily influence by your words and ways. Well might an angel flutter down from the skies to take a position, so advantageously environed, in which to serve and honor each winged hour, the God of Love.

"Rejoice," dear Julia, "in the Lord always," and while in gratitude you sing, "the lines are fallen unto me in pleasant places," occasionally also chant with serious resolution, "to whom much is given, of him shall much be required;"

"and again *rejoice*,"
for

"one drop of honey will draw more flies than a bowl of vinegar."

Let us ask for each other more and more of the Christ-ward attraction, of that "joy and peace," which comes of believing in Jesus.

And now with a kiss, dear darling, Good bye.

Your affectionate father,

SAMUEL F. GREEN.

I.

GREEN HILL, *March* 14, 1876.

MY DEAR BROTHER ANDREW:

. . . It is remarkable that your illness should occur just after my leaving. Did the presence of a physician keep what was imminent at bay, or did "Pilgarlic" leave behind morbific influence which soon culminated in ailment? I hope you are restored to your wonted health, comfort and vigor. What proof of constant and kindest care is the fact of our passing month after month without pain! Our complex, intricate mechanism surely needs the hand of the Former to keep it in easy working order. Let us daily praise Him in out-spoken ejaculation for His goodness. He declares to us that "Whoso offereth praise glorifieth me;" and what higher purpose can we at any hour fulfil than to glorify One who is really so gloriously worthy of the best we can offer? . . .

Most lovingly and gratefully and yearningly,

Your brother,

SAMUEL F. GREEN.

II.

GREEN HILL, *March* 23, 1876.

MY DEAR BROTHER ANDREW:

. . . Your brotherly visits, in one undesirable particular, are too much like angel's visits. Since I have had prolonged ocular evidence of your habitually severe pressure, I see the advisability and necessity of more relaxation for you. I cannot bear to see you voluntarily ageing so rapidly. . . . I have deep convictions as to this. I feel that such an entire break in the moil and toil of the week will tell powerfully and beneficially upon you physically, mentally and spiritually. The Bible being our only voice from heaven, we must, as we regard our souls, keep it fresh and warm by frequent and deliberate contact with it. As for the Rest-day, I feel bound to keep it "holy," 1st as an act of obedience, 2nd as a high enjoyment, 3d a profitable example. Why does the 4th commandment commence with "Remember?" It reminds of something previously enacted. . . .

As a brother I delight in you and have constant occasion to thank my Father for the companionship and for the tender kindness and the great liberality you have for so many years untiring shown me. Alongside our fraternal relations lies closely that of benefactor and beneficiary. The first place in this latter relation Providence has assigned to you. For all your favors I can make but slight return. But in both relations I wish to be true, and consequently I speak out my yearnings for your welfare. Were I now speaking to you, beloved, my last words, I would say, use your Sabbaths habitually, and your Bible daily, as one in earnest to secure salvation. . . . .

Yours affectionately,

SAMUEL F. GREEN.

III.

GREEN HILL, *April* 21, 1876.

MY DEAR BROTHER ANDREW:

What a marvel of Providence that amid such numerous and constant risks we measure our comfort and enjoyment by years, our suffering by hours or days. . . . Doing your duty by the Public, leave results to the Divine control. Things most pleasing in the present are not seldom least profiting in the end. There is no rest rival of that which rests in the Love which "sees the end from the beginning."

How selfishness is continually complicating the problem of life. From hour to hour the question should simply be that between right and wrong. But some ambitious scheme, some sinister aim obtruding, disturbs the current which might flow placid and clear. Truly, "They that observe lying vanities forsake their own mercy." . . .

Ever and affectionately,

Your brother,

SAMUEL F. GREEN.

IV.

GREEN HILL, *May* 25, 1876.

MY DEAR BROTHER ANDREW:

. . . We brought up one double roll of paper for the Library: the red paper, not the green. No paper sent for the front hall. I see in this some instruction as to the difference between regret and remorse. Supposing me responsible wholly for the miscarrying of the hall papering, it can easily be seen how far greater would be the mind-trouble than if I only stood sharer with you in the loss and delay. If regret may be represented by rheumatism, remorse must be set down as gout. I cannot forbear thinking how far severer the state of the lost is than if it were merely one of regret. One wantonly in perdition must be intensely incensed against himself. There is for regret the alleviation of sympathy; for remorse there can be none. Every one of us is lost till he is saved. . . . Of these earthly annoyances we can gradually be rid, by passing "on to the next," and on and on. But perdition must be, at best, I fancy, a permanent, brooding, sullen, gloomy chagrin in which one welters and flounders inextricably. . . .

I am, as ever,

Your affectionate brother,

SAMUEL F. GREEN.

NEW YORK, *Sat.*, 21 *Oct.*, 1876.

MY PRECIOUS CHILDREN:

I would fain write you severally and formally; but circumstances disfavor.

You are daily on my heart, and I have much joy in every intimation, "that my children walk in the truth." To the natural eye, Jesus is invisible; but the eye of Faith sees Him, clearly and ever near. Darlings, it is only while we are looking at Him, that these things around us, which are sometimes so pleasant, sometimes so troublesome, that these will work any lasting good for us.

Once, some little eyes were "watching for Papa." Papa is watching for the day and the hour, when again he may meet and greet, if the Lord will, those beaming eyes, and loving hearts.

Love from us both to each.

Affectionately, your father,

SAMUEL F. GREEN.

NEW YORK, *Sat.*, 4 *Nov.*, 1876.

MY PRECIOUS DAUGHTER MARY:

I was looking at the Republican torch-light procession till nearly eleven o'clock last evening. Previous to this, I had seen two other similar shows within a few days. As I was looking at the torches, with their flare and glare, I caught sight of a brilliant star; which, though seemingly but a dot upon the sky, with its clear and steady radiance, transcended them all. Nor less did the hurrahs and bustle, contrast with the quiet of those serene depths, in which our star and its fellows swing around unperturbed. The intensely fervent excitement, now agitating this community, will we hope in four days be lulled by the still ballot. The doings of the World are fitful and shallow, as compared with proceedings based on the Word of God. Nestling in Christ, we can exulting ask, "Why do the people imagine a vain thing?"

I feel very glad over your kind letter. I see that you will probably grow into an interesting correspondent. I am pleased that you do not attempt to write too much; for I would rather that you, by active sports in the sun and air, lay on an ounce of flesh, than that you, by staying indoors, should pen me a page.

My dear Birdie knows that I wish her to be one of the most happy, helpful lasses in the world. She knows the sweet story of Mary of old, and that nothing would more gladden Papa, than that she should in herself display the like inclination and choice.

Give love from Mamma and me, to each of the Sisters and the Brother.

Hoping ere long to greet you and them, I remain,

Your affectionate father,

SAMUEL F. GREEN.

Although Dr. Green's recuperation was slow, he desired to spend his strength in work for the Tamils. "I wish," said he in June, "to see the Chandlers before they sail in August. We hope to follow them within a year. Although powerfully weak we multiply half strength by tenfold demand and get the result of fivefold usefulness." When August arrived he said: "About going to India, I wish to feel acquiescent to the Lord's will. I would not prefer to stay here or to go there. I simply wish the indication as to duty perfectly clear. For aught to the contrary, a restoration to a good degree of vigor would be a clear indication to resume work there; work in which I have been much prospered; work most important; work about which not a tithe of the able and willing hands cluster that press around every Christian utility here."

Besides revising, at Green Hill, manuscript translations, Dr. Green prepared some religious tracts and popular scientific monographs. Of the latter he sent to the Mission for examination, and, if approved, for publication, four during the year, —entitled *The Eye*, *The Ear*, *The Hand*, *The Mouth.*

CHAPTER XX.

1876–1878: ÆT. 54–56.

AFTER attending the Annual Meeting of the American Board at Hartford, Dr. and Mrs. Green made a short visit with Mr. and Mrs. Knudsen at South Norwalk, and then spent several weeks with the sister and brother at New York, where they were recipients of great courtesies from several of his professional brethren, and whence they returned to Green Hill after an absence of about two months and a half.

GREEN HILL, *February* 14, 1877.

MY DEAR BROTHER:

. . . I have been latterly thinking repeatedly of morality. It seems to be only the second part of that Love which is the fulfilling of the Law. It may be most punctilious in all concerns between man and man and while recognizing with rigid exactness the claims of his neighbor, may ignore the ever present God who is first and most to be recognized. Morality *per se* is only an earthly blessing. Only as vitalized by faith in Jesus can it transcend the bound of time in any lasting good to the soul; for "without faith it is impossible to please God." Do we not see in the Scripture that faith is a *sine qua non?* The source of faith is infinite, and so is its freeness. Each of us can have all he will appropriate. You may have already more than I have. I think I have some, though it is lamentably weak and unsteady, as I see only too clearly. May I say that I long to gain more assurance as to your possession of this inestimable quality. One cheering sign would be a more spiritual use of the weekly Rest. . . . I am as ready to admit, as you could possibly be to declare, that this is a matter between yourself and your Maker.

Your high toned morality as a man, your loving kindness as a brother, constrain me to break over reserve and entreat you to see to it that as you abound in human excellences you pray and endeavor to abound in this crowning excellence of faith also. . . .

Ever and most affectionately,

Your brother,

SAMUEL F. GREEN.

TO DR. VAITTILINGAM.

GREEN HILL, *March* 23, 1877.

MY DEAR CHAPMAN:

Your last letter, giving the necrology of our common acquaintance, and the fatally diseased condition of several others among them, was as interesting as sad. May the Lord, the Spirit, work within those thus sentenced to earlier departure, that faith and repentance which shall prepare them for entrance on the glory of the coming kingdom of our Lord Jesus. We thank you for any and all the news you can communicate to us from our loved Jaffna. That little dot of earth, we long to see thronged with loving, humble, devoted followers of the Saviour Christ.

I have just finished revision of your last parcel, and have now to wait ten days for another. Can you not, with Mr. Howland's help, arrange to give me a parcel every week instead of every fortnight? . . . I can *easily* attend to the revision of *twice* as much as now you supply to me. . . .

The several Glossaries were prepared one after the other. All the while experience and acquaintance with the work of nomenclature were growing. Therefore the latest should have precedence of any made previously. First came the Midwifery, secondly the Surgery, thirdly the Anatomy, fourthly the Physic, fifthly the Chemistry, and now sixthly the Physiology. There has been a gradual change in the style of Terms and, I feel, a steady *improvement.* In any subsequent editions of the books, this should be regarded, and the Terms throughout the books severally, and in the Glossaries, should be conformed to the latest phase, the most advanced and improved style. The most *radical* change in the Glossaries was giving the English preference over the Sanscrit as a source for Terms.

. . . .

With kind regards for and from all,

Yours truly,

SAMUEL F. GREEN.

GREEN HILL, *March* 27, 1877.

MY DEAR SISTER LUCY:

. . . In my nightly round of fastenings I wander through deserts of garnished rooms, and when at the end I reach one which though empty has signs of current occupancy, I feel freshly struck with the truth that number has much to do with enjoyment. As "population is the wealth of a nation," so is number the strength of a family. Among the lesser mysteries of Providence is the problem of this beautiful and commodious Home. Who shall throng its stairways, who crowd its board, who repose in its secluded spacious rooms? The who and the when will all be disclosed by the gradual unrolling of the scroll in our Father's hand. As long as any of us have aught to do with it, may it be the abode of love, pure, fervent and unfeigned . . .

Ever and affectionately,

SAMUEL F. GREEN.

GREEN HILL, *April* 21, 1877.

MY DEAR BROTHER ANDREW:

It is delightful to me to contemplate you at ease for a day or two in the home and company of our sister Mary. The sensation of being at leisure must be almost strange to you, but I hope it will be less and less so till the exception shall grow into the rule. Our Heavenly Father has made us for enjoyment, and our inner self must be out of order if we are not happy. We are never truly happy till we are happy independent of externals. The man that could look up to the Lord and say, "All my springs are in Thee," had found the secret of joy. What a boon to have in us a fountain of water springing up into everlasting life! A blessing this within the reach even of the weakest and the worst. May you be steadily and growingly happy.

Yours lovingly and gratefully,

SAMUEL F. GREEN.

GREEN HILL, *May* 29, 1877.

MY DEAR BROTHER ANDREW:

I drove to town yester-afternoon with dear Sister Julia. We made several lively calls. Among other places we called at Mr.——'s cottage. He has recently gone to live as it were in a corner of the elegant grounds where once he occupied the central residence. How surely earthly possessions depart, either by our losing them or by our passing away from this transient world. Some one was speaking of Mr. Lockwood's place on which he spent millions. This soon slipped away, by various mutations, from his family, and passed for a few thousands into the hold of strangers. The man who lately held it has suddenly been summoned hence.

How generally men seem to forget that responsibility is the ever attendant shadow of possession. Our Saviour's precept and example both show us that the most is to be got out of our goods by making the most happy, others as many as we can. "Though He was rich, for our sakes He became poor." He is, we must suppose, the happiest Being in the universe, and is so because He makes the greatest multitudes happy. Among property holders, those seem to me the noblest who save to give, while those who save to hoard are of all most miserable. Of that nobility our venerated Aunt Betsey always seemed to me a conspicuous example. She spent little on herself; she gave munificently. I fancy she impressed herself on our sisters. We can never be too thankful that for years such a genius, presided among us. It is perhaps well that we have not her life-size full length portrait. Looking on us from the wall, it might over-tempt us to saint-worship. Even to a stranger's gaze, what a queenly presence it would show. Her worthy quality imparted has grown, through the years, into all the wealth of generosity and devotion in a sisterhood whom we count our joy and crown.

The children have completed the planting of their gardens. They undertake a larger plat this year. They have each a flower bed and vegetable bed; the latter in the same spot where our beets, parsnips, etc., grew in our boyhood. I have begun to go round about all the bounds of the farm with them. They are favored beyond any children in town, I think, in having such range and seclusion. We plan our excursion to Long Pond this season —a fishing pic-nic.

My young friend Sanders is to be "ordained" next Tuesday. I am named as one of the Council; so I think to go for old acquaintance's sake. It has long seemed to me that the higher ordination pertains to every Christian, each cognizant of the "good news" being supposably impelled to inform others also. The event is to transpire at Hartford, and that points to South Norwalk and on to New York. Sister Julia proposes to go also, and take little Mary. So we rejoice in hope to see our dear sisters and our dear brother soon face to face.

With much affection,

S. F. GREEN.

After the ordination of Mr. Charles S. Sanders at Hartford, Dr. Green proceeded to South Norwalk where his sister Mary then resided, and to New York, returning after a few weeks to Green Hill.

GREEN HILL, *June* 15, 1877.

MY DEAR BROTHER ANDREW:

. . . . As to my going to Ceylon again for awhile. Theoretically there is much to do here, but practically next to nothing. The uncertainty of life aside, there seems a fair probability of ten or fifteen years yet for me. As to the needs and modes among the Tamils, I have ceased to be a novice. As to man's doings, I think "Surely they are disquieted in vain," except so far as directly or indirectly their endeavors advantage minds and souls. Your long and able administration of the Park has indirectly this advantage largely, for it favors virtue in multitudes for generations. Your arduous struggle with political corruption also has presented an edifying spectacle to many. Though I am not strong—I never was strong—yet I have been sustained to accomplish twice ten years of hard and very necessary work; work which, though less energetic, may be no less effective towards the elevation of a degraded people. Although I cannot emulate your example in providing liberally and tenderly for relations, perhaps I may and should emulate it in attempting the good of others, even with impaired vigor, as you are now doing. . . .

Ever and affectionately,

SAMUEL F. GREEN.

To the inquiry of the Secretary of the A. B. C. F. M. in May, "What are your thoughts at present in reference to a return?" Dr. Green replied, "We are praying, waiting and hoping . . . We trust to be on our way within a year." In July, inquiries were made, to which he returned answer as follows: "I propose to return with Mrs. Green, leaving the children in America, all of them. We would propose to remain away for ten years, more or less, as long as life and health granted may warrant. I would like to complete the series of Medical Text Books if circumstances favor. For this two or three years would probably be required. After this I would like to do what I can in the production of religious books. Of course I should count all medical work as merely accessory to evangelization. In the Medical Class, in the Dispensary, etc., it is always the aim to give a distinctively evangelistic character to all that is done. Should the work so develop that I could ultimately delegate all but the direct teaching and preaching of the gospel, I should be only too glad to avail of the higher privilege."

Within a week of this reply, the Secretary wrote: "So after a careful consideration of the case, having in view your children and your own health, the advanced condition of the Medical Department in Ceylon in consequence of your past labors, and the adjustment made there in your long absence, the Committee did not think it expedient for you to return."

Dr. Green reported the substance and result of the correspondence to the members of the

American Ceylon Mission, saying, "Nevertheless, in heart and till death we wish to be accounted as members of the same Mission with you."

In August Dr. Green informed the Secretary of the Ceylon Mission that he had in hand the last pages of the Physiology for revision, giving detailed directions about printing it, and asking the decision of the Mission as to printing this, and as to translating and printing the next two volumes in the contemplated series.

His little work *The Soul's Abode* was furnished with the following prayer in English and in Tamil, one to be inserted at the beginning and the other at the end, in the second edition, which illustrates the way he endeavored to impress the readers of his scientific treatises with their intimate relation to Christianity:

"My Father in heaven, I come to Thee through the mediation of Jesus Christ, and praise Thee for so fearfully and wonderfully making me. I praise Thee for preserving this body, so complex, amid the many perils which constantly menace it; for constituting my senses inlets for so much knowledge and pleasure; for the comfortable occupancy of my body and for the enjoyable use of its various functions and members.

"I render Thee the acceptable offering of a broken heart and a contrite spirit, and humbly confess all my sinfulness, and pray Thee to pardon and cleanse me for Jesus' sake.

"I adore Thee for adding to thy goodness that wondrous love manifested in sending Him, thine only Son, to redeem me from the slavery, the guilt and the punishment of sin. Accept Thou my body as a living sacrifice. Aid Thou me diligently to observe temperance, cleanliness and every means to its health, and enable me to keep it pure from every selfish or vicious use.

"Pervade me so fully that my eye, my tongue, my hand, my every faculty, shall act ever kindly and helpfully. Do Thou so mold all my habits and dispositions that I may, with all meetness, pass from out this mortal body into that spiritual body which Thou wilt bestow on each one who loves Thee.

"And Thine for ever shall be the glory, through Jesus Christ. Amen."

On receiving the completed translation of *Dalton's Physiology*, the Mission decided to publish it, and also to publish the *Pharmacopœia of India* and *Taylor's Medical Jurisprudence*, when these also should be translated. Dr. Vaittilingam, *alias* Chapman, was justifying expectations to a good degree by his perseverance in translation and by the general excellence of his work. He began to translate the *Pharmacopœia of India*, and thus furnished Dr. Green with important work still to do for the Tamils. But on account of various interruptions, particularly the "reading and re-reading and re-re-reading" of the proof-sheets of the Physiology as it slowly passed through the Manepy press, nearly three years were consumed in the translation. Though the progress was very unsatisfactory to Dr. Green, perhaps it was fully compensated for by other advantages; it relieved him from being driven beyond his strength, and left him time for translating *The Believing Tradesman* and *The Shepherd of Salisbury Plain*, besides making improvements with reference to a second edition of his works.

For several weeks in January and February Dr. Green was away from Green Hill, visiting his friends in Connecticut and New York City, "enjoying much," besides profiting from the cessation of work. Yet at New York he was at home almost as much as he was at Green Hill.

GREEN HILL, *March* 26, 1878.

MY DEAR BROTHER MARTIN:

I hope you are having a real good time. I am expecting your visit to prove a triple refreshment to you, and may the great Ruler so cause it. The change is so entire, the society you will have so ennobling, and the scenes so interesting and varied. Surely those so favored as are you and I should not only be very happy, but steadily advancing in the best things.

I believe there is a purpose to follow up the Bible readings here. I imagined you last Sunday hearing Dr. Deems with our beloved nephew, and one of the Plymouth Brethren with our sister. I hope also you may once go to Olivet Chapel. I am surprised that for the far greater portion of my Bible apprehension I am indebted to the remarks of men. I see in this the utility of converse on Scriptural topics. I see one of the advantages of the "communion of saints." Had we better not be growingly unwilling to allow Earth overmuch of our discourse, and increasingly intent that spiritual themes shall form its staple?. . . .

I am your affectionate and grateful brother,

SAMUEL F. GREEN.

TO REV. WILLIAM EVANS OF LIVERPOOL, ENGLAND, ON THE DEATH OF HIS WIFE.

GREEN HILL, WORCESTER, MASS., U. S. A.,
March 26, 1878.

MY DEAR MR. EVANS:

Allow me, for myself and for all your friends at Green Hill, to express to you our lively sympathy with you in your recent bereavement. I well know how poor is human sympathy; that it can only speak to the ear; but I still can rejoice that the Comforter does condescend to use even the feeblest agency in his consolatory dealings with the wounded heart. We wish to commend you earnestly to the Lord and the word of His grace. We ask that His word, read of you beneath the shadow of affliction, beam out with new significance in the many promises pertinent to seasons of sorrow, and that they may flood you with serenity while you sit under His shadow, delighting yourself in the Lord.

As children of God, it is our privilege to exceed resignation under the Lord's permissive providence, and to rest in the assurance that such experience is but the will of God in Christ Jesus concerning us. Though in these sharp trials the love of God may momentarily be obscured, our faith, fed on His word, will soon again rejoice in Him and gratefully own that He is good and doeth good. We shall not only say as reasoners, "The Lord gave and the Lord hath taken away," but as loving children we shall add, "Blessed be the name of the Lord." What opportunity to magnify the grace of our Heavenly Father is afforded by these trying dispensations in the exhibition of a meek and quiet spirit. While we give sorrow its due and shed tears, as did the blessed Jesus himself, we can leave our departed in His presence, and therein with them rejoice all the more. We may contemplate the fragments of our broken schemes long enough to realize the significance of the divine dealing, but early use our privilege to admire the results of the seeming disaster; to the liberated how glorious! to the bereaved how blessed! Let us learn to regard death more and more as the entrance on the life eternal, try to realize the greetings of the "just made perfect," as the bright side of the sighs and tears of those left behind. As the soul released passes beyond earth-born clouds, how must it catch on its pinions the radiance of the then fully disclosed Sun of Righteousness, and sweep upward all refulgent to enter the streets of gold!—May the Comforter whisper to you sweet consolations out of his own Word, and so cheer your hours of loneliness that you shall be less and less lonely by being filled with the divine companionship.

As afflicted in your affliction, we remain in tenderest sympathy your friends,

SAMUEL F. GREEN, AND OTHERS.

TO DR. LANE.

GREEN HILL, *April* 17, 1878.

MY DEAR DR. LANE:

I am much interested to learn of your entrance into the Medical Profession. Allow me to extend you a hearty welcome, and to wish you a long and useful career.

I was re-born a physician thirty-three years ago. I have never desired to change my vocation. I have yet to see another calling a better way to usefulness. I am glad to have relieved bodily suffering, and gladder to have found, in course of professional ministry, opportunity to speak a word to those that are weary or to those out of the way.

Your position on the frontier is no doubt laborious; but all things, through providence, work in compensation. I hope you may see one reward of your hardships in the privilege of influencing a nascent community for all that is virtuous and noble. When we may in the next century look down from the skies, we shall, I expect, see the name Lane numerous and esteemed throughout the heart of our country.

Were it not sinful I could envy you the large investment vouchsafed you in the population of our land. May the Giver of the precious group give you daily strength to train them for His service on earth and His presence in heaven. "Unbending firmness, unwearied love," is a formula I have found helpful. The word of God commends to us patience as the way to perfection; and so it must be a powerful adjuvant to perfect our children. I have felt helped by the sentiment, "We must be ourselves what we would have our children be." Regarding the Bible as "the greatest book of morals," I feel the daily gathering of the family around the word of God, to read it deliberately with prayer and song, as so powerful a mean to the highest development, that I have grown to consider this method a *sine qua non.* —With love from us each to every one of you, I am yours fraternally,

SAMUEL F. GREEN.

GREEN HILL, *April* 23, 1878.

MY DEAR BROTHER ANDREW:

. . . . We had a very interesting letter from the oldest member of the Jaffna Mission last evening. Our fine old premises at Manepy are left vacant and forsaken. It would be a joy to me to have had some of the pictures in our life there actually observed and experienced by my sisters and brothers. I imagine some of your Trinidad scenes you would like framed in the galleries of sisterly and brotherly memory. These pictures are of our lasting heritage on earth, for the outward is ever changing and passing away. We are impelled repeatedly to "improve" even some of the dearest of them from our sight for ever; for example, eradicating homestead, banishing heirlooms, etc. Change is the very tissue of our existence, and were change to halt, misery would begin. Let us adopt it then as an abiding factor in all our plans. The greater any change, the greater may be the gain. What gain for the body to change from the natural to the spiritual, from the vile to the glorious! What gain for the soul to change in the Zenith moment of regeneration from self to the Saviour, from sin to holiness, from the death eternal to the everlasting life! . . .

Ever and affectionately,

Your brother,

SAMUEL F. GREEN.

TO THE REV. W. W. HOWLAND, TILLIPALLY, CEYLON.

GREEN HILL, WORCESTER, MASS.

May 7, 1878.

MY DEAR BROTHER HOWLAND:

We were rejoiced by the arrival of your letter of 26th March last evening. . . . I feel heartened by your speaking so sanguinely as to our returning. I had a letter recently from Dr. Clark. He says: "How are you now? We received not long since very warm expressions of regard for you from the Ceylon Missionaries, and the expressed desire that you might return. . . . I have informed them of our respect and high regard for you, and that it was a question of health with you and your friends." In a letter to Brother Hastings you will see our own opinion as to the adequacy of our health. Our opinion we had corroborated by experts, and made our offer of return in perfectly good faith.

Were the Committee generally to proceed upon the basis of the expostulations of relatives, I should not have returned to Ceylon in 1862; neither would you, nor would Brother Hastings. Surely those to whom relatives can be indifferent are not likely to prove the most acceptable and effective workers abroad. I hope the Mission will see it expedient to put more or less of the logic of all this very kindly before the Prudential Committee. As you saw a providence in our detention in 1862 from going by the *Resolute* to go in the *Star of*

Peace, so a providence may ultimately appear in our being delayed from 1877 to 1879. It would seem that if you all direct attention to the facts as to our health, the last obstruction . . . may be removed. I do not wish to be wilful in this matter; but if it may please "the Lord of the vineyard" to put us alongside our dearly beloved and longed for among our adopted people, we shall rejoice, and hope for another term, through His goodness, effective and completory.

We have been favored with somewhat of a revival lately. "Fervent in spirit" has been the human agency in it. Fancy one lighting up the lamps with an icicle. The icicle may be well shaped and brilliant, but it will only leave the house or street dark and cheerless. When we get empty wholly of self and filled with the Holy Ghost, then we are fit for the Lord's use in His great ever-present and continued work of rescuing souls. Get rid of the spectre of self so that its shadow shall not obscure the radiance of the Sun of Righteousness within us; then we can let our light shine, for we shall have indeed the light of life to emit. . . .

With love to all four from us each and all,

Affectionately,

SAMUEL F. GREEN.

GREEN HILL, *May* 17, 1878.

MY DEAR BROTHER ANDREW:

. . . We cannot reach the highest development save by deciding for God against the *world*.

For any worthy superstructure we must have a proper foundation. So long as in us is the rottenness of unforgiven sin, we have no right basis upon which to upbuild. We never can get the requisite forgiveness while we prefer the world to God. We must come to the choice of the better, the enduring, in the relinquishing of what may be pleasing but is transitory and treacherous. Although you have had a deal of hard work, and have had to pass through much contumely, still on the whole the Good Father has vouchsafed you an extraordinarily prosperous career, and I believe you are gratefully conscious of this. I fear, however, you are to some extent unconsciously beckoned toward that *world* which is in revolt against God, and which by its various blandishments is leading you from Him. Those influential, pampered, pompous ones who procured the rejection of Jesus for Barabbas, were the gentry of the place and time. Their dinners, their operas, their style were the daily environing of those who could applaud Jesus the Philanthropist and Philosopher, but would scorn Jesus as the forgiver of *their* sins. Through all ages humanity is at heart the same, and we are to decide each for himself which company we prefer.

If amid winning carolling and jocosity the name and work of Jesus sound incongruous and find no welcome, then what business has His follower there? If he prefers this, then is he not a follower of the *world?*

But paper fails; let us talk it—better, let each

be much over the Gospels and Epistles, and attend to what the Spirit shall utter.

Ever lovingly,

SAMUEL F. GREEN.

GREEN HILL, *June* 4, 1878.

MY DEAR SISTERS:

. . . I imagine you three enjoying each other's presence vastly. And yet how each human life is alien to each other human life. We only grow into sound union as we grow into God. He would seem to be the grand Cementer of all good or redeemed spirits of the universe. Our oneness as children of the same family by blood is oneness because the God of Nature has made it so. Pleasant as this oneness is, it only hints the unification of His children, which he will accomplish by grace. The trinity of God exists also in His Power, His Wisdom and His Love. The first characterizes His volume of Nature, the second His volume of Providence, the third His volume of Grace, although in each all three of these qualities are clearly seen. Each of us has as much of God as he wills to have. Whoever will have the Love of God has all three. Whoever will have but the Power will lack the other two. How terrible, at the instant of disembodiment, to feel but the grasp of Power clinched into every crevice of one's being. How blessed to feel the enfolding of Love, and to know it enwraps one forever. . . .

Affectionately,

SAMUEL F. GREEN.

GREEN HILL, *June* 6, 1878.

MY DEAR BROTHER ANDREW:

I went to-day, with all my family, to Greenville*. . . . We looked thoroughly over the old garrison house. All then drank from the well. House built in 1711. . . . We went quite through the village, so as to see how it looks beyond the churchyard. . . . We read the epitaphs of our venerated progenitor and his wife. We saw the place where lie the remains of "Father Dunbar." . . . We all looked at the traditional spot where the cow defended her calf, and afforded milk to the lone settler in his fever. . . . The weather was most propitious, and we exceedingly enjoyed the excursion.

It is a continual marvel to me that in a sin-cursed earth we should have so much of happiness. Gaussen speaks of our preservation as a continuous creation. How the goodness and mercy of the ever blessed Lord Jesus unceasingly environs, enwraps and enfolds us! And this will be in

*In Leicester, Mass., where his great-grandfather had built a church, and was for thirty-five years its pastor.

closest contact forever. If gratefully accepted, what bliss it will constitute; if coldly ignored, what inextricable misery.—We are all well, and all join in much love to your dear self.

Ever and affectionately your brother,

SAMUEL F. GREEN.

GREEN HILL, *August* 14, 1878.

MY DEAR NEPHEW:

I hope you are having a very profiting and a very enjoyable time. Ranging with special advantages among so very much that is interesting and instructive, you must be daily adding to your mental stores. Knowledge is primarily outside of books. A book, if it be worthy, is but a dip from the vast ocean of knowledge. Who knows what eventually you are going to dip out and diffuse for the benefit of your kind.

A child once answered me, to the question, What is the difference between knowledge and wisdom? that knowledge knows truth and wisdom uses it. The majority, perhaps in a degree all, know more than they use. Our Saviour says, "If ye know these things, happy are ye if ye do them." Allow me a suggestion towards greater wisdom. Order is the balance wheel of business, and punctuality is the pivot of order. As preparatory to business, I desire that you cultivate punctuality always and in every way. You seem admirably punctual in your attendance at school. I wish you would try to be equally so in the family. Regard each appointment which calls the household together in common as obligatory, and ever determine to meet it with punctuality. Particularly when breakfasting with the whole family be one of the first present, and more particularly on Sundays—when the hour is later and when we can honor the day. I would be happy to help you in this if you request me. I could call you timeously if you desire me to do so. Think on this: You can please Jesus; you can please many friends; you can foster a valuable habit for your business life; you may one day be the head of a household and need it. You can assist yourself to this punctuality by retiring earlier the evening previous. "Even Christ pleased not himself."

Receive lovingly and use wisely what is spoken lovingly by your loving uncle to his beloved and loving Nephew. May blessings increasingly rest upon you by your "Walking in the Spirit." For each age in our life and for every condition Jesus is our model. Would the youthful Jesus be a prompt and punctual member in the household at Nazareth? Come home when you have completed your visit, and give us occasional and quiet narratives of one thing and another.—With love from all,

Ever and affectionately,

SAMUEL F. GREEN.

As early as May, Dr. Green learned that by "the interposition of the Mission" the Prudential Committee had been induced to reconsider their decision as to the Medical Department. Encouraged perhaps by this, and by the assurance that the vote of the Committee against his return was "solely on the ground of health," he requested a reconsideration of that decision: "In view of the urgent call of the Mission, and encouraged by the experience of Mr. Tracy, Mr. Howland and others who returned feeble, we feel it our duty and privilege to propose again a return to our adopted people. I feel some confidence that my health is now such that I could comfortably and with a good degree of efficiency meet the claims of the position." Having received an early acknowledgement of his application, he ventured to add; "I am happy to find that I have ever been in harmony with the Board in systematic and prospered endeavors to advance the Medical Department of the Mission towards entire self-support. The greater the expenditure of time and money, fostering any beneficent enterprise, may have been, the more desirable and important it would seem to be to secure the legitimate results. It should not be finished by dropping it, but patiently completed by the requisite finishing touches. May the Divine example, which combined Healing with

Preaching, duly sway the Committee in dealing at this crisis with an enterprise just now entering with great promise upon its closing stage. As its foster-father I ask for it 'the benefit of any doubt'."

The Prudential Committee, however, had already been considering the question of sending out some young Christian physician and giving him the use of the premises at Manepy, on condition of no further support from the Board. In view of the possiblity, Dr. Green wrote his Mission: "Then I could remain here and work at translation, God willing, till the completion of the series, now near; and at revision as new editions might be required."

Before leaving Ceylon in 1873, Dr. Green doubted the willingness of the Prudential Committee to continue support to the Medical Department much longer, even if he should soon be able to resume the charge of it. When the question of his return came up, they decided, on the carefully considered report of a sub-committee, that it was inexpedient to spend anything more upon that Department in Ceylon. The general policy of the Board required its relinquishment. Yet in view of his own desire to return, and the Mission's desire that he should return, they finally offered to pay the passage out for himself and Mrs. Green, and to give him the free use of the premises of the Department, on condition of the Board incurring no further pecuniary liabilities. In view of all the circumstances, therefore, he did not deem it prudent to assume the burden of supporting himself by medical practice while the completion of his literary enterprise would require so much of his time and strength.

CHAPTER XXI.

1878–1880: ÆT. 56–58.

ANXIETY for the continuance of the Medical Department had led Dr. Green to send a circular letter to the Mission, giving his views of the policy to be pursued respecting another Class, the application to be made to the Government for continued assistance, and the relation of the hoped for American physician to the Mission and Hospital; and he was now waiting prayerfully for the result.

GREEN HILL, *January* 18, 1879.

MY DEAR BROTHER OLIVER:

I listen occasionally to your very interesting remarks on men and things. What you say of your own dear self and of your affairs especially lays hold upon my heart.

I notice here and there expressions of depression, of discouragement with yourself. Should we not think lowly of ourselves, as much so as we think highly of the Saviour? Let us keep working at the magazine of Salvation, storing in the knowledge of Jesus Christ. What is human knowledge, what accomplishment, apart from faith in Jesus? A godless man of culture and learning is as a corpse perfumed and attired. Let us look at things as God looks at them, ourselves included. We are just now reading in course the 11th chapter of Hebrews. We are much sense-bound. There is no worthy walk but the walk of faith. We are to use matter as subservient to mind, the body as the servant of the soul. The natural man is condemned and only waits execution and burial. Having died to sin, we are in all things--little daily matters—to walk in newness of life. Let us be constantly in communion with the ever present Saviour, "enduring as seeing Him who is invisible" to worldlings. We are more than half through our race; let us run the rest with patience, by God's grace enduring to the end.

With love for and from each and all,

Ever and affectionately,

SAMUEL F. GREEN.

GREEN HILL, *February* 24, 1879.

MY DEAR BROTHER ANDREW:

Were my letters the tithes of my thoughts of you they would be more frequent. How much even the nearest of kin are outsiders to each other. Human mind can impress itself on human mind, but can never, as the Divine mind, enter upon and blend with a soul. Jesus offers to do thus for each of us. What a glorious reality to have Him in His infinity of wisdom, power and love mingle in our being, and be to us the fullness of these attributes. He seeks the occupancy of our will. The will is the central citadel of the man. It seems among the faculties as the head among the members. The door is thrown open for the admission of the eternal life, not by admiration, not by reverence, not by mere sentiment, but solely by submission, by unconditional surrender. We give up self wholly and become filled with Christ. We cannot, to any practical purpose, understand this without the Spirit's teaching. "The things of God, knoweth no man, but the Spirit of God." "No man can call Jesus Lord (i. e. Master) but by the Holy Ghost." How importunately should we cry for the gift of the Spirit then, as we can only through his light and presence even begin the spiritual life.

The ditty has it, "I dreamed I slept in marble halls." The dream for me and mine is surpassed in the reality. "The lines" for us have indeed "fallen in pleasant places." For this I thank first the Lord and secondly yourself and the sisters. I yearn to have you happy, first at heart and then in your surroundings. I sorrow to imagine you dejected and worn. Is there not danger, think you, of a crowded life becoming with you a second nature? Having secured, as you have, a comfortable competence, why not remit, and use a larger and larger proportion of leisure? It would seem this policy would afford you more enjoyment current, and unquestionably more favorably bear on your future. If God has given us all our time, first for Himself, second for our soul, and thirdly for other things, what shall we say to Him if we use it mainly for the tertiaries? Put on the brakes and live longer and live happier. . . .

Ever and affectionately,

Your brother,

SAMUEL F. GREEN.

TO DR. MUZZY.

GREEN HILL, *March* 22, 1879.

MY DEAR ARTHUR:

. . . Don't, because disappointed, be discouraged. "Try, try again." "Why art thou cast down? hope thou in God." Use your utmost endeavors for success, but cheerfully allow the Lord to choose for you. Perhaps He sees you bent on self-promotion and intimates to you that you are to seek other ends in other lines. The word says, "Ephraim is an empty vine, he bears fruit (now?) to himself." "Seek first the kingdom of God"—within you, around you.

Have you duly weighed the Medical Mission work; duly considered the imperative call for Christian physicians among the darkened and degraded of other lands? If you think yourself unworthy so honored a work, and feel it would be high privilege to consecrate all your powers to the cause of the Great Healer, in the position of patron-physician to some tens of thousands in one of the many wide wastes of Heathendom, then offer yourself for His acceptance and use.

Resolutely face the present situation and go forward, serenely trusting in the Lord ever near yet within the believer's heart. He will vouchsafe you all the success that is good for you. But while looking to Him solely, still work for the blessing, recollecting that "obstacles exist to be overcome." You will find much promised "to him that overcometh." See close of each of the seven epistles to the seven churches, in the Apocalypse, chapters second and third. There is perhaps nothing so powerful as struggling to develop character. So, hopefully and courageously struggle on, but ever in communion with Jesus. He is ready to take any one of us into His company and to put His resources at our disposal. "He that spared not his own Son, but delivered Him up for us all, how shall He not with Him also freely give us all things?"

Hoping some day not distant to congratulate you on the barriers surmounted, the success achieved, the desire accomplished, I remain

Your friend,

SAMUEL F. GREEN.

To Dr. Vaittilingam.

Green Hill, Worcester, Mass.,

April 29, 1879.

My Dear Chapman:

We are always glad to find in the envelope of translation a few lines of news as to our friends, acquaintances and others in our chosen Jaffna. Anything about the Medical Graduates interests us. We shall specially rejoice over any leading unselfish lives; walking before the Lord Jesus in purity, honesty and kindness. . . .

Let us recollect that the purpose of our life from day to day must be testimony for Jesus, and that the way to witness for Jesus is to be in communion with Jesus. No communion, no testimony; no testimony, no life. "Ephraim is an *empty* vine, he beareth fruit unto *himself*." The unselfish loving life is truly life; the selfish life is death. We are good for nothing apart from Jesus. Let us then be always praying, or praising, or adoring Jesus in our thoughts. Then will our mouth also show forth His praise, and sinners shall be converted unto Him.

With kind regards for and from each,

Truly,

Samuel F. Green.

GREEN HILL, *May* 2, 1879.

MY DEAR BROTHER OLIVER:

You are much on my mind, and I find real comfort in commending you to the great Lover of souls. Household arrangements, sickness in the family, business claims far and near, the inner life struggles, all combine in pressure on your will. Could we not say, "The Lord is the strength of my life," "I can do all things through Christ who strengtheneth me," we should often falter in our pilgrimage. "The joy of the Lord shall be your strength." What a cordial—tonic this is! Let us each morning pray over the Scripture and kindle up a glow of spirit; then, joyful in the Lord, we shall sail as at flood tide through the cares of the day. Having Jesus on board, we shall make, each evening, the port of Peace.

I have been reading lately some of Mr. Andrew Juke's thoughts, and still more recently some of Mr. C. H. Mackintosh's thoughts. Both seem followers of Jesus and devoutly studious of His word. I feel instructed by them, and yet I feel jealous lest I may be led disproportionately by man and too little by the Bible. "Be not carried about by divers and strange doctrines." "It is a good thing that the heart be established by grace." Grace comes not from man, but from God through the channels He has appointed for us. We have just as much grace as we will live, and we live just in so far as we love. . . .

Affectionately,

SAMUEL F. GREEN.

GREEN HILL, *May* 14, 1879.

MY DEAR BROTHER ANDREW:

The "peep frogs" we captured have broken jail. We proposed keeping them till they had peeped in your hearing. We found they would peep twenty to thirty times at once. I had supposed always a single peep answered by a neighbor's, and so in the many shrill pipings, fancy peopled the swamps and pools with hundreds of happy denizens, where now one is forced to recognize but tens. Were it not for the conviction that truth is on the whole more the source of enjoyment, one might deprecate the dissipation of his pleasant illusions. But let us ever have the substantial before the showy. How our dear father always preferred the sound, broad, liberal thing in all his arrangements. The older I grow the more grows upon me a sense of his nobility.

The spring is upon us in all its blossoms and verdure. The song of birds, the hum of bees, all is fresh, wakened from the sleep of winter. How steady the circling of the seasons. How surely return in order seedtime and harvest, according to that word which is firmer than the hills. Dear Brother Martin is stirring all over the domain; ditching, walling, plowing, planting, all in process together. He is indefatigable, and amid the press of occupation his inherited vivacity lightens care.

I took a ramble with the younger children, while the older were in town with their aunt, learning the art of "shopping." The children took up entire several varieties of flowers for their "wild-flower garden." They find abundant around them to enlist their daily interest. I am glad and grateful that they can thus grow up close to Nature. These simple joys are so much better for the mind and heart than the giddy excitements of man's devising.

I wish you were nearer, so that oftener you could participate in the many advantages of the dear old homestead. You plan and place at other's disposal what you yourself scarcely enjoy with them, save in distant ideal. Will it ever be that you will take to a quiet life, and we be boys together again? Two rustics, we could drive about among the neighbors, and extend our trips in widening circles till we should familiarize ourselves with the villages nestling around us.

I recently received from dear Mr. Knudsen a new revision of his method in "spelling reform." His tenacity of purpose is remarkable, and one can not but admire the real skill he manifests in conceiving and developing his enterprises. In the use of his observatory, where he has mounted your gift telescope, he does much to elevate the taste and broaden the mind of many in his community. Our late friend Mr. Rand was a man of much discernment, and he expressed the highest opinion of Mr. Knudsen's intellectual ability, of his thorough balance of character. I increasingly value him as one who wears well in acquaintance, and I feel deeply indebted for the influence of his quiet, steady, straightforward life.

The sudden accession of great heat is trying to most of us. I hope you remit somewhat of your labors, till gradually adjusted to the change in weather. Let us remember that our powers are definitely limited, and that we gain only loss by over-taxing them. There is wisdom generally in "taking it easy," and particularly so at certain crises. Some one has said that "the body will bear much if the mind be at ease," and we have the "surer word" that he shall be "kept in perfect peace whose mind is staid on God."

We are all well, and all unite in love to you, to dear Sister Lucy, and to the dear Nephew and Niece. Hoping ere long to sit beside you and to ramble with you, I am ever and affectionately

Your brother,

SAMUEL F. GREEN.

TO DR. LANE.

GREEN HILL, *August* 22, 1879.

MY DEAR DR. LANE:

The dear friend who crowned you and entwined the darling children, has now proved her well wonted pinions in soaring and speeding among the denizens of the world of light, where the adoring melodies ever roll through an atmosphere of highest love. Those she has left bereaved are, we will hope, comforted growingly as time lapses, and will with advancing years more and more experience the good that is intended in affliction. In God "we live and move and have our being" naturally. This condition is constant and is an unconscious experience. So must we grow, under the Lord's discipline, to have our spiritual existence in Him, as well as our natural existence. We are screened from God by the interposition of a material body. We have to grow to the endurance of the unveiled presence of Him who is to all sin "a consuming fire."

How little can we bear any unusual manifestation of His nearness. When the Lord Jesus showed His real glory, the apostles fell into a death-like swoon. The prophet Daniel fell before the lesser light of Gabriel. The Lord is leading us into glorious perfection by a way we know not. The next step in our progress will likely be as much in advance of our present state as is our matured manhood beyond our fœtal life.

In the very nature of the case, we must be expectant. "First the flesh and then the spirit." We haste towards the higher "as fast as time can move." The closing of the present stage seems to sense the end of all, but faith sees in it a great promotion. Once "in Christ," and all things are ours, and we go on from strength to strength to take possession.

I hope through constant watchfulness and prayer you keep very near the Lord. We must ever bask in his rays. We soon chill if we wander into shadows. Faith grows dim and love grows cold. The gist, is to "endure to the end" and to "overcome." More is He that is for us than all that can combine against us. He is our leader, and He goes on "conquering and to conquer."

TO THE REV. W. W. HOWLAND.

GREEN HILL, WORCESTER, MASS.,

Sept. 22, 1879.

MY DEAR BROTHER HOWLAND:

. . . . I feel very thankful to you for your great kindness in giving me so much of your so fully engrossed time, strength and attention. Every page of that long letter was keenly appreciated,—not to say the same of the briefer ones. . . .

Let me advise that our future Medical Vernacular book printing be done at Nagarkoil. It will be the lesser of two evils to have a long list of Corrigenda in each volume than to have our translator's time frittered away in reading and re-reading and re-re-reading proof for a local press. I think this will expedite the completion of the long-talked-of series more than any other practicable measure. . . .

Let me suggest that the notes and emendations on the Christian's medical Tracts be severally copied and attached to each its original printed pamphlet, so as to have two sets, one in your own hands and another in the hands of the Secretary of the Jaffna Religious Tract Society. Thus make certainty doubly sure. . . .

When the time comes, the Anatomy, Physiology and Hygiene school-book should be thoroughly revised and reconstructed. I shall be glad to serve in this if all convenes. I think much could be worked in from Miss Beecher's *Physiology for Schools.* That seems eminently pratical. I have not seen Mr. Bruce's book. . . .

We hope that Mr. Joseph Anthony Sanders can graduate in Medicine and Surgery in April, 1881, and soon thereafter be with you. I hope that the Lord may see fit to keep for us the present Medical Government Grant of Rupees 2000; for Joseph can with this, and the other Rs. 1500 named by Dr. Kynsey, get along comfortably, I think. . . .

I think Mr. R. C. Hastings carried out the cuts for *Shepherd of Salisbury Plain.* Please get of him. I am glad to learn that *The Body* and *The Believing Tradesman* have been approved. I wait with interest the fate of the good old *Shepherd of Salisbury Plain.* Can you pick up any stray copies of *Hints to English Beginners in Tamil?* If so, please send me some dozen or more. My stock is low now, I had twenty-five or so. . . .

I hope, with the help of greater experience, vigorous recruits, and the forthcoming new English version, that what will be best to the ultimate Tamil Bible will be produced. I hope the true God will have in it His rightful *name*, and not share a title with Siva and the rest. . . .

I hope and pray that Dr. Mills (and Dr. Paul and Dr. Clives) may be so practical in their teaching as to encourage the continuance of the Medical Government Grant. It would be well to invite

Dr. Kynsey (and his representative *in loco*) to occasionally examine the Class, and be present also at regular examinations. . . . We are all in usual health, and all join in much love to each and all of the quaternion at Uduvil.

Ever and affectionately yours,

SAMUEL F. GREEN.

GREEN HILL, *October* 23, 1879.

MY DEAR BROTHER OLIVER:

I think of you and yours daily. But how little does man's thinking avail, and how very much does the gracious Lord's thinking for us avail. Man's thoughts are shadowy, are shallow and evanescent. The Lord's thoughts are substance, are profound and effective. We surely have reason to bless the Lord that His thoughts are not our thoughts, as are His ways not our ways. When we for each other "think the Lord's thoughts after Him," then we are oft-times honored to trace in edification some lineament of the Lord's upon a fellow soul; and what higher employ could stir the holy ambition of an angel?

I have repeatedly thanked you for the sentiment of the lamp and the window in the human being, as you cited it from the Evangelist Pentecost. Such a truth has the savor of God's own truth; it has also the flavor of the individual interest of the communicator, all the spice of life-long acquaintance and affection. Pray occasionally bestow similar cheer and helps; speaking something of the Gospel that has pressed strong upon your own heart and shall come thence, warm and earnest, upon one looking together with you for food to the good Shepherd of our souls.

I congratulate you on the safe return to you of your very interesting son. He is a diamond committed to you for polish. May he prove a jewel radiant with heaven's own luster. How well it is that we have ever near One who will continually supply not only grace, but from hour to hour the particular grace, requisite for developing the crescent character, into the fulness of perfection. Were we less this help, we should utterly and miserably fail in our children. Let us hourly cast ourselves upon Jesus, first for our own souls, next for our children's. He will never fail us. We must habitually try to be what we wish our children to be. The Scriptures intimate gentleness to be greatness, and quietness to be strength. Patience ever wins. Order is the balance wheel and punctuality is its pivot.

Our Father trains us by withholding from desires as well as by conferring. Firmness should hold calmly the ground between sternness and fondness. Fear should abide as an undertone in love. God is preparing each of his children, by giving rule over a few, to bear rule hereafter over many. The relation of parent and child is a mutual benefit arrangement. Where it is sustained according to God's word both parties receive effective help toward the better life.

There is much in environment. Our nearest is our body; next our family, and so on in several widening circles. The will is the core of being. It is not left naked, but girdled so as to brace and bear it onward with more of certainty to the right. We must to our utmost environ our children with conditions favorable to virtue. Our will, controlled by the divine, must, with the least of the imperious. dominate theirs. In our associate as in our individual life the way of obedience is the sole way to blessing. The precepts given in the Word for the training of children are the only safe rules to follow ourselves, would we lead them aright and with them arrive at the Home of the Blessed. In this we have no option; we neglect or we contravene at our peril. Frequent and prayerful recourse to the holy Oracles on the one hand, patient and felicitous utilization of the truth on the other, must constitute the tissue of our family life from day to day. Jesus must be openly, avowedly, habitually welcomed and domiciled as the One we would chiefest cherish. His presence should be constantly recognized, with equal reverence and delight.

In many things we all offend; but piling failures under our feet we must still aim upwards, ever eying Him who leads us in our struggle away from self and sin. Because He lives we shall live also, and in His victories we shall share.

There is neither help nor merit in disparaging ourselves. Such is not magnifying the Lord. It is well to feel our faultiness, but we may rejoice that our Lord knows us far better than we know ourselves, and where there is more felt need will there give more grace.

Let us therefore, "forgetting the things which are behind and reaching forth unto those things which are before, press toward the mark for the prize of our high calling in Christ Jesus."

There seems no end to the trains of thought when one lets such themes sweep through the mind. Giving ourselves to the Spirit's power we shall experience His living breath, throughout our hearts and minds, quickening and strengthening us for every need. To Him let us daily commend each the other.

With unwavering affection.

Your brother,

SAMUEL F. GREEN.

To———.

1879.

You prove, we fancy, the truth of the saying that, "The stars are brightest in dark nights." How many compensations our Father mingles in with every trial He has to lay upon us. We may confidently expect to understand hereafter that, "All His ways are mercy and truth," and that He "withholds no (really) good thing from those who walk uprightly."

I am glad you have had Christian converse. . . . As we progress in the spiritual life we see more and more the value of what is spoken of as the "communion of saints." Although we may meditate with much comfort and delight on the word of God, yet when conversation with the living pilgrim is added, how vastly is the impression strengthened and the emotion substantiated.

I thank our Lord for that view of the "inner self" which He has given you. There is naught so forcible to urge us to the great Healer as the disclosure of "the plague of our own heart." Having conviction of the desperation in our case, let us continually look away from self to the Saviour, ever following on after Him as our Pattern, our Leader, our Deliverer. He declares Himself to be "the first and the last," "the Author and Finisher of our Faith." Our salvation is to grow up into Him in all things. While the old nature, evil till the last, remains stubborn and unchanged, the newly implanted nature is the stronger and is ever gaining upon the old. The whole matter seems to be in the will. While we may resolve and determine for the right, we must heartily enthrone the Lord Jesus within. All our resolutions amount to little apart from His abiding presence. "Without me ye can do nothing" is the instructive word to us. "Our life is hid with Christ in God;" in Christ within us. How powerful, how serene the new life! The source of it is within us. There, in the chamber of our will, is the hiding of our power. An elected theocracy. When Christ abides He looks from our eye, He sways our hand, He tunes our song and tones our speech. We need not waver for He bears us on and bears us through whatever He plans for us. Our life will be "fruit in season;" patience, when that is tried; courage, when that is called for; wisdom, when needed for ourselves or for counseling others. We learn by habit to draw every needed grace from out His fulness, according to the requirement at hand.

It is delightful to contemplate your family worship. Let it be regular and punctual. Let it be as deliberate as practicable. Let it be as familiar and informal as can consist with the injunction, "Decently and in order." Encourage prattle and chat about the portion read. Refer to maps and dictionary. Sing, by all means, and keep all sunny and attractive. It will be as a blessing of the Lord settled down right in your midst. Encourage the children to propose petitions. Let them learn many of the texts exhorting and encouraging to prayer. Let them in time, occasionally two or three at a time, lead in prayer. Teach them to be free, explicit and brief in supplication. As for their private devotions, encourage extempore prayer; tell them to embody praise and thanks, confession and supplication, remembrance of relatives, acquaintance, neighbors, etc., in intercession. They will range according to their years. Baby prayers are, no doubt, as acceptable as the prayers of the aged. The Father's ear likes the prattle of the child.

Keep the hold of love upon the darlings. Let nothing divide for an hour, much less alienate. When discipline is required, let it be alone, tender, firm, and with prayer. If castigation is needed, let it be out of sight and sound; let it be followed by audible prayer together, and this by loving embrace and kiss and a return in sunshine to the rest of the group. Castigation will seldom be called for if tact avoids collision. Obedience must be prompt and cheerful. Exact this quietly and habitually. One will must rule, and that one with all the rest, reverently bowed to the Divine will, daily and openly recognized in the family worship.

Let us hope that no separation may be necessary; but only occur through the maturing and dispersing as Providence shall call to usefulness and independency. "What God has joined together let not man put asunder" holds here too.—I have written on, and leave you to winnow and gather any grains of the "good seed" which "the Spirit of truth" may bring before you, even in such a vessel as this note.

TO DR. KANAKADATTINAM, (*Tamil*)

alias, LEVI SAMUEL STRONG.

GREEN HILL, WORCESTER, MASS., U. S. A.,

April 3, 1880.

MY DEAR SAMUEL:

On the 18th of March last I received your kind note with the picture of nine of my old acquaintances. We are happy to greet even the shadows of you all, and we would greatly enjoy an hour's conversation with each one of you. The re-acquaintance with you gains every time we study the picture. We feel thankful that you all took pains to assemble before the Photographer. This shows fraternity among yourselves, and kindly regard for us.

We judge that you are all prospering in your business concerns, for which we are thankful. We desire above all things that your souls should be in health and prosper. Show your faith in our blessed Lord Jesus by your daily endeavor, in his strength, to walk in purity, honesty and kindness. He sought us even before we sought Him, and He will manifest Himself as a very present help in trouble. Inspired by His example and strengthened by His Spirit, live the noble, the unselfish life.

Remember us kindly to your and our common acquaintances among the Medical Graduates. We hope that each of you may prove not only a centre of Christian influence, but that you may in particular fasten and further in the community correct ideas of life and health; of Hygiene and Sanitation. Each of you can and should leave your several circles of acquaintance wiser and better in these matters; and, after you shall have departed, have many to rejoice that you have lived to bless them and theirs.—With special and kindly remembrance to yourself and wife, to your parents, to the Asburys—all, and to the Cookes—all,

I am yours ever and truly,

SAMUEL F. GREEN.

SOUTH NORWALK, CONN.,

Thurs., 24 *June*, 1880.

MY DEAR SON:

I think of you daily, and I feel that you do of Papa, and that we pray for each other. These ties of relationship embody much of joy, and when ennobled by love toward Jesus, they seem earnests of that higher life, in the better land for which we look, and into which we may enter any day. I hope my little man is constantly endeavoring to live the self-denying life, which is ever considerate of others, and happiest in scattering smiles of gladness over surrounding faces. I am thinking of the pleasure I had last year, with your dear sister Mary here, and similarly anticipate the coming here of her brother, next year, if his parents then should think it best for him to journey and visit awhile.

You have heard of the severe illness of your beloved aunt Julia, and I doubt not are rejoicing with us, that the Lord of life and death yet spares her to us all, and seems restoring her to comfort. There is a constant tendency to die within us, and we only continue, because He "holds us in life." Strong or weak, sick or well, we unceasingly near the termination of our animal life. The believer in Jesus sees in this the beginning of a far better life; a life inexpressibly glorious and blissful. Let us ever commit ourselves to Jesus, and let Him keep fast hold of us, for none can pluck us out of His hand, and so deprive us of the glory He owns and shares with us.

I imagine you and your sister Mary, enjoying the rockaway, with dear Mamma, very much. I hope you have driven around the head of the lake together. I am wondering how your gardens flourish. I suppose the drought is as severe with you as at "Fridensbolig." You have no doubt looked at the babies nigh you, and given them each the smile of welcome to the great family of man, and to Green Hill in particular. I hope they and many others, now babes, may have occasion to say, "I think Mr. Nathan Green is a very nice man, he is so kind to every one."

You must be interested in the procedures at the dam. Perhaps you picture already the rippling pond, the rocking boat, and the dripping fish, hopping and flopping in the hold. If Uncle develops all this, I shall hope for an invitation to accompany you on a row and a haul. How glad we would be to spread an occasional dish of English carp before him and your Aunts, to say nothing of your Mamma, quietly relishing the treat, and saying, "Why Tambi, how sweet these are."

When I begin to talk with you, my darling, it seems as if my pen would not stop; but I must drop it, for the heat forbids me to further ply it, and you would say, "Never mind, Papa, we will sit down and talk the rest." Very well, my dear; I will hope ere long for such a privileged interview.

Ever and affectionately,

Your father and friend,

SAMUEL F. GREEN.

In the Spring of 1880 his children had the Whooping Cough, and Dr. Green took the disease and suffered from it for several months. This may have quickened into greater activity the malady which had so long preyed upon him, but which had not generally prevented him from calling himself well,— for, in his view, health was but a relative term at the best. While thus suffering he went with his sister Julia and two of his daughters to spend a few weeks with their friends in New York City and South Norwalk, Ct., and while at the latter place his sister was seriously ill. She ventured to travel home in a comfortable compartment of a railway carriage, and "seemed at times near death." After reaching home she seemed to be improving for a few days, and then became more ill. His care and solicitude for her—while prostrated and suffering, yet patiently enduring, and confidently looking for the coming of her Saviour—greatly affected and weakened him. In giving the absent an account of her, he said: "Our beloved sister is redeemed and, having faith, is, through the present great suffering, being sanctified. Only one more step remains for her, and that is to be glorified. With her how many of us believe in Jesus and are 'hasting on from grace to glory.' Surely we are a remarkably favored family to have so many members partakers of the heavenly calling." On the 5th of August "she passed away very peacefully in full assurance of the eternal life."

He thus recorded her departure in the Book of Green Hill.

"Aug. 5, Thursday. At half past ten, in the morning, our beloved Sister Julia departed this life, in the faith of Jesus; rejoicing in hope of the glory of God. She had been occasionally ill for months past, and more frequently and severely during the past few weeks. On Tuesday night, signs of approaching death supervened. She lingered in 'the valley of the shadow of death' for over thirty hours; of this, near the last, one hour was passed in mortal agony; when she afterwards fell asleep most peacefully as to the body and most trustfully in Him, who 'is the Resurrection and the Life.' For us it is irreparable loss; for her it is unspeakable gain. 'Blessed are the dead who die in the Lord.'"

Though he deeply felt his bereavement, yet he rejoiced for her. He had no need that others should point him to the source of consolation, for he was realizing again what he had said before: "When one of our candles goes out, let us open the eastward shutter a little wider; the Sun of Righteousness is ever aglow, and we have but to admit His rays."

Dr. Green's benevolence was very disinterested; he was as ready to deny himself for the cause of Christ among the Tamils as he was to ask others to do the same. Notwithstanding the generosity of his brothers and sisters in offering funds to defray the expenses of travel in Europe on each return from Ceylon, to help him in his literary enterprise, to support him and his family so largely at home, to enable him to visit his friends here and there at his pleasure and to spend the inclement season in a warmer climate, he rejoiced in their willingness to contribute still further towards the welfare of his adopted people, if they were moved by a higher motive than for his own sake. On the 27th of August he wrote to his brother Andrew: "I thank you much for your kind note as to Jaffna College. . . . The 'Green Scholarship' fund of a thousand rupees is very nearly made up and should be wholly filled by Tamils themselves. As for a 'Green Professorship' of Natural Science in the Vernacular, I do not feel specially called to found it. I would wish the name attached to it solely, if at all, as expressive of sympathy with the cause of Christ among the Tamils."

CHAPTER XXII.

1880–1883: ÆT. 58–61.

THE translation and revision of the *Pharmacopœia of India* was now drawing to a close. The last instalment of manuscript was soon received and returned ready for the press. The next work contemplated had been one on Medical Jurisprudence, and Dr. Green would have rejoiced to enter at once upon its preparation. For some reason it was not then undertaken. So far as the series of text-books was concerned, his work of translation and revision was now done. Henceforth there was nothing to urge him beyond his strength except his love of work. He could give himself to such varied usefulness as Providence might offer him, and to that rest and recreation which might be needful and agreeable. Yet he could not but watch with solicitude the slow progress of the Pharmacopœia through the press, the work and welfare of the mission and of his Tamil friends. He kept up his correspondence with near and distant friends, imparting counsel and consolation, admonition and encouragement, as he thought the one or the other might be needed.

In view of some surprising statements as to the prevalence of caste in the Ceylon Mission, the Secretary of the A. B. C. F. M. addressed Dr. Green as to the truth of them, and received this reply.

GREEN HILL, *November* 6, 1880.

MY DEAR DR. CLARK:

Your letter of the 4th inst. names four points: 1. Caste perhaps is just about as prevalent in the Jaffna churches as it is among professing Christians in America and England; I think it is not more so. 2. The Seminaries, Boarding Schools, and College are freely open alike to every Caste. 3. At public worship the natives all sit on one level. There is some segregation, as here we notice; the wealthy occupying the better pews. You will recall the struggle at Tillipally as to arranging for settees in the church,—happily settled with equal privilege for all. 4. The missionaries, in common with the children of God here, would regret the show of pride and exclusiveness in any guise.

The general intermingling of Castes, and the free interchange of intimate socialities, will only occur in the course of generations. The progress is slow but steady, and ultimate unity is certain.

With very kind regards from us all for yourself and your family, I am,

My dear Dr. Clark,

Yours fraternally,

SAMUEL F. GREEN.

Dr. Green took great interest and unwearied pains in the education of his children—three daughters and a son. Instruction was begun as early as they were capable of receiving it, and steadily adapted to their growing capacity. It was not confined to books, but extended to everything useful and interesting to know, as opportunity arose or suggested. The little world around them was made one of their text-books. The flowers which delighted by their colors and fragrance were explained,—their names, growth, structure, uses, seasons, history, significance, reproduction, divine origin, and claim on man for gratitude to their Author. In like manner they were instructed about the insect, the bird, the crawling and creeping things, the quadrupeds and man. Thus while in daily contact with nature they were growing in the knowledge of natural history in that way which was the most interesting. By witnessing dissections of plants, insects, fishes, birds and animals, they received explanations in anatomy and physiology in a way to apprehend and remember them. The microscope was used to reveal to them its field of beauty and wonders; as they looked through it upon a frog's foot, they learned more of the circulation of the blood than the wisest Tamil physicians, uninstructed in medical science, ever knew. They witnessed with great interest, as sometimes did older spectators, dissections, as of the eye of an ox, learning the superhuman mechanism of the wonderful organ, and lessons of the wisdom, power and goodness of the Creator.

As the most favorable hours for study were devoted to his labors for the Tamils, Dr. Green spent a little while in the morning and again in the evening in hearing his children read, and in questioning and explaining the language and sentiments. In the afternoon he gave them a lesson in the Bible, and in drawing and writing, generally from 2 to 4 o'clock. Mrs. Green taught them in the forenoon, while he was at his literary work. Whether with his children in the house or in walking or driving, his instruction was constant, embracing every subject that came to sight or mind. It was doubtless partly because of this favorite method that he regarded the freedom and seclusion of the homestead as inestimable blessings to them.

He taught his children the things to be regarded in letter writing; the general style, the natural order, the gradation of terms according to acquaintance, the requisites of various occasions. Occasionally he took them to manufactories, to show the working of machinery, and the processes of producing various things; for example, the grinding of grain, the making of brushes, the weaving of carpets, the reduction of bars of iron to wire, the turning of tortoise shell into jewelry, the converting of leather into boots and shoes.

For eight years after their return to America Dr. and Mrs. Green taught their children at home. But when his sisters proposed to provide them a private teacher, he declined, saying: "I have strong doubt as to the expediency of teaching them by themselves. This method may beget such peculiarities as shall impair their usefulness, not to say their happiness in life. I query whether it will not be better to put them by and by into the public schools, and let them meet the world earlier, and while under counsel and control at home. Say, the eldest two this fall in the preparatory class of the High School, and the younger, if spared, into the same when they may be ready for it; meanwhile teaching them at home."

The sense of parental responsibility was very strong and constant, and he was ever glad to correct or confirm his own views. "While I would for myself," said he to a friend, "have the Bible for my first and last handbook in home-training, I think well also of *Gentle Measures*, by Jacob Abbott; also of *Our Nurseries and Schoolrooms*, by Miss Hooper; as I believe they embody in a suggestive and helpful way much Scriptural wisdom." In family training, "unbending firmness, unwearied love" was his motto.

Dr. Green preferred health to learning for his children. He wrote to a brother: "If superadded to regeneration and its fruits, how would the following gradation of acquirements do for a character? namely, pleasing manners, correct language, a good handwriting. And no more of these than can consist with sound health. A moderately educated worker is better than a learned invalid. If you let your son go to public school, don't stimulate him overmuch to keep up to grade."

To the Rev. W. W. Howland.

Green Hill, Worcester, Mass.,
April 4, 1881.

My Dear Brother Howland:

On the 16th ultimo I sent you the Tract entitled *The Body*, with notes and emendations. Permit me now to send you *The Believing*

Tradesman's notes and corrections. May I ask you to have them appended to a copy of that Tract, ready for another edition. . . . .

If you do not succeed to get any copies of *Hints to English Beginners in Tamil*, please to let me know, that I may issue another edition. With this information, a copy with your opinion and your suggestions towards more utility would be very welcome. . . . .

I am surprised that the note, showing the unscripturalness of going in debt, should have been omitted. I feel strenuous that it should appear in the next edition. . . . .

We are all well and all send love. I wrote Dr. Chapman a note of condolence on the 19th ultimo.

Gratefully,

S. F. GREEN.

In June and July, Dr. Green and his family spent four weeks with their friends in Ledyard, Ct. He gratefully acknowledged his brother's invitation to visit New York also, and reminded him of "the dream of 1837—of a room to ourselves with a fire in the grate—realized!"

GREEN HILL, *October* 10, 1881.

MY DEAR BROTHER ANDREW:

I need not say that you are much on our hearts at this crisis, when "friends" may endeavor to persuade you to public office. If beckoned to any new burdens of trust, I hope the indications may be clear as to the Divine will. If led into relations by the Lord, we can count on His strength to meet the responsibilities. Position, profit, and power are gifts of Providence, and, while appreciated, should be less esteemed than gifts of Grace; for at best how transitory and tainted they are. Let us care first and always to please our enduring Friend, and let others come in afterwards in our regards. . . . .

I am, with much of favor to muse upon, just gliding into the sixties. How very near the glad Haven must be! . . . Shall we repine because we are made so great! because nothing finite can content us!

. . . . Within and without it seems, as a recent guest here said, like Paradise. "What shall we render to the Lord for all His benefits?"

With much love from every one of us,

Ever and affectionately,

SAMUEL F. GREEN.

The relation of Dr. Green to the members of his own and of other missions, to Tamil and Sanscrit scholars, to authors and publishers of scientific and medical works, to his graduates engaged in his enterprise for a Tamil medical literature, to physicians in America and Europe, to printers, and to the American Board, occasioned a multitude of letters written with care and often of great length because of many details. The notes of revision on the many parcels of Tamil manuscript alone required a great many letters, not only to the translator, but to those members of the Mission who superintended the Medical Department in a general and non-professional way. In the fifteenth letter, from October 18th to April 20th, to Mr. Howland alone, he remarked of the list, "You can say he here confesses to prolonged taxing of my time and patience." The time between mailing a letter and receiving a reply made it needful to mention letters written meantime, in order to know whether any had been lost.

To the Rev. W. W. Howland.

Green Hill, *December* 7, 1881.

My Dear Brother Howland:

We received tidings direct from you on the 11th April up to 23d February, 1881; and on the 16th July up to the 28th of May; and on 24th September up to 10th August, by your wife; and on 24th September, from D. W. Chapman, to 10th "July" (probably 10th August).

I wrote you 16th July about yonr watch, etc.; also 7th September, 1881. I wrote Chapman on the 29th September, in reply to his, giving us a sketch of the last days and hours of his lamented wife.

To-day is just a year since my last receipt of manuscript from Dr. Chapman. Working through Dr. Chapman, so as to spare your eyes and head, could you inform me whether, or no, *all* the parcels of *Pharmacopœia of India* manuscript notes (from No. 1 to No. 44 being on the English book up to page 430) sent by me have been received. To know this would lessen by so much my uncertainty as to the Enterprise. I feel a very great desire to have the *Pharmacopœia of India*, now it is translated and revised, printed carefully in an edition of two hundred and fifty copies, and distributed to *all A. C. M. Medical Graduates*, and to *all the Libraries* of the Government, and of Missions in Tamildom, as per list left by me. . . . .

If the Manepy press is so dilatory as to cause so much delay to Dr. Chapman's work, I should consider this *decisive* for doing our (Medical) printing at Nagarkoil.

We have the A. C. M.'s Medical Department much on our heart in these days. We ask that the Great Medical Missionary shall influence the Brethren to do concerning it what is of Faith—what is judicious. We wait the results of your annual meeting for business with much interest, especially on this matter.

Even should the Mission decide to take no more Classes, I should wish the Pharmacopœia completed and distributed.

On the principle that a crumb is better than no bread, I hope a carefully selected Class, though in small number, might be kept along; certainly so long as the Government Grant can be retained.

. . . The condition of each one of the favored band concerns us. . . . We are all well and prospering. The Lord deals very graciously with us. . . . . . Love for all the five at Oodooville from all at Green Hill.

Ever and affectionately,

S. F. GREEN.

GREEN HILL, *March* 18, 1882.

MY DEAR BROTHER ANDREW:

I have thought that less is printed than is written, less is written than is spoken, less is spoken than is thought. Then what a tide of thought there must be in the average human being throughout all his waking hours. This thought is of all kinds and qualities, and the variety inconceivable. It is no doubt well that much of it dies unuttered. It is all aloud to the conscience. How significant this word con-science. God knows and self knows and they (con) together know every thought. To the Divine eye we are each just rolled inside out. Who could stand the gaze of men upon his interior? Aye, what man but would stand aghast at the clear exposure of his neighbor's every emotion? Young says, " God spares all beings but Himself that awful sight—a naked human heart."

Ever and affectionately your brother,

SAMUEL F. GREEN.

For a time during the spring Dr. Green suffered somewhat from an affection of the throat. On the 4th of June he wrote his brother briefly: "I have resumed voice. What a faculty it is! David calls it, I think, 'my glory.' I have no vivacity to-day." He was not restored to former strength, however, and was sensible of debility, if not of a slight physical deterioration during the summer. A hint of this is contained in the following letter.

GREEN HILL, *August* 18, 1882.

MY DEAR BROTHER ANDREW:

We are happy in being enabled to report to you our prospered arrival at the dear Homestead, after our six weeks of varied and favored experiences. All this while, though moving among slumbering perils, our only cognizance of tempests and disasters has been the perusal of what has befallen our fellows. You will, we presume, join with us in thanksgiving to Him whose presence has proved our constant shield.

The spacious and elegant look within, and the broad and beauteous look from various sides around, have the zest freshened to us by absence. . . . . . We look that our physical gain appear now soon after our return.

I find here a pair of Dr. Williams'* portraits addressed to me. I am very glad to possess them. I admire him, but we must adopt no standard but the blessed perfect One Himself. It is no small advantage, surely, to have a faultless Model to work to.

We hope you are quite well again and enjoying much in various ways; not least in "a heart at leisure from itself to soothe and sympathize."

Ever and most affectionately

Your brother,

SAMUEL F. GREEN.

A few days later he wrote his brother: "We propose, if all favors, to remain here next summer and have our change in visiting Wachusett Mountain, Purgatory Chasm, and Long Pond; this, with home picnics, will suffice very well for one season."

On the anniversary of the Family Re-union he said, "We look about on much remaining of outward good; on some vacancies in our ranks, their promotion to the higher service, and realize we are far nearer the better Home."

*Dr. Wm. R. Williams, an eminent Baptist clergyman of New York.

GREEN HILL, WORCESTER, MASS.,

September 11, 1883.

MY DEAR BROTHER OLIVER:

We are all well, and are all reaching out after you since you encouraged us to hope for your appearing. Hearts yearn for you, comforts await you and may the Lord of all motives prosper your way to us.

Marvellous are His dealings. While He orders all, how differing the lot and way of each individual. Through all He ever beckons us nearer, ever seeking to re-establish the union of will in the creature with the Creator. Let us inmost say, "Draw us, and we will run after Thee."

Love for and from each and all.

Ever and affectionately,

S. F. GREEN.

GREEN HILL, *September* 13, 1883.

MY DEAR BROTHER ANDREW:

. . . Ten years ago to-day, the dear sisters and you accorded me and mine such a welcome to the dear old Homestead as can never fade. The recollection of it is as a memorial of praise and thanks to the bounteous Author of so prolonged and so abounding favor from the most loving relatives.

How few decades fill out the longest earthly career. Should all or most be spared for another, the carried will likely become the carriers. May they emulate and reciprocate the unvarying kindness and consideration shown them, and be prospered to meet in faithful gratitude the claims of growing infirmity. . . . .

Affectionately, gratefully, and ever,

SAMUEL F. GREEN.

Under Dr. Green's administration of the Medical Department of the Mission, the Government of Ceylon gave for many years fifty pounds annually towards its support; then for a few years one hundred pounds, and afterwards for about ten years two hundred pounds annually. When the A. B. C. F. M. felt unable and unwilling to continue their support of the enterprize, it was thought needful that the grant-in-aid by the Government should be doubled in order to carry it on. But the Government did not feel willing to increase their annual appropriation unless assured of a thoroughly competent physician at the head of the Department. Finding no such provision was to be made, the Government decided to reduce their appropriation for 1883 to one hundred pounds, and thereafter to make none at all. Such long-continued liberality shows the estimate, by the Government, of the value of Dr. Green and his services to the public.

The long list of Dr. Green's publications in Tamil is a remarkable demonstration of what may be accomplished by patient, persevering, systematic labor for Christ's sake, in circumstances very discouraging, and in spite of obstacles very formidable. In translating a work into a foreign language, which has an abundance of terms for the expression of every thought, the work is always difficult; but how much more difficult when many thoughts require the coining of new terms in that language; and how much more difficult still when the coining of terms has to be done by one to whom that language is not vernacular. This was the task which Dr. Green undertook and accomplished. His Tamil assistants were obliged to use scientific terms which he gave to their language, and of which they had first learned the meaning, in many instances, from his explanations of objects and relations, and from his demonstrations of effects, before their eyes. Their translations were apt to be grammatical but too literal, and too full of technical terms or of inadequate circumlocutions; but they were very valuable to him, as showing how Tamils apprehended the meaning of Western science as expressed in

Tamil words of his own making. It was inevitable that his revision of their versions should require a vast amount of labor to put them in proper shape for publication. Though the revision sometimes became almost wholly a re-translation, yet he most generously, on the title pages, ascribed the works to their respective Tamil translators, taking to himself only the revision and emendations. They, however, as generously speak of the printed text-books as his translations. It should be remembered, too, that instead of merely translating these American and English books, he made omissions, additions, and alterations, according as his own experience and knowledge suggested.

The following is a list of his works, original or translated, published in Tamil.

I. Text Books.

1. Cutter's Anatomy, Physiology and Hygiene. Second edition. 204 pages, 12mo. 1857
2. Maunsell's Obstetrics. 258 pages, 12mo. 1857
3. Druitt's Surgery. 504 pages, 8vo. 1867
4. Gray's Anatomy. 838 pages, 8vo. 1872
5. Hooper's Physician's Vade Mecum. 917 pages, 8vo. 1872
6. Wells' Chemistry. 516 pages, 8vo. 1875
7. Dalton's Physiology. 590 pages, 8vo. 1883

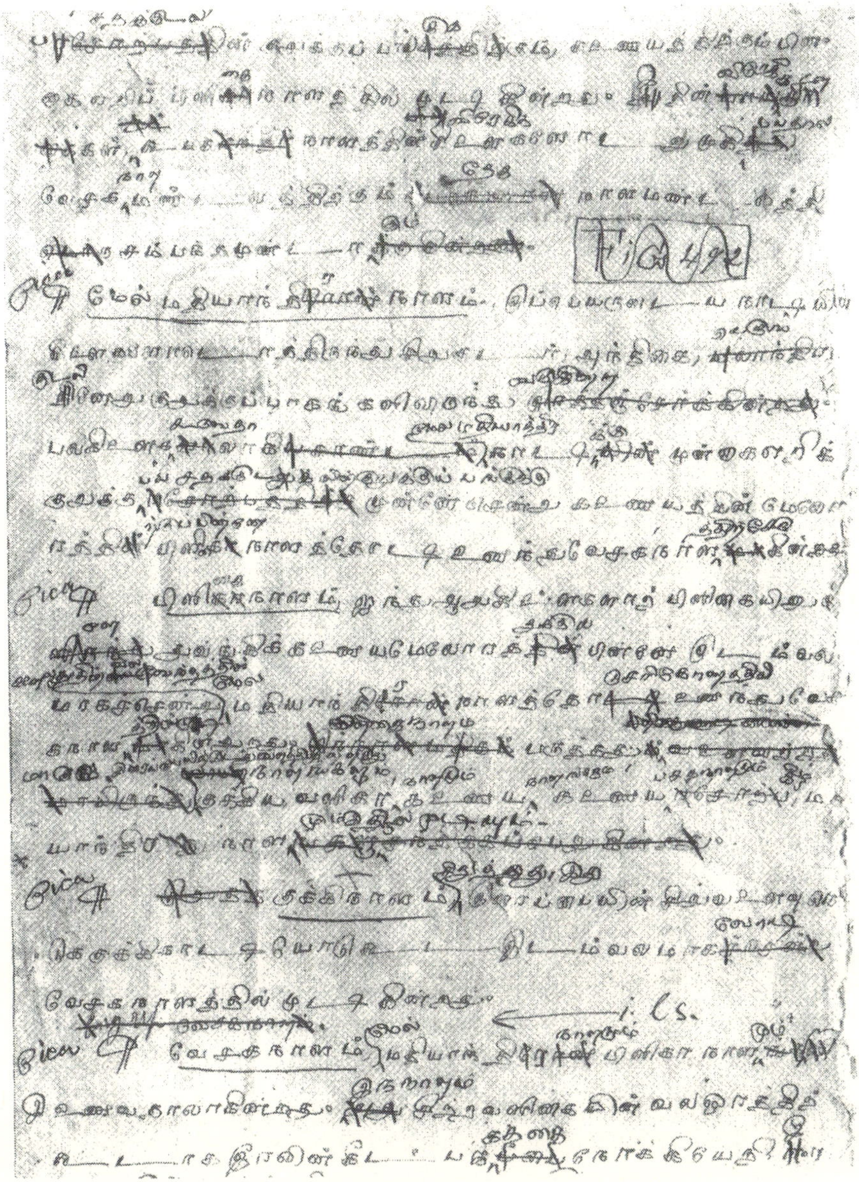

SPECIMEN SHOWING THE LABOR AND METHOD OF CORRECTING MANUSCRIPT OF DR. GREEN'S VOLUMES AS THEY WERE PASSING THROUGH THE PRESS.

ARTOTYPE, E. BIERSTADT, N. Y.

8. Waring's Pharmacopœia of India.
574 pages, 8vo. 1884

II. Vocabularies.

1. Physiological Vocabulary. 134 pages, 1872
2. Vocabulary of Materia Medica, Diseases of Women and Children, and Medical Jurisprudence. 161 pages, 1875

III. Popular Treatises.

1. Secret Vice. 24 pages, 32mo.
2. The Soul's Abode. 44 pages, 18mo.
3. The Mother and Child. 44 pages, 18mo.

IV. Religious Tracts.

1. Lot's Choice. 22 pages, 18mo.
2. Lucy and her Chickens. 12 pages, 18mo.
3. The Shepherd of Salisbury Plain. 56 pages, 18mo.
4. The Believing Tradesman. 28 pages, 18mo.

V. Original Treatises.

1. The Eye. 11 pages, 18mo.
2. The Ear. 11 pages, 18mo.
3. The Hand. 11 pages, 18mo.
4. The Foot. 12 pages, 18mo.
5. The Skin. 16 pages, 18mo.

6. The Mouth. 12 pages, 18mo.
7. The Body. 15 pages, 18mo.
8. Be Clean. 4 pages, 18mo.
9. Hints for Cholera Times. 20 pages.
10. Government Tract on Cholera. 11 pages, 12mo.
11. The Way of Health. 4 pages, 12mo.

According to his own estimate, the whole list of his works printed in Tamil amounted to very nearly 4500 pages octavo. In the earlier part of his missionary life, Dr. Green contributed to a New York Medical Journal an article on Tamil Obstetrics, and one on Tamil Surgery. After his final return he prepared a Tract, of 3 pages 8vo on Hints for English Beginners in Tamil.

The small Anatomy, Physiology and Hygiene has been adopted in the Schools of Ceylon and Southern India. Dr. Vaittilingam says the Obstetrics, which "is learned by several of our educated women, is all used up;" and that "of the large *Anatomy, Surgery and Physics* [Vade Mecum] there are so few copies left it is necessary to revise and edit them all."

It is much to be grateful for, that very many persons heard the gospel from Dr. Green once, even though they may never have heard it again from any one. A reminiscence, furnished by Mrs. Green, shows the value of even the most seemingly hopeless opportunity to point a lost sinner to Christ. "One day while staying at the seaside for the benefit of one of his children who had typhoid fever, Dr. Green went out in the early morning, as was his habit, on horseback; the tide being low, he rode on the beach for nearly two miles, when he came to a native's house, where he saw a woman pounding rice in the yard. He spoke to her, and found she was blind. She said: 'I know who you are. You are the missionary Doctor. Fifteen years ago I had a fever, and was carried to your Dispensary at Batticotta. You told me about Jesus Christ. I have prayed to Him ever since, and have not worshiped idols.' The patient had been forgotten, but the good seed sown had taken root."

How grateful to the ear of the poor blind woman must have been the gentle voice which had conveyed to her the glad tidings that were blessed to her translation out of spiritual darkness into the light of Him who is the Light of the world!

CHAPTER XXIII

1883–1884: ÆT. 61–61+.

FROM November it became more and more evident from month to month that Dr. Green was near that event which he had long contemplated with calmness, and sometimes with desire. His conscious approach did not change in the least the feeling and view of it he had so often and so confidently expressed when it seemed more distant. His was the path of the just, which is as the shining light that shineth more and more unto the perfect day.

GREEN HILL, *December* 20, 1883.

MY DEAR BROTHER ANDREW:

. . . . I was lately thinking that our little sphere, in its careering along and about in the universe, never doubles its track; for though it circles about our sun, the sun is in rapid flight around some greater centre. We are borne constantly through new regions, and shall be perhaps untold cycles in return to any former course. And so our own personal microcosm,—physical, mental, spiritual,—from strength to strength, from glory to glory. Oh how we need the strong grasp of the pierced hand, as in our littleness we toddle forward the interminable journey. Joy, that it is ever stretched out towards us to cherish and to cheer. . . . .

Affectionately,

SAMUEL F. GREEN.

During the weeks that followed, his decline was constant. In February it seemed to become more rapid. A few extracts from his notes to his brother Andrew indicate his own view of his condition.

11th,—I am thankful to report myself much better to-day of the last added ail. The swallowing is less a distress. Yesterday I neither looked into a book nor hardly out of a window. To-day I am able to be a little at my desk. The will of God is the mightiest and most glorious among all things of the Universe. In sickness to see it is most helpful, for the logic of it is comforting.

14th,—I hope to get out and about again when we have settled sunshine.

15th,—I have a very acceptable and encouraging letter from Jaffna to 26th December, 1883.

20th,—I can hardly thank you duly for your very liberal offer of residence at the South. I feel no climate with exile discomforts can excel home comforts in one's native air.

25th,—I thank you for kind thought about respirators. I could make no use of one.

The following letter indicates at the beginning a very feeble and trembling hand, somewhat steadied in the sequel by his thought and affection.

GREEN HILL, *March* 24, 1884.

MY DEAR BROTHER ANDREW:

I have for long been hoping each succeeding day to write you and tell you how deeply I appreciate your repeated messages of loving interest. I sweetly realize that "A brother is born for adversity."

"The outward man perishes, but the inward man is renewed day by day." We can live but one life at a time, and as there is such full assurance that the next life is to the believer in Jesus such a vast advance in various advantages over the present, one cannot but desire to reach it. All in due time, all in the Lord's time, all in the best time.

It is a great pleasure to think of you enjoying active life, and contributing to the happiness of so many. I am frequently overcome by the great kindness and tenderness shown me. I see in it the Lord Jesus at His unvarying employ of "doing good." How can I sufficiently thank Him for so environing me!

Ever and affectionately,

Your brother,

SAMUEL F. GREEN.

Early in April, Dr. Green seemed to decline so much less rapidly that his friends thought he might live till autumn. The expectation was cherished till within five days of his decease, when he penned his last letter, closing abruptly, without sentiment or signature, as if exhausted by the effort.

GREEN HILL, *May* 23, 1884.

MY BELOVED BROTHER ANDREW:

I set pen to you with joy after long waiting. The torpor is great, and the tire greater. So farewell.

I would be proficient in the art of conversation, seasoned *always* with grace, as with salt.

I rejoice with you in at last reaching the falls and pools all along the ditch. This season seems to really treat you with a look at various desirable results after waiting and working thereto.

On the same day he took a short drive with his brother Martin, enjoying for the last time the freshness of the fields, the beauty and fragrance of the orchard. The morning of the 28th was nearly spent when he called for his friends and bade them farewell. When asked if Jesus was near him, he answered with emphasis, Yes, *very* near. Then, with the sun and the Sun of Righteousness at meridian, he passed to the inheritance of the saints in light.

Record of the Book of Green Hill.

May 28, 1884.

Our precious and most dearly loved brother Samuel died at fifteen minutes past twelve o'clock this afternoon.

The day was rainy, the apple blossoms were in their full sheen upon the orchards. The trees in the bounteous freshness of their new leafage, and the fields smooth and bright in the luxuriant verdure of their carpeting. The whole landscape seemed animated by the vital forces of the resurrection of Spring—all about was peaceful and still.

One of the children, Lucy, came, in seeming haste, to me, and said, Papa wishes you to come, and was afraid he might die betore I got there.

As I stepped into the room and approached the bed-side of the dying brother, he said, "Call the sisters and brothers to come in, one by one, and then Margaret and the children;" then, reaching his hand to me, he said, "'The Lord bless you, and keep you: the Lord make his face to shine upon you, and be gracious unto you: the Lord lift up his countenance upon you, and give you peace,'—peace based upon pardon, and pardon upon penitence. I will say farewell to you, brother Andrew, but you stand by till all are through, and we will so form a trio."

Sister Lucy then came in, then sister Mary, then brother Martin, then Margaret his wife, then his children in order of age, Julia, Lucy, Mary, Nathan. Each he bade good bye, with a few brief words of tender affection.

He evidently spoke as one who knew that no moment was to be lost. To one of the servants who had come in he turned with his uplifted hand toward heaven.

Serene and composed, he asked to be aided to turn on his side, then shortly turned his face upward; and in a few minutes, without a struggle, his loving, gentle spirit winged its flight to the bosom of Jesus who was his all; to that city which none can enter " but they which are written in the Lamb's Book of Life."

The religious services were conducted by the Rev. Daniel Merriman, D. D., pastor of the Central Church, with which the family were identified.

Mr. Cutler of the Union Church gave a brief account of Dr. Green as a missionary, introducing it by an extract from his Will.

"I wish that my funeral may be conducted as inexpensively as may consist with decency and order. Let the exercises be simply to edification; and of the dead, speak neither blame or praise.

Should I ever have a gravestone, let it be plain and simple, and bear the following inscription: viz.,

SAMUEL FISK GREEN,

1822—188

MEDICAL EVANGELIST TO THE TAMILS.

Jesus my all."

These requests, which I read from the will of our departed friend, written during his final illness, are characteristic. They are few and brief, delicate and circumspect. They betray his habitual preference of others to himself, his dislike of extravagance and display, his delicate sense of propriety, his shrinking from obtrusiveness, and his spiritual mindedness. For himself he would as soon his mortal part should rest in oblivion; for his friends he would have it in remembrance; to the world he would have it still speak the teaching of his life; and for his Lord and Saviour he would have it bear witness to his faith and hope, his love and devotion, his assurance and his joyful anticipation. The remembrance of his life gives special significance and force to these simple expressions of his desire in regard to his funeral, and the marking of his grave. His wish is sacred, and must be regarded. It does not, however, exclude his desire that "the exercises" should be to the "edification" of those who should be present. He shrank from censure, and he deserves none. He was averse to eulogy, and he needs none. But his supreme regard for Jesus, his All, would not allow him to wish for silence in respect to the power of His grace and the glory of His name.

It seems almost presumptuous for one who only saw him occasionally to attempt to portray his character and work to anybody, but especially to those who knew him in the intimacy of daily intercourse. It is not, however, to give information, but simply to gather up in few words the main features of his life, that we may take leave of him intelligently, and hold him in grateful remembrance.

In his physical constitution he was frail even from his infancy. But by the consequently greater care on the part of others and on his own, his life wanted less than half a score of three-score years and ten. He who destined him for his work graciously preserved him through frailty, illnesses, and dangers till his work was done; and done so as to present the fullness and completeness that are naturally expected only of those who are more robust and have a longer term of years.

Having chosen the medical profession and qualified himself for it, and having consecrated himself to the service of God in aid of the welfare and redemption of his fellow men, he gave himself to the work, at twenty-four years of age, under appointment by the A. B. C. F. M., as Medical Missionary to the Tamils.

This was in 1847, when the journey to his field of labor consumed four months and a half. The first thing to do was of course to acquire the language of the people. Beginning the study of it before his embarkation and devoting himself to it with assiduity on his arrival, he was soon able to make himself useful as a physician ; and by occasion of his professional intercourse with the people his mastery of their tongue, colloquially, was greatly facilitated, and his preparation for his evangelistic duties was proportionally hastened.

His field was now a wide one, embracing the missionaries within a radius of about twelve miles, the English residents, and all the natives to whom he could get access, or who could get access to him. To heal diseases of the body while endeavoring to heal that of the soul was the method of the great Physician whom he had taken as his model. In ministering thus to the physical wants of the people he rapidly gained their confidence, and great influence over them, until he was welcome everywhere among the high and the low as their devoted friend, and as their physical and spiritual benefactor.

How exactly fitting to his character was his position as the superintendent of the Jaffna Friend-in-Need Society's Hospital, in which several thousand patients were treated annually. But his main work was in connection with the American Mission Dispensary, where the number of patients treated exceeded two thousand a year. Here, as everywhere, he took the opportunity to give religious instruction in connection with his work as physician and surgeon. In the report of the Ceylon Mission of the A. B. C. F. M. for 1852, it is said: "We believe that much good is being accomplished among the people in connection with this department of missionary labor, not only in weakening the power of their false and superstitious notions concerning the healing art, but in spreading a knowledge of the gospel. It is arranged, that those who come for medical attendance may hear the discourse delivered daily at the appointed hour, in which the way of salvation and kindred topics are dwelt upon, and many are conversed with individually." What a tax upon a constitution never strong, and alive with the tenderest sympathies.

His labors were even yet more abundant. He early saw the importance of educated native physicians, and proceeded to gather suitable Tamil young men under his instruction, carrying them through a regular course of study, and graduating them with diplomas which not merely certified their qualifications, but made them sought for the English stations in the country. His graduates as physicians and surgeons numbered no less than seventy. All these he imbued as far as possible with his own moral and religious principles, that they also might do their work as they saw him trying to do his.

After eleven years of service, he found it needful to return to his early home. On the way he took the opportunity to enlarge his knowledge by visiting Paris, London, Oxford, Edinburgh, Dublin and other places. After an interval of about five years in his native land, he was married and went again to Ceylon. This was in 1862, in the latter part of which he had a narrow escape from death by the falling of the tiled roof of his house, as he had in 1855 by the cholera. After devoting eleven years more to his work, he was constrained again to return to America, by failing health, in the hope that he might after a period of repose find himself able to resume his work in India. In this he was disappointed. Thus our friend had about twenty-two years of service among the Tamils. But what of the remaining eleven years here at home? Though absent in the body, he was still present in the spirit with the people to whom he had given his life-service. Here he continued the work of translation, compilation and composition of a vast amount of knowledge needful to them, placing them nearly if not quite abreast with Europe and America in respect to the science and practice of medicine and surgery. Of the seven volumes, containing from three hundred or four hundred to nine hundred pages each, five were completed by him before leaving

India, the remaining two, with other minor works, after his return to this country. These publications bear witness to his unflagging industry, patience, self-denial and benevolence, as well as to his knowledge and skill. These books are in India and Ceylon recognized as standard authorities. Yet how few among us were aware of the great service that was rendered that people by this quiet, methodical man, who seemed more like an invalid who needed all his care to preserve his own health! The literary work was accompanied by an immense correspondence in securing from publishers in England and America permission to use their illustrations of the various parts of the human body, as in health or affected by disease, and of instruments, means and methods of treatment — all as important to the Tamil students and practitioners as to those of Europe and America, as well as by correspondence with the agents of the English government and with the English and American missionaries.

What may well increase our estimate of his labors, is the fact that his means were always limited, and that he wrought on content that Providence had so environed him.

Still he found time to write religious articles or tracts, to distribute them where he thought they might be useful, and to converse with all he met long enough to point them, in his delicate, inoffensive way, to the privilege and duty of living, not for themselves, but for others, and to Him who died for them and rose again. It is believed that he has found and is to find a great number of persons "turned to righteousness" by his instrumentality.

Of his domestic relations we may not speak except in the most general terms. When a brother of large experience and observation can testify of him as the completest approximation to the Christian ideal, all that need be said, or can be said, is said by implication and with emphasis. Imagination can draw the picture of the reciprocally loving and beloved, and of the numberless offices by which that reciprocity was expressed. His example and his counsels, his consideration and unselfishness, his constancy and strength of affection, constitute a richer legacy to them than any material good which Providence might have given him.

It is grateful to our feelings that his intellectual powers were unimpaired and unobscured to the end, and that his assurance and anticipation of the world to come were such as to make the prospect of a possible continuance here, even for a few months more, a disappointment. Though not yet an old man, he knew his work was done.

He would be the last to characterize it as perfect; but to us it seems as well-rounded and finished as possible with his limitations.

"Blessed are the dead which die in the Lord; Yea, saith the Spirit, that they may rest from their labors; and their works do follow them." His impress on the Tamils will not disappear with those with whom he came in personal contact. Moral and Christian, as well as professional influence, are reproductive. The forces may cease, after a time, to be recognized as proceeding from their proper source, or even to be at work at all. But though silent, and undistinguishable by us from those influences which seem to be radiating from immediate and visible sources, they are perpetuating themselves so that their author "being dead yet speaketh."

The name of Dr. Green will bring to our recollection the man as he lived and moved among us — the Christian gentleman, abounding in good will, in sympathy, in friendly feeling, in charity, in genuine and unaffected courtesy. Sincerity and heartiness were the obvious and spontaneous expression of his whole bearing. "Wisdom maketh a man's face to shine." His face was radiant with that wisdom which cometh from above, and which makes the recipient reflect the gift.

For all that he was, however, and for all that he accomplished, he would have said, " Not unto me, not unto me, but unto thy name, O Lord, be the glory." He had the common infirmities of the race, and, like every one else, had natural obstacles to withstand and overcome. He knew this, and felt his dependence; but he realized in himself the sufficiency of that "grace to help" on which he relied. By this grace he attained to great self control, tranquility and joyousness of soul. Clear in his apprehensions, honest in his convictions, he knew how to differ from the opinions of others without giving offense, and without losing his self-respect, or the respect of others for him. With the tenderness and delicacy and tact of a woman, he adhered to principle with a winning tolerance but a masculine firmness.

These remarks may seem very close to eulogy, but I trust they have not transcended his expressed desire; for the "edification" he suggested seemed to require a plain statement of the leading features of his character and facts of his career, in order to give his Lord and ours the glory of that grace of which he was a manifest subject, and of that good to others of which he was the ever humble and grateful instrument. He certainly would not conceal the fact, or his satisfaction with the fact, that he had been permitted to spend his mature years as Medical Evangelist to the Tamils; nor would he have had anything omitted that might be through him to the glory of his Master.

You who are bereaved have great reason to be thankful for such a life. You have to bear your sorrow, each in the degree to which it affects him, alone; none, with however much sympathy, can help you. But there is One who by reason of His sinless character and human experience, and by reason of His exaltation to that throne where He is invested with all power in heaven and on earth, and where he ever liveth to make intercession for us, can realize to you the sympathy and support you need. To Him I commend you; for you cannot seek in vain of "Him who in that he himself hath suffered being tempted is able to succor them that are tempted."

Record of the Book of Green Hill, May 30, 1884.

The funeral of our loved brother Samuel was from the House at Green Hill, at two o'clock in the afternoon. Many relatives and friends were present, and his remains were laid in the family ground at the Rural Cemetery.

"Certainly this was a righteous man."

A composition of his boyhood at school, deprecating " the love of praise," disclosed a sentiment characteristic of him to the end of life. Though when it was written he was but a moralist, yet after he became a Christian it was sanctified into a spiritual habit. While he disliked praise, however, he was not given to self-disparagement among his fellow-men, beyond the consciousness that without Christ he was nothing; but with Christ strengthening him he felt competent for any task providentially assigned him.

While a considerable portion of important communications from missionaries and physicians has been incorporated in the narrative, a few extracts from those more recent will not seem inappropriate.

From the Rev. Henry Martyn Scudder, M. D., D. D.

Dr. Samuel F. Green was one of the noblest of men. He possessed a clear, keen, cultivated intellect, sparkling with wit. He was large-hearted, sincere, generous, unselfish. He was an earnest, faithful, zealous, fearless Christian. I loved him when living, and shall ever revere his memory.

. . . . . Dr. Green gained a great reputation in the country, and his services were sought by

From the Rev. E. P. Hastings, D. D., President of Jaffna College.

all classes. He was kind and affable to all and won their confidence and good will. It was his practice to speak with those who came to him, and with many whom he met, about their souls and their need of a Saviour; and no one could doubt that, while willing to do all he could to relieve men's physical infirmities, he desired still more their spiritual good. He was a *missionary* physician in the fullest sense, subordinating his profession to the service of Christ. He accomplished a great work, especially in the training of young men to the practice of medicine, and in preparing in the vernacular language useful medical works. He was highly esteemed and beloved by those associated with him in the Missionary work, and his departure from the field was regarded by all as a loss not easily repaired.

From the Rev. W. W. Howland, missionary in Ceylon.

Dr. Green was eminently skilful as a physician and surgeon, and devoted himself to his profession with much enthusiasm; while thoroughly acquainted with the science and practice of medicine, ... he was ever ready and anxious to learn everything new and valuable in theory or practice from any source; . . . ingenious and courageous, yet with the gentle touch of a woman, some of his operations seemed to the natives most wonderful.

His great desire and the prominent object to which he devoted himself was to replace the miserable quackery of the country by the diffusion of true medical science and by training skilful practitioners. At first the instruction was in English, the classes using English text-books; but finding that these thus trained went into positions under government and foreigners, he decided to educate in the language of the people. He commenced the translation of medical text-books. In this he had the assistance of students already trained, himself superintending and revising their translations, for which he was remarkably well fitted, having obtained a very thorough and critical knowledge and use of the Tamil language. The books thus translated are a most valuable bequest to the people.

. . . . . A man, who had heard the truth till past middle life and yet continued a heathen idolator, when taken with cholera was attended by Dr Green and his assistants, and recovered. He then became and continued a consistent Christian through his life; giving as a reason for his change that the devotion and care of Dr. Green and his assistants, when others would not help or come near him, convinced him that theirs must be the true religion.

Dr. Green was a genial companion, a warm and thoughtful friend, a true Christian gentleman and a devoted missionary. His love and devotion to Jesus were very marked. He recognized Jesus not alone as Saviour and Friend but as King and Ruler, controlling every event, whose aid should ever be sought and depended upon, and to whom all praise and honor are due. In all his medical works he has a prayer to Jesus, in the preface and at the end of the book—one in English and the other in Tamil.

His influence is most marked and manifest as it was impressed upon his students by example and precept.

From the Rev. Edward Webb, formerly missionary in Southern India

. . . . My acquaintance with him (Dr. Green) began on occasion of a visit to Jaffna for health in 1848. A little incident exhibits his cheery pleasantry. It was the custom at Father Spaulding's breakfast-table for each one to repeat a Scripture verse. His verse was, "Be not forgetful to entertain strangers: for thereby some have entertained angels unawares." The application was made in a smile all around and a glance at the brother and sister from Madura. Another thing occurred there to which my thoughts have often turned. We were speaking of our religious experience, he and I alone. I remarked, "When I wander away from Jesus for a time, how blessed to return and find Him as loving as ever." His reply was as specific of his piety as the other incident of his pleasantry: "I have no experience of that; I have never left my Saviour for an hour since He first became mine."

I had been on the mission field for about two years, he for less than one. Both of us were hard and greatly interested students of the native language. We studied together then. He used to say I helped him so much; and, to express his respect and gratitude, had the fashion of raising his hat and bowing almost reverently whenever we met. I could not understand this treatment, for I felt I received quite as much as I gave. But humility and reverence were distinguishing graces in his religious life. He used to underestimate his power and correspondingly overestimate that of his brethren. At one time I used to think that his reverent salutations were marks of his quaint humor; perhaps they were in part, but he was too sincere and childlike in his make-up to put on or affect anything of the kind.

That visit was the beginning of a loving and intimate friendship. I greatly prized the correspondence which followed, and which did not cease till the pen dropped from his trembling hand. A few days before his death, he wrote on one of his own visiting cards: "With loving salutations and farewell. The outward man perishes rapidly." I have carried this with me ever since.

Of his missionary fidelity and self-denying labor, of his literary works in his professional department, of the unusual and very remarkable proficiency he acquired in speaking and writing the Tamil language, of his great success as a teacher and professor in the training of native physicians, there is perhaps no need that I should write.

The memory of your precious husband is among the most inspiring and elevating to which I can turn. I thank God for honoring me with such a friend.

From the Rev. James A. Bates, once a missionary in Ceylon.

Our Ceylon acquaintance was brief; we only met occasionally, and then mostly when he came to doctor me or mine, or when all our intercourse was professional. My idea of him is that as physician he was always very careful in expressing an opinion, but very quick in forming one for himself.

On one occasion, when we had ridden together to a village in the Chavagacherry field not often visited by foreigners, I looked on with wonder at the rapidity with which he prescribed for one, and then performed a surgical operation on another. As I remember it, I should think he must have disposed of fifty cases in an hour.

It was a wonder to me, too, how the news that Dr. Green was in Chavagacherry, or was coming, would go out among the people, so that sometimes he would find a crowd of the sick and the lame and the blind waiting for him to heal them when he drove up. Then the natives thought he could do anything and everything.

From the Misses Leitch, of the Ceylon Mission.

The late Dr. Green used always, after prescribing, to kneel down and offer prayer for God's blessing. The heathen respected him for this, and many heathen will to-day speak of him with grateful love, pointing out the spot in their house and saying, "It was there that Dr. Green knelt and prayed for the recovery of my child."

From Mr. Frank K. Sanders.

Mr. Frank K. Sanders, son of a missionary in Ceylon, and five years a teacher in Jaffna College, Ceylon, said at the annual meeting of the International Medical Missionary Society in New York in December, 1887: "I was in Jaffna and became acquainted with the people in their homes; and after I understood their language I began to hear them talking of Dr. Green, which showed to me the wonderful way in which his life had taken hold of the people of that country. His memory is just as strong as ever, and I don't see any chance of its fading out. His plan was to train up doctors from among their own people. The result is that to-day the leading doctors all over Ceylon are Dr. Green's men. These men all feel a love for him, and feel it incumbent upon them to carry out his views. Very many have told me that they were brought to the Christian life by Dr. Green."

From Dr. Waitillingam, Assistant Colonial Surgeon.

Dr. Green always, as a rule, commenced to attend on patients after first preaching to them Christianity. He had a large heart glowing with sympathy for the world, and self-interest was never found in him. . . . . His success in the surgical operation* he performed, first induced me to study medicine, and that too under him.

From Dr. Sivapragasam Pillay.

Although English medicine was introduced long before by others, ... it was reserved for Dr. Green by his general skill to produce in the minds of the ignorant a faith in English medicine. For people then thought that, just as Jesus Christ

*See Chapter 3, under October, 1847.

introduced his religion by curing deseases, so then these missionary doctors had also come to do the same; and when any of these attended on a sick patient, the idea of one's transition from his father's religion to Christianity was also associated with it.

Dr. Green's perseverance and zeal may be best seen in the number and character of his graduates, who are at this moment doing immense good in various parts of Ceylon and India.

His affability and hospitality, combined with his knowledge of the Tamil language and the characteristics of the natives in general, endeared him so much to them that their recollection of him still retains its vividness. . . . . The cheerfulness with which he helped the poor made even children cling to him as their father. . . . . His anxiety to win souls for Christ was not inferior to that of any missionary. He knew when and how to speak to the people about their indifference to cure diseases of their souls. He was indeed a successful preacher of Christianity.

From Dr. Ethernäyakam, *alias* C. T. Mills, Practioner and independent Medical Teacher.

Dr. Green was an earnest Christian worker; he used to speak of Christ to all and every one. He was very kind to all . . . . "The Gooroo Doctor"—the Missionary Doctor—is a household word among all people. . . . .

He is an undisputed authority in

Medicine and Surgery among the Tamil people, yea, even among the country doctors. He shall be our illustrious "Agastier" in future all over the Tamil lands. His translations of Western Medical Works into the Tamil langnage will secure him this distinction. . . . .

In an occasion of typhoid fever, in the family of a native Christian lawyer whose five children were laid up, myself and a colleague of mine were the attending phycians. On a certain night, the lawyer, after observing the care and attention bestowed by us on his children, gave vent to the following remark: "If Dr. Green has not come to this country, and if he has not trained up a few of our young men in the art of healing, the idea that the European Medicine shall ever be useful to us, and that we shall ever be able to avail the services of such men, is an impossible thing."

From Dr. Kanakadattinam, *alias* L. S. Strong, Government Health Officer.

I am afraid I cannot pay due tribute to a true Christian and as true a patriot, Dr. Green, whose consecrated life combined with rare talent, accuracy, piety, ability, fidelity and excellent Christian character; who though dead is still in the hearts and lips of thousands in Ceylon and India; and whose medical and scientific works, combining Western theories and Eastern practice, are left behind for the benefit of future generations. . . . . When a respectable native gentleman remarked to him that all which could be spared must be spent in English medical education he replied, "I must have the satisfaction, at the close of my work, of leaving behind this very useful study to the Tamil nation in their own tongue, as an abiding thing, and not in a foreign language which may in the lapse of time depart from the land."

We learned more from copying his life than from the lessons he taught us. He lectured to us, not from a platform, but near the bedside. He had the task of making the patients laugh even when the tears were flowing from the pain of operations.

. . . . . The Doctor desired that I would select a place in Jaffna and make it my place of usefulness. I have come down here (Point Pedro) and settled for the last twenty-one years. During the time I had to attend to nearly 8000 people affected with cholera, 3000 with small pox, besides 25000 of ordinary sickness that came under my care and treatment in my Dispensary.

His work is still incomplete; who will carry it out? Is there not in all America one who can sacrifice his comforts and follow the footsteps of the departed, glorified, sainted doctor of souls and body, whose name is engraved in the hearts of the people?

From Dr. William Paul, a Tamil, now resident Surgeon of the Jaffna Friend-in-Need Society's Hospital, Jaffna.

My personal acquaintance with Dr. Green extends only to four years, commencing from the period of his return from America in 1862.

At the time we numbered eleven and were nearly completing our first year's course of study under one of his former pupils. The Doctor took upon himself the sole management and teaching of the Class, and we were put under strict discipline and regular system. Although he was strict and exacting, he was so impartial and just that we admired his skill.

He expected every one to be punctual and diligent. Exactly at 9 o'clock in the morning he had the roll called, and joined the Class in prayer. A chapter of the Bible was regularly read, verse by verse, by every one of the students, which the Doctor explained, and admonished. He took great pains to inculcate moral principles and Christian character. Those who were not Christians were not in the least forced to accept the religion, but every effort was made to convince them of the truth.

He devoted one hour in the morning and one in the afternoon to hear recitations. His knowledge of the subjects was vast, and his explanations clear and lucid. Those who were ready with their lessons fared well, but those who took no pains were marked and had to face his displeasure.

So far as I have known, he rarely allowed an opportunity to slip without telling a word or two about the Great Physician. When he visited the sick in their houses, he generally squatted by the bedside of the patient according to Oriental custom, and by his funny words and cheerful looks generally made even the worst of his patients to smile.

All colloquial and common phrases and expressions he committed to memory. His free intercourse with the mass of the people enabled him to acquire a thorough knowledge of the colloquial language.

As a surgeon he was *par excellence.* He had not the equal in the Island. During his absence in America a patient was operated upon, but as is generally the case in operations of that kind there was a defect left unremedied. After his return from America he saw the patient, and we noticed him for hours together sitting in his study in deep thought and contemplation. One day his face beamed with delight, and he told us that he had hit upon a remedy. We were then students in our second year, and were not able to follow the minute descriptions he gave about it. He said he failed to find in books of reference any operation mentioned to relieve the poor man's defect, but that he has now hit upon a plan which he hoped would answer. He sent for some of his former pupils, and successfully performed the operation. The man is still alive—a living witness to his skill and ability.

During our course of study the Doctor made arrangements to teach a Class in the Tamil language. . . . . He engaged four of the students to assist him in the work and it fell to my lot to be one of the teachers. Requested to chose one among his pupils to be sent as Medical Officer in charge of the Government Immigration Service at Pamben, he told me that he wished to see me in Dr. Spaulding's study at Oodooville. In the presence of Dr. Spaulding he said to me, "William, I have decided to send you to Pamben. To spare you from the work I have commenced is very inconvenient to me. But I must not stand in your welfare. I have been a task-master and made you work hard. You have done your duty satisfactorily. Had I commended you before this, I would have spoiled you; but now, on the eve of your leaving me, I do not hesitate to say so. You can now serve under any strict master. Are you willing to accept?" I replied that if he wished to to send me I will go. Then he said, "I will give you three advices; First, keep up your study; second, sustain your moral character; third, forsake not your religion." He commented at length upon each of these subjects, and I promised to endeavor to abide by his advice. Then Dr. Spaulding, laying his hand upon my head, prayed; and I was dismissed with his blessing.

I was indeed very sorry to part with my benefactor and patron. I continued to help him, while at Pamben, in finishing the translation of the book. I often corresponded with him as a son would with his father. He took great interest in the welfare of his pupils. . . . . His work and the good he did to the country still ring throughout the length and breadth of the land.

From Dr. Vaittilingam, *alias*, D. W. Chapman, Translator and Physician to the American Ceylon Mission.

I knew my beloved teacher and spiritual father, Dr. Green, from the year 1862. I was with him for ten years almost every day except Saturdays and Sundays. . . . . When he left Jaffna he put me to act in his place.

The Doctor had in view to educate and give a physician to every ten thousand of the ten millions Tamil population. He has educated seventy-two men directly and sixty-two indirectly . . . . The Vernacular graduates have turned out successful practitioners.

The Jaffna Friend-in-Need Society's Hospital, from its commencement up to the present time, was supplied by medical officers from among Dr. Green's students. This Hospital accomodates about thirty in-door patients, and receives on an average fifty out-door patients daily. The Doctor was visiting this institution bi-weekly, promptly getting there at 9 o'clock A. M., when a very large crowd of sick people would be anxiously waiting his arrival; he politely received them one by one into the room, and prescribed for them after examining their complaints. The routine of Hospital business is, first, out-door patients; secondly, issuing provisions; thirdly, indoor patients; fourthly, surgical operations; fifthly, inspection of Record-books; sixthly, out-door patients again.

The Government appreciated the Doctor's work; in all matters of importance, such as appointment of medical officers and sanitary measures, he was consulted.

Although the whole Island had its Capital in the town of Colombo which is the residence of the Governor, Dr. Green's station, Manepy, was to some extent the capital, as long as he lived there, in being the headquarters of medical science and training. Throughout the Island, and even in India, he was considered one of the greatest men who lived in this century. . . . . . He was able to talk Tamil very easily and fluently; had the command of words, phrases, idioms and proverbs. The Tamil maxims he was daily using more freely than an ordinary Tamil man can do. . . . .

Although he was absent from Jaffna for the last eleven years of his life, his heart was here with his adopted people and on the work that is being carried on here. He writes: "We should aim to give our foster-sons, the Medical Students, in Tamil each several books as perfect and as full as prayer and painstaking can make them. . . . I hope each father of a volume in the series will cherish it and see that in due time it re-appears in a *vastly* improved edition. This most important enterprise we have had in hand many years. I hope you may be prospered to bring it all to a satisfactory conclusion. . . . . . The Lord seems to have fitted you for this important work. Do not lightly decline His call. Whatever you do, do all for Him, earnestly, filially, desiring to honor Him, and He will bless you. . . . .

"It seems incumbent on you and your confreres to maintain the Medical Mission in Jaffna. Get what help you can from the Government and from the Mission, and combine among yourselves to perpetuate the practice and propagation of a system of medicine so much needed in that community in a sanitary, hygienic, and curative way.

"My daily prayer for long has been, 'O Lord, stir and constrain Chapman, Mills, and Paul to do all they may and all they should for the maintenance and perpetuation of medical mission work for Christ in Jaffna, and enable them each, and each of the medical graduates, to walk in purity, in honesty, and in kindness. Please mention this to friends Mills and Paul with my Christian fraternal love.'

"May Jesus the Sun of Righteousness bless His servant's work, enabling his numerous students to follow the footsteps of their tutor."

MAXIMS.

PREPARED AND WRITTEN BY DR. SAMUEL F. GREEN

FOR HIS CHILDREN.

1877.

Growingly rejoice in the constant presence of Jesus.

Displace self by copying the Saviour.

With a well studied Bible link good manners and correct speech.

Where Love leads, all prospers.

Show love by cheerfulness and patience.

Win rather than drive.

Those attached by kindness are easily ruled.

Evince kindly interest, but avoid intrusiveness.

Speak kindly of people, just as if they were present.

Be free to commend and slow to blame.

Rarely threaten, never scold.

Defer reproof till cool.

Reprove briefly, mildly, seldom and alone.

Never take nor allow liberties.

Be always polite; occasional politeness is mannerism.

Be patient, cheerful, and obliging.

Be frank, in word and act.

Equanimity is more helpful than officiousness.

Playing tricks is contemptible.

Ridicule seldom, if ever, and cautiously.

Beware of the Flatterer.

Slang tends to impurity and profanity.

Speak, as the Sensible and Cultured speak.

"Think, before you speak."

In social converse, be discreet, unaffected and cheerful.

Be as ready to listen as to speak.

In argument, say little and hear much.

Shun bad company.

Be reserved with the opposite sex.

Be slow to form intimacies.

Good thoughts at sleeping time bring good thoughts on waking.

Purity is the first excellence in character.

Begin the day quietly and calmly.

Rise promptly, so as to dress without hurry.

Dawdling and hurry are equally wasteful of time.

Never mix work and play.

Punctuality and promptitude exclude hurry.

Hurry is the mother of Impatience.

Shun alike hurry and worry.

First, health; afterwards, learning.

Rather keep comfortably warm than comfortably cool.

Save to give, not to hoard.

Give habitually, judiciously and liberally.

Extravagance and penuriousness are equally selfish.

Practice is the substance of Theory.

In learning prefer what is practical.

Be slow to promise, sure to perform.

Prompt beginning saves hurried ending.

By cheerfulness serve God and your neighbor.

MISSIONARIES IN CEYLON

CONTEMPORANEOUS FOR SOME PERIOD WITH DR. GREEN.

REV. AND MRS. BENJAMIN C. MEIGS,
" " " DANIEL POOR,
" " " MIRON WINSLOW,
" " " LEVI SPAULDING,
" " " GEO. H. APTHORPE,
" " " HENRY R. HOISINGTON,
" " " SAMUEL G. WHITTELSEY,
" " " EDWARD COPE,
" " " JOHN C. SMITH,
" " " ADIN H. FLETCHER,
" " " WILLIAM W. HOWLAND,
" " " WILLIAM W. SCUDDER,
" " " EUROTUS P. HASTINGS,
" " " JOSEPH T. NOYES,
" " " CYRUS T. MILLS,
" " " THOMAS S. BURNELL,
" " " MARSHALL D. SANDERS,
" " " NATHAN L. LORD, M. D.,
" " " MILAN H. HITCHCOCK,
" " " JAMES QUICK,
" " " JAMES A. BATES,
" " " WILLIAM E. DE RIEMER,
" " " THOMAS S. SMITH,
MR. " " EASTMAN S. MINOR,

MISS ELIZA AGNEW,
" HARRIET E. TOWNSEND,
" HESTER A. HILLIS.

TAMILS EDUCATED IN MEDICINE

BY DR. SAMUEL F. GREEN.

CLASS OF 1848–50.

Joshua Danforth,* J. Dennison,*
J. Waittilingam.

CLASS OF 1851–53.

J. Town, N. Parker,*
C. Mead,* A. C. Hall,
S. Miller.*

CLASS OF 1853–56.

T. Hopkins,* G. Mc. Reid,*
C. McIntyre, A. McFarland.*

CLASS OF 1856–59.

J. H. Bailey,* A. Blanchard.
J. P. Harward, F. Latimer,
J. Wilson,* J. Ropes,*
J. Flud,* D. P. Mann.

Class of 1861–64.

Kartthekaser,	*alias*	M. Hitchcock,
Ethernäyakam,	"	C. T. Mills,
Swaminather,	"	S. W. Nathaniel,
Kanakadattinam,	"	L. S. Strong,
Vaittilingam,	"	D. W. Chapman.
S. Navaratnam,		Sivappiraksam,
A. Appapilly,		William Paul,
J. B. Shaw,		L. Spaulding.

Class of 1864–67. The First in the Vernacular.

K. Elyapillay, Kandapper,
S. Sittambalam, A. Sivasidambaram,
V. Sittambalam, S. Sinnappu,
Samuel David, Samuel H. Murugasu,
Daniel Vettivalo,* R. S. Welopilly,*
S. Mandalam.*

Class of 1867–70.

A. Appapillay, A. Appuckutty,
Arumugam, S. Sarawanamuttu,*
V. Senivasagam, S. Saminather,
S. Kandavanam, Edward Lovell,
V. Vannitumby, Visuvanathan,
S. Vinasitamby.

Class of 1871–73.

J. Amerasinger,
S. Arunasalem,
M. Ramalingam,
V. Catheravaloo,*
V. Sadasivam Bates,
S. Sarawanamuttu,
S. Sinnatamby,
S. Sinniah,
K. Tilliampalam,
K. Vaittilingam,
K. Wellopilly.*

Class of 1872–75.

A. Amerasingam,
R. Ambalam,
T. Kanagasaphy,
C. Kumaravaloo,
Richard S. Adams,
Benjamin Lawrence,
V. Sellappah,
N. L. Joshua,
N. Tambimuttu,
M. Nannitamby,
Abrabam V. Nitsinger,
Joshua K. Pereatamby,
V. Ponnambalam,
K. Ponnambalam,
S. Ponnambalam,
Mutiyah S. Ropes,
N. Mutatamby,
V. Vetteawanam.

*Deceased.

The class of 1875 had not completed their course when Dr. Green left Ceylon.